Cuisine Minceur

Michel Guérard was born at Vétheuil, to the west of Paris, in 1933. Drawn early to cooking, he served his apprenticeship at Mantes under Alix Kléber, and there mastered all the classic techniques of cooking and pâtisserie. After doing his military service in the navy he joined the 'brigade' at the Hotel Crillon in Paris, where he was first a pâtisserie chef and sauce chef. After several years as chef in a private household, he worked with Jean Delaveyne at the Camélia at Bougival.

In 1965, bored with the classic disciplines, he set up on his own in a small restaurant at Asnières, on the outskirts of Paris, 'Le Pot-au-Feu', which soon became a favourite haunt of gastronomes from Paris and all over the world. It was there that he perfected his 'Cuisine Gourmande' (literally 'greedy cuisine') helped by his friends and colleagues among the great contemporary cooks. Since 1972 he has worked at Eugénie-les-Bains in south-west France, where he has developed his Cuisine Minceur in the peace of the countryside.

Caroline Conran is a cookery writer for *The Sunday Times* and the co-author, with Susan Campbell, of *Poor Cook* and *Family Cook*, now published together as *Bumper Cook*.

Michel Guérard
Cuisine Minceur

translated and adapted by Caroline Conran

and adapted for Australia by Elise Pascoe

Pan Books in association with
Macmillan London

La Grande Cuisine Minceur
Les recettes originales de Michel Guérard
© Editions Robert Laffont SA, Paris 1976

This English translation and adaptation first published 1977
by Macmillan London Ltd
First published in paperback 1978 by Pan Books Ltd,
Cavaye Place, London SW10 9PG
in association with Macmillan London Ltd
9 8 7 6 5 4 3
© Macmillan London Ltd 1977
ISBN 0 330 25517 7

Printed and bound in Great Britain by
Cox & Wyman Ltd, Reading

Michel Guérard's *Cuisine Minceur*
with drawings by Michel Guérard and photographs by Didier Blanchat

Contents

List of illustrations

Colour plates

Creamed Eggs with Caviar No 50 (Oeuf poule au caviar)
Fresh Tomato and Spinach Tarts with Thyme No 58, Carrot
Gâteau with Chervil No 55 (Tarte de tomates fraîches au thym, Gâteau de carottes fondantes au cerfeuil)
Potted Salmon with Lemon and Green Peppercorns No 61 (La hure de saumon au citron et poivre vert)
Terrine of Sea-Bass with Asparagus Tips No 64 (La terrine de loup chaude aux pointes d'asperges)
Mussel, Saffron and Lettuce-heart Salad No 70 (Salade de moules au safran et aux coeurs de laitue)
Veal Kidney 'in a Green Waistcoat' – braised in spinach and lettuce leaves No 106 (Rognon de veau 'en habit vert')
Steamed Calf's Liver with Sweet-Sour Leeks No 107 (Foie de veau à la vapeur aux blancs de poireaux en aigre-doux)
Bananas 'en papillote' No 161, Little Pear Soufflés No 169 and Light Apple Tart No 159 (Bananes en papillote, Soufflé léger aux poires, Tarte fine aux pommes chaudes)
All photographs by Didier Blanchat

For Christine

Part One
Michel Guérard introduces
Cuisine Minceur

I have been a dreamer for forty-two years. Sometimes I dream at night, more often during the day. But one particular morning I woke up in a sweat, having slept heavily and sluggishly. All that night, as I did so often, I had been trying to escape into my dream, but this time it was hopeless. My poor body, heavy with the residue of so many rich and delectable sauces, was so well covered that it weighed me to the ground, where dreams cannot take flight. Round my waist, the centimetres had covered a considerable distance since I was that young first communicant in the old photograph, with the knobbly knees, hollow cheeks, sticking-out ears . . . So this was what my occupation had brought me to.

I should mention here that in the same way that some people are landscape gardeners, I am, both by temperament and circumstances, a cook-gourmand – not that this was handed down by my father – and I am never quite sure which has the upper hand, cook or gourmand.

Anyway, the evening before, the mysterious and lovely Christine, who had doubtless already made up her mind to marry me some months later, had whispered in my ear, very softly and nicely: 'You know, it would be a good thing for you if you could lose a few kilos.'

What a jolt – I had to swallow my pride and lose some of my corporation to win Christine's heart (I did not know at that time that she would be the inspiration of this book, nor how much she would help me with the writing of it). My great pleasure in the joys of the table was about to be given a beating, starting with a sharp blow in the taste-buds.

So I began my long trudge through acres of grated carrot and other equally agreeable delicacies, destined to push me eventually to the very edge of despair. The ritual 'plainly-grilled steak and boiled haricots verts' left me gasping. Already I was unable to feel the vibrations that made my senses, eye, nose, palate, and touch sing when a really successful dish appeared. I felt isolated, cut-off, surrounded by a closing wall of frustration.

It was too much; I could not take it without trying to solve what was, after all, not a new problem. People had been preoccupied with keeping a sound mind in a healthy body and had been writing diets into their cookery books since before the days of Louis XIV. It was a long-felt need, so I decided to try and fight back, just for the hell of it, and to do it by modifying some of the fundamental rules of gourmet cooking that have been handed down to us.

So, this is what I did, for weeks on end, sometimes with pleasure, seldom with ease. Then, having found the path I wanted, I explored it day after day to make myself familiar with my new cooking technique, which I was gradually beginning to master. Eventually I managed to find the exact formula for my recipes, in rather the same way as a painter will find precisely the right tone by mixing the colours on his palette.

Having jettisoned several kilos on the way, I finally emerged at the end of the tunnel a different man – the man I was before. It was a great triumph; but there is many a slip betwixt cup and lip, and if you don't know how to cook you will certainly spoil the broth, and so I have written this book to help all like-minded gourmands. Use it often, look upon it as a friend, and cooking will lose its mystique.

The book is intended to let you into the secrets of the kitchen and give you a basic knowledge of the chemical and physical interaction of the ingredients and elements you will come across there. Also, and this is my favourite part of the book, I have put down all the moss I have gathered over the past three years – methods, devices and detailed recipes. I did not, however, set out to make a book of unconnected recipes. On the contrary, I wanted to produce a complete festival of light meals for slimming, with salads as fresh as children's laughter, gleaming fish, the heavy scent of forbidden peaches, and roast chickens as deliciously perfumed as those of my childhood picnics.

Michel Guérard

How to use this book

It is important that this book should not be used in the same way as other recipe books. You should not treat each recipe in isolation but should decide that once, twice – or ten times – a year you will have a week entirely devoted to Cuisine Minceur.

You should compose your menus in advance and, during the weekend immediately before, make up the basic ingredients (especially the stocks) which you will use throughout the week. As a guide, pages 14–16 give fourteen menus similar to those I serve at Eugénie-les-Bains.

Ideally both wine and spirits should be wholly avoided during a Minceur week. If the temptation is too strong, ration yourself to one glass of a light table wine at each meal. You should also scrupulously make use of the Eugénie tisane, with its scent of flowers and herbs. It should be drunk as an aperitif or between meals.

Eugénie Tisane

Equal amounts of heather flowers, maize silk, horsetail, uva ursi (bearberry leaf) and cherry stalks (all obtainable from herbalists).

Take one level tablespoon of this mixture for each 25 cl ($\frac{1}{2}$ pint) of water. Proceed as for a classic tisane. During the infusion, add to the water half a lemon, half an orange and a small bunch of fresh mint. To serve, strain and serve in a tall glass with ice cubes. Sweeten with sugar substitute to taste. Add the juice of half a lemon, decorate with attractive fruits in season and a few fresh mint leaves.

Breakfast is a very important part of a Cuisine Minceur course, and must not be neglected. You can adapt it in the three following ways:

Tea with lemon and a poached egg (No 48)
Black coffee and low-fat fromage blanc (see page 29) with red fruits (strawberries and raspberries)
Hot Eugénie tisane and a boiled egg served with asparagus tips to dip into it.

Finally, if you are brave enough and can spend a relaxed day, have a 'journée-bouillon' eating only vegetable soup (No 17).

However, if the spirit moves you – and I hope it will – forget what you have just read, and don't hesitate to serve a Minceur dinner for your friends. They will be astonished by its delicacy and lightness.

A Cuisine Minceur week at Eugénie-les-Bains

Monday lunch Tourte aux oignons doux
(Sweet Onion Tart No 57)
Gigot de poulette cuit à la vapeur de marjolaine
(Chicken Drumsticks steamed with Marjoram No 115)
Julienne de légumes
(see No 87)
Gelée d'amandes aux fruits frais
(Almond Jelly with Fresh Fruit No 165)

Monday dinner Soufflé aux tomates fraîches
(Fresh Tomato Soufflé No 59)
Sabayon de Saint-Pierre en infusion de poivre
(Peppered John Dory with Sabayon Sauce No 91)
Purée d'artichauts
(Globe Artichoke Purée No 133)
Banane en papillote
(Bananas en Papillote No 161)

Tuesday lunch Mousseline de grenouilles au cresson de fontaine
(Mousseline of frogs' legs with watercress No 63)
Gigot d'agneau cuit dans le foin
(Leg of Lamb cooked in Hay No 110)
Confit Bayaldi
(Confit Bayaldi No 141)
Blancs à la neige au coulis de cassis
(Floating Islands with Blackcurrant Sauce No 166)

Tuesday dinner Soupe à la grive de vigne
(Soup of Vineyard Thrushes No 21)
Truite en papillote à l'aneth et au citron
(Trout 'en papillote' with dill and lemon No 86)
Mousse de champignons
(Mushroom Purée No 132)
Sorbet au thé
(China-Tea Sorbet No 150)

Wednesday lunch Salade de cerfeuil à l'aile de pigeon
(Pigeon Salad with Chervil No 76)
Poulet en soupière aux écrevisses

(Chicken served in a soup bowl with Crayfish No 114)
Orange à l'orange
(Caramelized oranges No 162)

Wednesday dinner Bouillon de légumes d'Eugénie
(Light Consommé with Fresh Garden Vegetables No 17)
Turbotin clouté d'anchois à la vapeur de safran
(Saffron-Steamed Turbot studded with Anchovies No 93)
Oignons Tante Louise
(Tante Louise's Stuffed Onions No 137)
Soufflé aux fraises
(Wild Strawberry Soufflé No 170)

Thursday lunch Terrine de poisson aux herbes fraîches
(Fish Terrine with Fresh Herbs No 62)
Sauce grelette
(Sauce Grelette No 32)
Aiguillettes de caneton au poivre vert
(Fillets of Duck Breast with Green Peppercorns No 118)
Gratin du pays de Caux
(Normandy Apple Gratin No 143)
Petit pot de crème à la vanille
(see No 152)

Thursday dinner Gâteau d'herbage
(Gâteau of Green Vegetables No 54)
Bar en cocotte sous les algues
(Bass cooked in Seaweed No 92)
Purée de cresson et d'oseille
(Sorrel and Watercress Purée No 131)
Clafoutis aux pommes d'Aurélia
(Apple Clafoutis No 158)

Friday lunch Salade de moules au safran et aux coeurs de laitue
(Mussel, Saffron and Lettuce-Heart Salad No 70)
Rognon de veau 'en habit vert'
(Veal Kidneys in a Green Waistcoast No 106)
Marmelade d'oignons au vinaigre de Jerez
(Onions cooked in Sherry Vinegar No 136)
Ananas glacé aux fraises de bois
(Iced Pineapple with Wild Strawberries No 167)

Friday dinner Crème d'oseille mousseuse
(Foamy Cream of Sorrel Soup No 19)
Le grand pot-au-feu de la mer et ses légumes
(Seafood pot-au-feu No 95)

Tarte fine chaude aux pommes reinettes
(Light Apple Tart No 159)

Saturday lunch Caviar d'aubergine
(Aubergine Caviar No 53)
Ragoût fin d'Eugénie
(Eugénie Mushroom and Sweetbread Ragoût No 109)
Purée d'épinards aux poires
(Pear and Spinach Purée No 129)
Fruits au vin rouge de Graves
(Fresh fruit steeped in red wine No 160)

Saturday dinner Gâteau de carottes fondantes au cerfeuil
(Carrot Gâteau with Chervil No 55)
Homard à la tomate fraîche et au pistou
(Lobster with Fresh Tomato and Basil No 81)
Granité de chocolat amer
(Bitter Chocolate Granita No 151)

Sunday lunch Salade de crabe au pamplemousse
(Crab Salad with Grapefruit No 72)
Grillade de boeuf aux appétits
(Grilled Steak with Herb Relish No 96)
Mousses de haricots verts et de céleri-rave
(Purées of French Beans No 128 and Celeriac and Parsley No 125)
Paris-Brest au café
(Paris-Brest Coffee Ring No 168)

Sunday dinner Oeuf poule au caviar
(Caviar with Creamed Eggs No 50)
Foie de veau a là vapeur aux blancs de poireaux en aigre-doux
(Steamed Calf's Liver with Leeks in Sweet/Sour Sauce No 107)
Soufflé léger aux poires
(Little Pear Soufflés No 169)

La maison d'Eugénie

Introduction
by Caroline Conran

Michel Guérard, one of today's six acclaimed masters of French cuisine, inventor of Cuisine Minceur and author of this book, is a slim, bright-eyed, gourmet of forty-three, passionately involved with his food and drink.

You may say that by the nature of things, middle-aged gourmets who spend so many long hours over generous dinners have no right to be slim, well and bright-eyed. But Michel Guérard has discovered, or rather invented over a period of years, a means by which people deeply interested in food can eat the lovely dishes they enjoy, continue to go without much exercise and still be the right shape. This invention he has called Cuisine Minceur, and it is a far cry from the traditional diet recipes – the oceans of raw grated carrots, the mountains of plainly grilled meat.

Michel Guérard, as he describes in the foreword to this book, stared certain facts in the face – facts unpalatable to a chef who makes his living by selling exquisite food to the discriminating. It was clear that while life had changed and become far less physically demanding, the things we eat have stayed the same as ever: it was time to change our whole philosophy of cooking and eating. So Maître Guérard has worked upon an alternative, doing away almost entirely with fattening and over-rich foods, and things heavy in saturated fats, while retaining the high standards of classical French cooking. His Cuisine Minceur, delicious and delicate, contains almost no butter, little cream, not much fat or oil, no flour, few egg yolks and no sugar. Instead, these elements are replaced with others which provide flavours and textures as savoury and succulent as before.

For example, a chicken roasted in the traditional way with lashings of butter and perhaps served with roast potatoes is now supplanted, in the recipe on page 193, by a roasted chicken kept juicy by a moist coating of 'fromage blanc' (one of the cornerstones of Cuisine Minceur) and parsley inserted under the skin, perhaps accompanied by a fragrant dish of gently simmered leeks flavoured with mint.

Instead of creamy sauces to accompany simply cooked turbot or John Dory, we now have light and foamy sauces made with a little egg yolk and wine or water and a lot of air, made on the same principle as a zabaglione and flavoured with pepper; or a moist layer of minutely fine strips of vegetables – perhaps mushrooms, celeriac and carrots, bathed in a parsley-flavoured stock.

Game, shellfish and vegetables appear abundantly, their sauces and liaisons brought to the right velvety consistency with a judicious mixture of mushroom purée and the light 'fromage blanc'. Puddings are sweetened with sugar substitutes. (In many recipes we are allowed more than enough sweetener for some palates, so these may need adjusting to provide the correct balance of flavours. As sugar substitutes vary considerably from place to place it is important that you test your chosen sweetener for strength and adapt the quantities accordingly.)

The dishes are always served and presented in Maître Guérard's own particularly careful and appetizing way; he offers them to his readers as he would to his customers. While this kind of presentation is certainly vitally important in a restaurant, it is not likely that many home cooks would find time to arrange the dishes as carefully as the book suggests. However, as long as they keep the appetizing colours and fresh appearance of the dishes, this is not really significant; the food tastes just as lovely when simply presented. Curiously enough, in France the plates themselves are often cold but Maître Guérard stresses *hot* plates and it is important to follow this rule.

Michel Guérard suggests that a course of Cuisine Minceur several times a year would be enough to keep you fit and slim, but you can by all means apply the principles to everyday cooking – the use of small amounts of oil in place of butter for basting chickens, fish and joints; the use of concentrated stocks and finely chopped or puréed vegetables to provide the necessary flavour and texture in sauces and stews, instead of the use of fats, flour or cream.

When planning a complete week or fortnight of Cuisine Minceur, however, it is important to go into the thing very thoroughly, and start from scratch. On page 14, Maître Guérard gives some of the menus served at his hotel at Eugénie-les-Bains and I give some suggested menus for the home cook on page 39.

When you embark on Cuisine Minceur for the first time, look up certain of the basic recipes and decide to make them in quantity. Once made, they can be frozen in small parcels and used as needed. The most important of these basic ingredients are:

1 Mushroom purée (No 132). Keeps several days in the refrigerator and up to a month in the freezer, without deteriorating.
2 Basic chicken stock (No 2).
3 Fish fumet (Nos 3, 5).
4 Sauce Américaine (No 10).

You can also make crème fraîche – the equivalent of the cream sold in France which keeps rather well and is perfectly delicious, having a much livelier flavour than ordinary cream – and a substitute for fromage blanc. I give recipes for both on pages 29–30.

There will also be things to buy for the storecupboard. You will need, for example, dried mushrooms (see page 28). You will also need skimmed milk powder, an artificial sweetener, green peppercorns (poivre vert) in tins and also truffles – if you can bear to part with the large sum required to buy even a very small tin (however, even a small tin will contain several truffles and they will last three weeks or more in the refrigerator, particularly if topped up with brandy after their own liquid is used up, and kept well covered).

Of course you will need herbs, and there are one or two of which Michel Guérard is fond, that are not easily found in this country. Chervil is one, sorrel is another. Luckily, both are exceedingly easy to grow. Plant them in your garden or ask a country friend to grow them for you, and then freeze them for later use. Incidentally, if you are growing your own tarragon, which, like chervil, is certainly immeasurably finer when fresh, be sure to grow the fragrant French variety *artemesia dracunculus* rather than the Russian *artemisia dracunculoides* which has no particular taste at all.

You will need red and white wine for cooking and a bottle of dry white Vermouth, such as Noilly Prat or Martini, which gives a very rich deep flavour.

As far as oils are concerned, Michel Guérard uses mainly peanut oil (arachide) and olive oil. However, some people may prefer to substitute sunflower oil for the oil of arachide as it has a much lower rating of saturated fats and mono-unsaturated fats with a higher proportion of favourable poly-unsaturated fats. Use olive oil where flavour is needed – it has been found, thank goodness, to produce no harmful effects, although not so high in poly-unsaturated fats as sunflower or corn oil.

In many of the recipes you will find 'miniature vegetables' made by carving up larger vegetables and 'turning' them into shapes. It looks very elegant but the dishes look just as pretty if you slice the vegetables quickly into small strips or sticks, and you will save a lot of time.

Many of the recipes for vegetables, fruit purées and sauces depend for their smooth velvety texture on being very finely puréed in a liquidizer. The ideal answer to this is a powerful flat-bladed blender which can cope with the toughest asparagus stalk and stringiest leek. Otherwise use a liquidizer or a Moulin-légumes, but these will give rather less satisfactory results.

Other equipment that may be needed includes, as well as the usual batterie of sharp knives, heavy saucepans and sturdy chopping boards (see pages 25–6); a steak-beater for flattening pieces of meat or birds; a steamer for the delicious recipes cooked over aromatic steam – a couscoussier with a wide bowl-like top and a lid is ideal. An ordinary steamer or even a fish-kettle will make a reasonable substitute. It is useful to have a fish-kettle anyway, as poached fish is always good and always difficult to lift from the pan unless you have a proper rack to lift it on.

For grilling, which Maître Guérard describes on pages 45–8, he uses a heavy ridged iron grilling-pan, but an ordinary overhead grill will serve just as well, though you will not obtain the attractive grid pattern or 'quadrillage'.

If you cannot find a sauté pan, which is a shallow saucepan, then use a frying-pan or a paella pan. Choose a heavy pan because you will find that thin pans are not ideal for Cuisine Minceur as, except where Maître Guérard specifies a gentle heat, everything is cooked in the true chef's fashion, at full flame. Chefs are usually in a hurry, and tend for example to soften onions, in a wide pan over a very high heat for a very short time, keeping them moving around with a wooden spoon all the time to prevent them from browning. Meat, poultry and game, as well as fish, are also cooked at high temperatures and for a short time. It is also very important to allow roasted meat to 'rest' for at least half an hour in a warm place before carving. This gives a much juicer and more succulent result. *Slightly* underdone fish is a revelation, and far more delicious than fish that we would normally consider properly cooked.

In certain recipes, such as Onion Tart (No 57) and Fish Terrine (No 62) the vegetables are cooked 'à sec', that is, without any fat or oil. This is done much more readily if you have a non-stick pan, as the vegetables will exude their juices without sticking or browning. However, care should be taken to keep the temperature low, and you will get the best results if you keep the pan covered and stir the contents from time to time while they are cooking.

Chefs like using gas – Michel Guérard himself says he uses it like the accelerator on a car – fast or slow as he needs it. Other forms of cooking make life more difficult, as the heat is slower to adjust, so preheat rings and ovens to the temperature you require before starting to cook, especially as many of these recipes tend to be rather wet if not cooked fast enough. In particular, liquids are reduced at a galloping boil. The sauces themselves are anyway inclined to be much more liquid than one has been brought up to expect a sauce to be, and this is intentional. Maître Guérard says sauce should not be mashed potato, it must be light, clear and delicate and be served beside the meat or fish, not poured all over the top like a blanket.

The size of the helpings too is a matter of some surprise. They are rather small; not ungenerous necessarily, but small. This is because they are supposed to let you leave the table feeling as light as you did when you sat down, and of course if you eat large quantities of food, no matter what it is, you are not going to lose weight.

Most people like to feel well and attractive, and it is for them that this book has been written. We should be able to eat normally and well most of the time, but take to Cuisine Minceur when we need to – which is, anyway, a pleasure, while the lessons and principles of Cuisine Minceur can be applied to everyday cooking, with delicious and beneficial results.

Batterie de Cuisine

white porcelain soup bowls

egg-dishes

earthenware cocottes

oval ovenproof gratin dish

dishes for both cooking and serving

heavy enamelled iron casserole

terrine

non-stick frying pan

sauté pan

heavy ridged iron grilling pan

pans for frying, sautéing and grilling

strainer

colender

wire sieve

implements for sieving and straining

mandoline   liquidiser   mouli-julienne

tools for shredding, slicing and purées

bain-marie & saucepans   steamer   couscoussier

fish kettle

pans for poaching and steaming

1
2
3
4
5

1 potato peeler
2 small knife
3 pastry brush
4 melon baller
5 channel cutter

10

11

12

scales and
measuring jug

weights and measures and small hand tools

6   7   8   9

6 roasting fork
7 large kitchen knife
8 skimmer
9 ladle

14

15

13

10 forcing bag
11 wooden spatula
12 metal spatula
13 rolling pin
14 steak bat
15 large whisk
16 small whisk

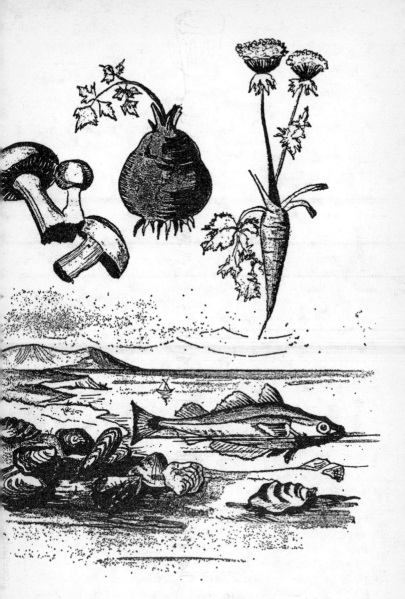

Le merlan à la julienne de légumes

Ingredients

Some ingredients may be unfamiliar or hard to find outside France. The following general notes may be helpful, but don't forget that with some ingenuity local alternatives can usually be found.

Crayfish   Freshwater crayfish, écrevisse in France, krefte in Scandinavia, are found throughout Northern Europe in clean chalk streams. They look like miniature lobsters about three inches long, dark mud-brown when alive, a beautiful fiery red when cooked. (They are not much eaten in Britain, but can be caught by baiting a flat net with rotten meat or a bloater and leaving it on the river bed at night. Go off to the pub for an hour or so, then return with a torch, pull up the net quickly still keeping it flat, and the crayfish will be clinging to it.)

If you can't catch them for yourself, Maître Guérard suggests substituting whole Dublin Bay prawns (otherwise known as scampi), which are also pretty but not such a glowing colour as crayfish. They are most easily available frozen.

Wild Fungi and Dried Mushrooms   Certain edible fungi beloved of the French are specified in the recipes, namely ceps, morels and millers. They are all to be found growing in Northern Europe, by those who have an absolutely clear idea of what to look for, but if you are in any doubt about a wild mushroom or fungi – leave it alone.

Ceps (French, *cèpes*, Latin, *boletus edulis*)   There are several varieties, but basically a cep is a fleshy, round-topped fungus with a thick, fleshy stalk, spongy yellowish or whitish pores underneath and a suede-brown, slimy-soft bulbous cap, to be found beneath pine trees and at the edges of forest rides. Ceps must be picked and eaten young. Discard the spongy pores as, at any rate to my taste, they are a bit too slimy. Ceps are also available – and very good – dried, the best place to look for these is an Italian grocer (or Italian airport), where they are called Porcini.

Morels (French, *morilles*, Latin, *morchella esculenta*)   These spongy-looking dark brown or beige fungi are rare, but are occasionally to be found in Britain, appearing in the spring. They are very distinctive in appearance, their uncommon honeycombed structure being ideal for the harbouring of sand and grit, so wash them very carefully. Dried morels are sold only in very top grocers as they are exceedingly expensive. However, their flavour is so special that they are worth an occasional fling. Soak them in warm water for half an hour before using.

Millers (French, *mousserons*, Latin, *clitopilus prunulus*) I have never seen this mushroom, but they are found in shady pastures or ferny banks and have a strong smell of flour. They are an opaque dirty white with soft thick white flesh, and are somewhat trumpet-shaped. They are also available dried. As they are rather uncommon, it might be easier to substitute ordinary field mushrooms.

Chinese (and Japanese) mushrooms The matsu mushroom (*tricholoma matsutake*), the shiitake (*lentinus edodes*) and the wood ear (*auricularia polytricha*) are all available dried from Chinese supermarkets. They need soaking before use in warm water.

Dried mushrooms are so delicious, adding a deep warm flavour to gravy or sauce, that it is surprising we do not make greater use of them. Although expensive, they are also very light, and what seems a tiny amount will swell to quite a decent bowlful when soaked. Use the liquid afterwards for flavouring, but strain it as a certain amount of dirt will almost always collect at the bottom of the dish while they are soaking.

Seaweed Seaweed is used in Cuisine Minceur, for instance in the recipe on page 170, as a humidifier in the cooking of fish. It adds a strong flavour of its own too, a flavour very similar to the smell that rises from seaweedy rocks when the tide goes out, rather pungent and salty. Use young Bladder Wrack (*fucus vesiculosus*) or Knotted Wrack (*ascophyllum nodosum*), the dark green-brown common varieties covered with oval bladders which pop when you stand on them. If you can't pick it yourself at the seaside, you can buy it at wholesale fish markets or, possibly, order it from your fishmonger, although he may be rather surprised.

Saffron This precious spice consists of tiny dried stamens of the Saffron crocus (*crocus sativus*). A deep red-gold in colour, these stamens dye food a beautiful pure yellow and impart a flavour dry, honeylike and warm. Only a pinch is needed, which is fortunate, as even a pinch will be costly. If you can find them, always buy whole stamens as the powder can very easily be adulterated – and most likely has been. Soak for a few minutes before using in a little of the warm cooking liquid or in white wine.

Fromage blanc is a fresh cheese made from skimmed milk and containing no fat solids. Traditionally made in Luxembourg, it has now become a mass-produced product, packed and marketed like yoghurt and very popular in France where it is eaten as a pudding with sugar and fresh fruit.

It is marketed increasingly widely outside France, but if not available can be replaced with a home-made version. Here are two alternative methods.

One

100 g (3½ oz) low-fat cottage cheese
125 g (4½ oz) yoghurt
3 teaspoons lemon juice
Blend very thoroughly in a liquidizer until shiny and smooth, and as thick as lightly whipped cream.

Two

Add 25 g (1 oz) of skimmed milk powder to 500 ml (scant pint) of milk. Heat to 65°C (150°F) and hold it at this temperature for five minutes.

Allow to cool to below blood temperature 24°C (75°F). Add 2 teaspoons of lemon juice and 2 teaspoons of low-fat yoghurt, cover the pot and leave in a warm place (24°C (75°F) or thereabouts) overnight. Chill.

This method, based on a cheese called Labeneh from Jordan, produces a smoother and less dry-tasting result than the previous method, but is more trouble, and does not keep well.

Crème Fraîche   Stir 1 tablespoon buttermilk into 500 ml (scant pint) of whipping cream in a saucepan over a gentle heat. Bring the temperature gradually up to 24°C–29°C (75°F–85°F), no hotter or it will not work; at this point the cream will still feel very slightly cool to the back of your finger.

Remove from the direct heat, pour into a bowl, cover and keep warm (at about 25°C (75°F)) either in a bath of water over the pilot light of a gas stove or in a warm airing-cupboard, etc. It will take from eight to twenty-four hours according to the temperature it is held at.

To whip crème fraîche, add one-third of its volume of cold milk, water or chipped ice, a little sugar to taste, and whisk.

Yoghurt

1 heaped teaspoon plain yoghurt
1 litre (1¾ pints) fresh milk (the amount of milk used makes the same amount of yoghurt)
Bring the milk to the boil over a high flame. When it starts to rise in the pan take it off the heat and allow to cool until you can keep your finger in while you count ten. Put the starting teaspoon of yoghurt in a bowl and stir in the milk. Put the bowl in a warm place, wrapped in a folded towel, and leave it undisturbed for six to eight hours. Overnight is ideal. Unwrap

the bowl. You should now have yoghurt with water on top; if not put it back for a while, otherwise pour off the water and chill the yoghurt.

The first batch is not always as good as it might be, because bought yoghurt has often been deep-frozen, but using your own yoghurt as a starter will make a good second batch – each subsequent batch will become increasingly weak.

Tomato Ketchup A strange thing has happened in France – French chefs have discovered tomato ketchup. They put it, rather discreetly of course, into all sorts of otherwise delicate sauces to be eaten with terrines of fish or with shellfish.

Ketchup is ketchup is ketchup, but I prefer to use, if anything, my own home-made ketchup. The recipe is quite simple and keeps extremely well.

2.75 kg (6 lb) ripe tomatoes
6 shallots
225 g (½ lb) sugar
1 teaspoon paprika
pinch cayenne
40 g (1½ z) salt
2 tablespoons wine vinegar (chilli or tarragon)
500 ml (1 pint) spiced wine or cider vinegar

Slice the tomatoes and peel and chop the shallots; cook covered until the tomato skins start to come away and the shallots are tender. Rub the pulp through a sieve, add sugar, salt, cayenne and paprika. Cook until the sauce thickens, then add the spiced vinegar and wine vinegar. Cook until the sauce thickens again to the consistency of thick cream. Pour into sterilized hot bottles and seal firmly. Leave to mature a month or two.

Note for Users in Australia

This edition has beeen adapted for the use of people in Australia and others who do not have access to ingredients and utensils available in Europe, and especially in France.

Most of such features are covered in Caroline Conran's Introduction, which should be read carefully before the book is used. However, some problems are peculiar to Australia, and these are summarized below. In addition, you will find suggestions for alternative ingredients appended in italic type to the recipes themselves and a page at the back of the book giving addresses of businesses which sell a wide range of utensils. In recipes where the principal ingredient is not available in Australia, a subheading naming a possible substitute has been included under the French heading.

Ingredients

The exotic nature of many of the ingredients, recipes and examples used in the 'techniques' section, is so much a part of the style of *Michel Guérard's Cuisine Minceur*, that it would have been vandalism to alter too many things or interrupt the flow of the author's prose with excessive annotation. Consequently, once the Introduction and this note have been perused, you should continue to bear in mind the need for imaginative improvisation.

Game
It is difficult in Australia to find much of the game that cooks in Europe take for granted. Some kinds are available from specialist farmers, but for the most part it will prove easier, and no less satisfactory, to substitute more commonly available kinds of meat. Here are some details:

Guinea fowl Fresh guinea fowl is available from March to July at major department stores, and from good butchers. At other times of year deep-frozen guinea fowl can be bought: and in case of difficulty we suggest you contact Olson Game Birds, Nyah, Swan Hill, Victoria. Small turkeys and chickens weighing about $2\frac{1}{2}$ lb (1.10 kg) are good substitutes in all recipes.

Pheasant The availability information for pheasant is exactly the same as for guinea fowl (above). None of Michel Guérard's recipes calls specifically for pheasant, which is just as well, because no other bird tastes quite the same. An average-sized chicken is a reasonable equivalent.

Pigeon Pigeons, such as the French know them, are difficult to obtain in Australia. Spatchcocks (chickens about six weeks old, weighing up to $1\frac{1}{2}$ lb (700 g)) will actually be preferred by many people.

Quail Quail is difficult to find, but is occasionally available from the best poulterers. Spatchcock is a good equivalent.

Thrush Again, spatchcock is a useful alternative, and additional herbs and spices will give a stronger flavour, closer to the original.

Rabbit The varieties of rabbit found in Australia are different from those found in Europe, to the extent that they are seldom found on restaurant menus. On the whole, they are coarser and stronger in taste, and therefore not suitable for use in Michel Guérard's subtle recipes. There is nothing to prevent the adventurous from trying whatever kinds of rabbit they can find, but a piece of yearling veal can be cooked in the same way as a rabbit with results that many might consider preferable.

Hare Hare is occasionally available from good butchers. In recipe No 124 it would probably not be advisable to substitute a less strong-tasting meat because the rest of the recipe would overpower it.

Fish

It is not possible to find exact equivalents of Atlantic and Mediterranean fish for Australia, but the variety of fish available in all States is so wide that all Michel Guérard's fish recipes can easily be used. We provide a rough guide to Australian equivalents of the fish used in the book that should be applicable to all States, but using this as a basis, you may wish to experiment with different fish of similar size, colour, texture and shape.

Salmon Salmon trout has a similar texture and some of the colour of the Atlantic salmon.

Sea Bass Young teraglin, perch or schnapper are fair substitutes but other fish of similar size can be used with good results.

Plaice Flounder is slightly heavier in texture than plaice, but is close in size and can be cooked in the same way.

Sole Flounder is a good substitute for Dover sole.

Turbot There is nothing in Australia very close to the subtle taste and texture of turbot, but once again flounder and schnapper will produce good results.

Sea Bream This is almost identical to Australian black bream.

Angler Fish and Monkfish Angler fish and monkfish are one and the same species (*Lophius piscatorius*). They have a large flattish head and a disproportionately small body. The flesh is white and although no closely related species exists in Australian waters, we suggest rock flathead, black bream or schnapper as substitutes.

Crayfish See Introduction, page 28.

Trout River trout in Australia is not significantly different from that found in Europe.

Whiting   This is very similar to Australian whiting in shape and texture.

Red Mullet   Red schnapper is the best Australian equivalent.

John Dory   The European John Dory is no different from the Australian.

Rascasse   Schnapper is the suggested substitute.

Oysters   Sydney oysters are similar in taste to the large flat oysters referred to in this book, but where the shell is required as a base on which to rest garnishes as, for example, in the recipe for Scallops and Oysters with Truffles, No 79, small scallop shells, easily available from fishmongers, will prove more practical.

Other Ingredients
Crème fraîche   See Introduction, page 30.

Gelatine   Leaf gelatine is used in several recipes. It is available from good Australian delicatessens and supermarkets, but in case of difficulty the powdered variety can be used. Two scant teaspoons of powder are equivalent to one leaf. It is particularly important not to overheat mixtures of which powdered gelatine forms a part.

Shallots   In New South Wales, spring onions (small shiny white bulbs with long green leaves) are also known as shallots. This is considered incorrect and real shallots look like small white onions with brown, dry skin. If real shallots cannot be found, substitute either white onions to almost the same weight or an equivalent amount of dried shallots, but *not* spring onions.

Foie Gras   Although expensive, this can easily be bought in Australia. It is important not to overheat it, as the less expensive kinds can separate.

Frogs' legs   Available tinned or frozen.

Fromage blanc   See Introduction, page 29.

Parsley   It is worth while distinguishing between the flat-leafed 'continental' parsley, and the more common curly-leafed variety.

Mushrooms and fungi   The European wild mushrooms are discussed on page 28. Outside Europe they present more of a problem. In Australia ceps, morels and millers are virtually unobtainable, and where a variety of mushroom tastes and textures is required, the best idea is to combine fresh mushrooms (field and cultivated) with whichever tinned and dried mushrooms you can find at a good delicatessen or supermarket. The oriental types described on page 29 can be obtained in dried form from Chinese supermarkets and good delicatessens in Australia.

Wines used in cooking It is obviously far from essential to use the French and Algerian wines referred to in some recipes. Australian red and white wines will produce excellent results, especially if you bear in mind that Australian red wine is usually heavier than the European equivalent, and adjust recipes accordingly.

Utensils
There should be no real difficulty in obtaining any necessary utensils you do not already possess. (See drawing on pages 25–6 and addresses on page 256.) As with ingredients, you will frequently be able to save trouble and expense with a little ingenuity.

Measurements

Since the introduction of metric measurements in the kitchen in Britain and elsewhere, cookery-book writers have been faced with all sorts of headaches, as it is now necessary to give two different measurements at once.

In this book the usual business of converting pounds and ounces to grammes has been reversed, but the problems remain the same.

The difficulty lies in finding sensible equivalents – one ounce actually equals 28.350 grammes, for example.

So to prevent situations where the reader is supposed to measure out 0.353 of an ounce (10 grammes), and so on, we have followed the usual practice of rounding the quantities up or down to the nearest number of ounces or pints.

However, even so, some measurements are distinctly fiddly, so we suggest taking the (eventually) inevitable plunge and obtaining metric scales and measuring cups and spoons – you can then use Monsieur Guérard's original measurements.

If this is impossible, use your own judgement as to whether it is important to be exact or not.

Conversion tables

Weight

Imperial avoirdupois	Recommended British metric equivalents	Recommended Australian metric equivalents
½ oz	15 g	15 g
1 oz	25 g	30 g
2 oz	50 g	60 g
3 oz	75 g	90 g
4 oz	100 g	125 g
8 oz	225 g	250 g
12 oz	350 g	375 g
1 lb	450 g	500 g
2 lb	900 g	1 kg

Liquid Measurements

Imperial	Recommended metric equivalents
¼ pint	150 ml
½ pint	300 ml
¾ pint	450 ml
1 pint	600 ml
1¾ pints	1 litre
2½ pints	1.5 litres
3½ pints	2 litres

In Australia, one metric measuring cup is equal to 250 ml. It is simpler and more practical to work with metric cups and spoons than to juggle millilitres, so here are some useful equivalents:

$$250 \text{ ml} = 1 \text{ cup}$$
$$125 \text{ ml} = \tfrac{1}{2} \text{ cup}$$
$$65 \text{ ml} = \tfrac{1}{4} \text{ cup}$$
$$60 \text{ ml} = 3 \text{ tablespoons}$$
$$20 \text{ ml} = 1 \text{ tablespoon}$$
$$5 \text{ ml} = 1 \text{ teaspoon}$$

Oven Temperatures

Setting °C	Setting °F	Gas mark
110	225	$\frac{1}{4}$
130	250	$\frac{1}{2}$
140	275	1
150	300	2
170	325	3
180	350	4
190	375	5
200	400	6
220	425	7
230	450	8

Replacement Values for Length Measurements

Inches	
$\frac{1}{16}$	2 mm
$\frac{1}{8}$	3 mm
$\frac{1}{4}$	5 mm
$\frac{1}{2}$	1 cm
$\frac{3}{4}$	2 cm
1	2.5 cm
$1\frac{1}{2}$	4 cm
2	5 cm
$2\frac{1}{2}$	6 cm
3	8 cm
4	10 cm
6	15 cm
7	18 cm
8	20 cm
9	23 cm
10	25 cm
12	30 cm
14	35 cm
16	40 cm
18	45 cm
20	50 cm

Cuisine Minceur Menus for the Home Cook

These menus have been developed with the home cook in mind. Most of the dishes will be found in the recipe section (the bold numbers indicate the recipe numbers) but I have also included dishes which combine simple ingredients – grilled meats, salads, fruits – with Minceur sauces and purées.

Winter menus

Monday lunch Grilled veal escalope with tomato sauce (see **103**)
Green salad, vinaigrette **24**
Fresh fruit
Monday supper Grated celeriac with mayonnaise **26**
Scarlet tongue with onion sauce **101**
Watercress purée **135**
Caramelized oranges **162**

Tuesday lunch Poached eggs with watercress **49**
Bananas 'en papillote' **161**
Tuesday supper Mussel, saffron and lettuce-heart salad **70**
Chicken in coarse salt (page 64) with béarnaise sauce **36**
Purée of leeks **126**
Light pear soufflés **169**

Wednesday lunch Carrot gâteau with chervil **55**
Fresh fruit
Wednesday supper Garden salad **67** made with button mushrooms
Bass cooked in seaweed **92** or grilled served with sauce vierge **34**
Hot apple tart **159**

Thursday lunch Grilled steak with herb relish **96**
Green salad with vinaigrette **24**
Bitter chocolate granita **151**
Thursday supper Eugénie vegetable soup **17**
Grilled pigeon with garlic sauce **120**
Normandy apple gratin **143**
Coffee creams **154**

Friday lunch Veal kidney in spinach and lettuce 106
Fresh fruit
Friday supper Avocado with vinaigrette 24
John Dory (or other fish) with a pepper sabayon sauce 91
Carrot purée 130
Apple Clafoutis 158

Saturday lunch Beef stew with baby vegetables 99
Purée of celeriac with parsley 125
Green salad with vinaigrette 24
Lime and grapefruit sorbet 147
Saturday supper Velouté of wild mushrooms 22
Duck with green peppercorns 118
Normandy apple gratin 143
Floating islands with blackcurrant sauce 166

Sunday lunch Leg of lamb cooked in hay 110
Leeks simmered with wild mint 140
Little coffee soufflés 171
Sunday supper Grilled steak with herb relish 96
Green salad
Orange custard creams 152

Summer menus

Monday lunch Glazed eggs with ratatouille 48
Fruit sorbet 149
Monday supper Fresh tomato soup with pounded basil 18
Steamed calf's liver with leeks in sweet-sour sauce 107
Little coffee soufflés 171

Tuesday lunch Tante Louise's stuffed onions 137
Melon
Tuesday supper Marine salad 69
Parslied chicken 111
Sorrel purée (see 131)
Fruit steeped in red wine 160

Wednesday lunch Tomato tart with thyme 58
Green salad with vinaigrette 24
Melon sorbet 148
Wednesday supper Asparagus with hollandaise
Grilled guinea fowl with limes 116
Maman Guérard's vegetable stew 142
Little strawberry soufflés 170

Thursday lunch Aubergine caviar 53
Apple compôte with apricots 155
Thursday supper Sorrel soup 19
Trout 'en papillote' with dill and lemon 86
Fresh raspberries

Friday lunch Raw fish salad 71 or terrine of rabbit with plums 123
Green salad
Fresh fruit
Friday supper Green bean and tomato salad with vinaigrette 24
Escalopes of salmon with sorrel 85
Melon sorbet 148

Saturday lunch Grilled bass (page 51) with lemon slices
Ratatouille niçoise 144
Fresh fruit with custard creams 153
Saturday supper Artichokes with vinaigrette 24
Duck breasts with fresh figs 117
Strawberry Chantilly 164

Sunday lunch Roast sirloin of beef with Minceur gravy
(have cold if very hot weather)
Green salad
Raspberry sorbet 149
Sunday supper Fresh tomato soufflé 59
Chicken liver mousse 65
Fresh fruit

A Cuisine Minceur Dinner Party
Velouté of wild mushrooms 22
or Fish terrine with fresh herbs 62
Pigeon pots 121
Green salad with vinaigrette 24
Fruit steeped in red wine 160

A Cuisine Minceur Buffet
Aubergine caviar 53
Potted salmon with lemon and green peppercorns 61
Bass cooked in seaweed 92 served cold with sauce vierge 34
Cold ratatouille niçoise 144
Salad of curly endive, chicory, fennel and thinly-sliced radishes with
vinaigrette 25
Iced pineapple with wild strawberries 167
Raspberry sorbet 149

Au commencement il y eut
la terre puis l'homme qui trouva le feu
alors il se mit à cuisiner . . .

The principal methods of cooking and their application to Cuisine Minceur

'Quel qu'en soit le mode, Mode Traditionnel : à la Cheminèe, sur le Gril, Rôti, Sautè, à la Friture, à l'Étouffée, à la Vapeur, Braisè, Pochè ; ou, Mode Futur, la cuisson est pour un aliment le passage de l'ètat cru à l'ètat cuit, phénomène qui modifie son aspect extérieur, voire sa couleur, sa mâche et sa saveur, faisant naître ainsi un halo d'odeurs qui éveillent à l'appétit. Le Feu, lui, en est l'auteur aux maints visages, bois, charbon, gaz, électricité, ondes ...'

The Two Great Laws:

1. Cooking by sealing

Sealing and browning   The method consists of crisping and browning the surface of the food all over, by applying heat either with or without fat or oil. The purpose is to seal and imprison all juices and nutritious elements inside the food to be cooked. It is used in grilling, roasting, sautéing and frying.

Sealing without browning   The same result can be achieved without browning the food by cooking it in boiling liquid or steam, or in a non-stick pan. The method is used for poaching eggs and for cooking pasta, vegetables, fish, chicken and meat.

2. Cooking by exchange

Exchange with browning   This consists of pot-roasting or braising meat, poultry, game and offal, first sautéing them briskly in hot fat or oil, to retain their juices and nutritive elements, and then moistening them to half their depth with wine, basic veal, chicken, game or fish stock or any other aromatic stock: the making of the basic fonds blonds also follows this principle.

The juices sealed inside the food are gradually released to combine with the cooking liquid and at the same time the food absorbs, and is enriched by, the various flavours of the liquid itself – hence the term 'by exchange'.

Exchange without browning This is the same as the preceding method but with one difference; the food may be sautéd in fat or oil but *not* coloured (stewed gently in butter, the principle of a fricassee), or soaked in water to remove every trace of blood (offal), and blanched for a few minutes if necessary, then sautéd in a non-stick pan before adding the moistening liquid, which will become the base of the sauce or gravy, due to the process of exchange.

On the other hand, unlike meat, the braising of fish is not started by sautéing, but simply by placing the fish on a dish which may or may not be lightly buttered, and then moistening it to half its depth with fish fumet, or with cold white or red wine and placing it in the oven covered with greaseproof paper or aluminium foil to prevent burning. This last is an excellent example of cooking 'by exchange without browning' as the fish quickly releases its juices and flavours into the fumet, which in return helps the food to become succulent during its cooking, by 'exchange'. This method is also used for the cooking of basic fond blond (veal or fish) consommé and the poaching of fish in a cold, well-flavoured stock (court-bouillon) which is gradually brought to simmering point.

Cooking on an open fire or barbecue

Man's first attempts at cooking were done on a wood-fire, and it is still a good place to start learning the art of cooking. I have written the next few pages specifically for all devotees of the open fire, for fledgling and weekend cooks. *With a little ingenuity they can cope with almost any form of cooking on an open fire.*

Cooking on a grill

This method is concerned with sealing and browning the meat on the top of a fire or stove. The source of heat comes from glowing embers, burning vine prunings or brushwood, fruitwoods and other woods (avoiding those that are resinous) or charcoal, and the only equipment needed is the grilling rack, on which you place whatever is to be cooked.

There are also, of course, effective modern grills which work by gas, electricity, infra-red rays, or which are simply a solid disc of iron, ridged on the top and slightly at an angle, with a handle on one side, which is put straight over the source of the heat (but nobody has yet managed to reproduce the wonderful effect of wood-smoke on food).

Red meat The grill must be clean and very hot, and the meat should previously have been allowed to come to room temperature and then brushed rather lightly with oil (olive or arachide).

Grilling 'bleu' – very rare The piece of meat is put on the grill and sealed on one side, then turned half-way round on the same side to obtain a criss-cross pattern or 'quadrillage', and also to give it a light browning and form a crust on the surface. The other side is then treated in the same way.

The meat is only left on the grill very briefly: test it by pressing it lightly with one finger on the crusted surface. If it offers no resistance, and remains soft, it is now 'bleu'. To make sure the meat is hot all the way through, take it off the heat, and put it on one side, covered, in a warm place for a few minutes.

Grilling 'saignant' – rare If you leave the meat on the grill rather longer, a light beading of clear rose-coloured blood appears on the upper crust. Lightly press the meat with your finger. If it meets with a slightly pliant resistance, it is now 'saignant'.

Grilling 'à point' – medium rare More thorough cooking needs a less fierce heat; keep the steak away from the hottest part of the fire; the upper surface will become heavily dewed with clear beads of blood. Pressing it with your finger, you will meet a firmer and stronger resistance than before; it is now cooked 'à point'.

Grilling 'bien cuit' – well done If you prolong the cooking, the beads of blood become rosy-brown pools all over the surface of the meat. The finger now meets a very strong resistance; the meat is now 'bien cuit'.

White meat and poultry, game – kebabs (brochettes) – charcuterie
The fire should be less hot, but the grill itself must be well heated before the food to be cooked is placed on it. The meat should not be left too long on the grill, as it has a tendency to become dry. In fact it is essential to finish the cooking before the meat has lost its succulence. A chicken, for example, should not be allowed to whiten all the way through, but should

still show a very pale rosy colour along the wish-bone, the sign of its being beautifully cooked, with a lovely melting quality to the flesh (pierce the breast with a needle, which should slide in almost of its own accord, and allow a bead of almost colourless juice to seep out). The same applies to game and lamb.

If the subsidiary ingredients of a kebab (brochette) include mushrooms, green or red peppers, bacon, etc. it is sometimes useful to blanch them in water beforehand (unsalted for bacon). The main ingredients – meat, poultry, offal, fish – are usually marinated before cooking (with oil, thyme, a bayleaf, parsley, slices of lemon, coarsely-ground pepper, etc.).

Fish   Oily fish (sardine, mackerel, herring, salmon) are more delicious when they are cooking on a grill as it helps them to lose some of their oiliness. The fish, which are sometimes marinated in oil beforehand, are first brushed very lightly with oil.

The grill is also oiled to prevent the skin sticking when the fish are turned and should be:

Very hot for small fish.
Very hot for larger fish, which are usually given a quick turn on the grill to produce a criss-cross pattern or 'quadrillage' and then put in the oven to finish cooking.
Hot for large fish which are to be cooked entirely on the grill.

Flat-fish (brill, turbot, skate, sole, plaice) should be grilled first on the white side and then on the dark.

Round fish (herring, mackerel, red mullet, bass, sardine) are put on the grill, all facing the same way, with their dorsal fins to the left, and then reversed.

Certain of the large fish (salmon, hake, halibut) can be cut in steaks or 'darnes' before grilling.

However, rather than cutting a salmon into steaks (the old French word 'dalle', meaning tiles or slabs is more appropriate) it can be cut lengthwise along the back into strips about 5 cm (2 in) thick. The skin is important and must be left on. The skin is then slashed in a trellis pattern and the fillet placed skin-side down on the grill and cooked without turning. The grilled skin permeates the flesh with a pleasant smoky flavour and keeps it amazingly succulent and tender. If you like, the salmon can be marinated in a Scandinavian marinade (No 15) before cooking. Oysters, scallops, cockles, clams, and other edible shellfish, all open of their own accord when put on the hot grill. They can be eaten just as they are, or with a few turns of the peppermill and some chopped herbs. (In the

Roussillon, in south-west France, they cook snails, already purged and cleaned, directly on the grill; they are served with little sausages, also grilled, 'boudin catalan', bread dipped in oil and Roquefort cheese.)

Grilling – Shortcuts and sleights of hand   One of the properties of salt is to extract the juices from meat and so to prevent it from browning and forming a crust. It is therefore better to salt all smaller pieces of red meat half-way through the cooking. With larger pieces, where the meat is to be cut in slices after cooking, or with a large fish, which is going to be filleted before serving, it is essential to salt a second time after carving or slicing, adding at the same time some freshly ground pepper. This is because the salt can never reach the heart of the meat or fish during cooking. This applies to all larger joints which are going to be carved: leg of lamb, rib of beef, loin of veal, loin of pork, saddle of lamb, and so on.

When you turn the meat during cooking, avoid sticking a fork into it, or you will lose valuable juices and blood.

Larger pieces to be grilled must be cooked more slowly to allow time for the heat to reach the centre, so keep them away from the hottest part of the fire. You can speed up the cooking by slashing the skin in several places, for instance with a leg of lamb or fish.

If the piece to be grilled is uneven in thickness, keep the thin part further away from the heat than the thick part.

If you are not worried about excess calories, the grilled meat or fish can be brushed after cooking with a little brush or a 'plumet' (made out of a small bunch of chicken feathers) with a little oil or melted butter, which makes it look shiny and appetizing. A grilled piece is usually served with the side which you have cooked first, uppermost.

After use and while still hot, the grill should be scoured with a metal brush to remove all the bits and pieces, which will otherwise burn next time you use the grill and give a bitter taste to the food.

Enclosed cooking on an open fire

The food is wrapped in greaseproof paper or aluminium foil and pushed into the hot ashes. The method is also called 'en papillote'.

Dry-cooking   Potatoes, mushrooms, asparagus, etc.

Rabbit, pigeon and smaller birds, etc. decked with parsley, chives, thyme, bayleaves, etc.

Apples, bananas, etc. (accompanied by vanilla pods).

Cooking with moisture   In this case a little liquid – red or white wine, or well-flavoured stock is poured into the foil case or paper bag, before it is closed, to cover or moisten the food to be cooked. The parcel can then be put on the grill, or even in the glowing embers; the liquid will be absorbed by the food, and at the same time prevent the paper from burning.

Steaming over an open fire

Cover the grill with a layer of seaweed soaked in seawater, or with the wild succulent herbs (cresses, wild mint, brooklime) that grow in the water-meadows. Place the fish on top and cover with another layer of the same plants. It will not take more than twenty minutes to cook a sea-bass weighing 800 g ($1\frac{3}{4}$ lb).

The lazy way of cooking on an open fire

Larger pieces of meat, such as rib of beef, leg of lamb, etc., can be cooked on a fire without using a spit. All that is necessary is to brown the meat all over on the grill, giving it the usual grid pattern, and then to place it very close to the fire on hot, but not glowing, ashes, being careful to slip a piece of aluminium foil underneath it first. This method of cooking takes longer than any other, because the temperature is that of a very cool oven, about 100°C/210°F/Mark $\frac{1}{4}$. Turn the joint from time to time, and don't be afraid to keep your leg of lamb there for two to three hours, according to its size. When you finally cut into it you will be staggered by its tenderness and the uniform rosiness of the meat.

Cooking in smoke on an open fire

It is important not to confuse this method of cooking with the process of smoking fish such as salmon, trout and sturgeon, and poultry such as goose, chicken and duck, which after seasoning (and sometimes mari-nation) are exposed to cool smoke. The tepid or cold smoking is similar to 'boucanage' or smoke-drying, one of the most important methods of preservation in the past. For this method, however, a good fire is built up with a deep bed of glowing embers. Put the wire grill on, to heat up, and then brown the chosen food (meat, poultry, or fish) without cooking it.

As soon as this is done the embers are smothered with damp branches or sawdust (oak, alder, poplar or fruitwood, never resinous woods). The sealed food, on the wire grill, is then laid on top and covered with a domed metal meat cover or other suitable 'cloche' and the hot smoke gently cooks the food, permeating it with a myriad of elusive woody scents and flavours.

Cuisine Minceur and the open fire

The various ways of cooking over an open fire or barbecue can be adapted to Cuisine Minceur, provided certain precautions are always taken.

If the piece to be grilled is brushed with oil in the usual way before cooking, to help form the crust on the outside, it can be sponged to remove any excess, before and after it is cooked, with absorbent kitchen paper.

It is also possible to dip the piece to be grilled into water in which you have infused a little thyme and a bayleaf before you place it on the grill, instead of using oil.

Another method is to put the food to be cooked on a bed of coarse salt spread out in a frying-pan and made very hot (wait till you hear the salt rustling before you add the food).

The skin of a chicken to be grilled or cooked on a spit, should be pricked all over with a needle, so that the subcutaneous fat is gradually released during the cooking.

To sum up – cooking over an open fire can give one's imagination a free rein and all lovers of cooking and, to my thinking, all cooks worthy of their salt, should have dabbled in this kind of cookery at least once.

Roasting

The roast

Roasting a food means cooking it by the direct action of heat, without moisture, turning it frequently. It is another way of cooking by 'sealing and browning'. To obtain the sealing and crusting of the food, it is necessary, as in grilling, to coat the meat sparingly with fat and oil (one-third butter, two-thirds oil). Roasting can be done in the oven, on a spit and even, in an emergency, in a large uncovered cocotte or braising-pan.

Roasting in the oven

The oven (which ideally should have a vent for the fumes to escape), should be heated beforehand, the temperature depending on the type of joint to be cooked and its size. The temperature should be high enough (240°C/475°F/Mark 9) to sear the food thoroughly and conserve all its juices.

The food (meat, poultry, game, fish) is very lightly coated with fat and oil, put, unsalted, into the oven either straight in the roasting-tin (à la ménagère) or in a shallow oven dish called in France a lèchefrite, with a rack to keep the meat above the level of the fat or sauce, or else on a bed of broken and lightly browned bones, or even – for a fish – on a bed of seaweed.

When the sealing and browning of the food is completed, slightly lower the heat of the oven and baste it from time to time with the juices which collect in the bottom of the roasting-tin (except where seaweed is used), until it is cooked. Now, it can be salted. White meats, poultry, game, and large fish, need a more moderate temperature, after the initial sealing, to cook successfully and retain their succulence.

Roasting on the spit

On a spit the cooking takes place over the fire, with the food uncovered, entirely surrounded by dry air, and rotating continuously. A roast cooked in this way is for some people more toothsome than one cooked in the oven.

The technique of cooking on a spit is the same as that of cooking in the oven, except that it is necessary to baste the joint more frequently with the juices which collect in the dripping tray below.

Roasting shortcuts and sleights of hand

How to obtain a tender roast   A joint, bird or fish, roasted on a spit or in the oven, is cooked by sealing and browning; the high temperature crusts the outside of the meat, imprisoning all its juices. These juices are driven inwards towards the heart of the meat through the complicated network of tiny blood vessels, allowing it to cook in its own juices without losing essential nutrients.

If you cut into the joint immediately after it is cooked, you will find first, an outside layer, which is very well-cooked, then another less well done, and finally, the heart which is 'bleu', and contains all the juices, which will run out. *Therefore it is essential to let the meat rest.* If the meat is taken from the oven or fire and kept warm on a dish, covered with a domed meat cover, large bowl or a layer of aluminium foil, the fact that the heat is no longer exerting its inward pressure towards the centre of the joint will allow the juices, by an inverse process, to flow back towards the outer layers of the roast, giving it an even rosy or red hue according to the length of the cooking. At the same time, the muscular fibres, contracted by the heat, relax and expand again, giving the meat the desired tenderness. *It is therefore preferable to finish the cooking of, say, a leg of lamb an hour before you sit down with your guests.*

Salt the meat during the cooking and salt it again as each slice is carved, adding a few turns of the peppermill.

Avoid piercing the roast with a fork while it cooks.

Certain of the dryer meats, such as game, are improved by being covered with a waistcoat of bacon or pork fat, which is removed before the end of the cooking to allow the meat to brown. Hare, rabbit and game birds, such as pheasant and partridge, can also, if necessary, be larded by inserting little strips of pork back fat into the flesh with a larding needle.

If certain parts of the meat, bird or fish are particularly delicate or easily burned (the knuckle of a leg of lamb, the tail of a fish for instance), wrap whole or part of the piece in aluminium foil.

The juices from the roast

The roasting juices are never better than they are at home, because the home cook instinctively keeps them simple and straightforward, whereas the professional cook often tries to make an elaborate sauce with them – something over-sophisticated, and, in my opinion, quite wrong.

Every piece of meat, poultry or game or even fish which has been roasted in the oven in a nice large dish, will have left in the bottom of that dish enough juice to make the gravy.

Shortcuts and sleights of hand   Remember to coat the joint with half oil, half butter – 30 g (1 oz) for every kilogram (2¼ lb) of meat (oil can withstand higher temperatures than butter and helps to prevent burning).

Put an unpeeled clove or two of garlic into the dish with the joint. Always preheat the oven.

After it has been cooking for ten minutes, baste the roast with the juices which have already collected in the tin, and turn it over when the top is nicely browned. Continue to baste, and turn frequently.

Take the roasting-tin out of the oven, remove the roast and keep it hot on a covered dish; make sure that the juices covering the bottom of the tin are sufficiently concentrated (do not on any account allow them to blacken, as this gives the gravy an irreparably bitter taste).

Spoon off most of the fat (about a quarter should remain with the juices and will amalgamate the gravy when it is boiled). 'Deglaze' the pan, that is, add twice as much water as you wish to make gravy and scrape up all the particles caramelized on the bottom of the tin with a spoon, dissolving them in the hot water. Allow the gravy to boil and reduce (leaving roughly two tablespoons per person).

Strain the gravy through a sieve, crushing the cloves of garlic with the basting-spoon if you like it slightly garlicky. You can at the end of the cooking, incorporate several little dabs of butter which are mixed in by shaking the dish with a rotary movement to give the gravy a velvety texture. A few drops of very good red wine vinegar will also bring out the character of the gravy.

How to improve the roasting juices   You can put a few broken-up veal bones round a joint of beef, or veal, or lamb bones round a leg of lamb or a loin, or one or two crushed chicken carcases round a chicken, and let them brown while the meat is cooking. When the time comes to make the gravy, you can replace the hot water with light veal, lamb or chicken stock (*see* Nos 1, 2, 4).

Roasting in Cuisine Minceur

If roasting in the oven or on a spit is done correctly, it can be used in Cuisine Minceur, because the fat and oil are used in very small quantities, and are there, once the meat has browned, only to prevent it from burning.

As in Cuiseine Minceur grilling, poultry should be pricked all over with a needle to release the fat lying between the skin and the flesh. To make the gravy, all that is necessary is to skim off *all* the fat that has collected in the roasting-tin (from the oven) or dripping-pan (from the spit).

Once you have removed every trace of fat from the roasting-tin or dripping-pan, put the joint to rest in a covered dish for fifteen to twenty minutes before serving. The juices which seep out of the roast can be used as the basis of an excellent Cuisine Minceur gravy.

In the Cuisine Minceur version, whatever the butcher may say, veal and beef should be cooked 'naked' and not wrapped up in layers of fat.

Sautéing

Sautés are a quick method for making dishes in savoury sauces. Their instant cooking by sealing is similar in principle to grilling and roasting, in that it consists of the rapid cooking in an open pan, a shallow sauté pan, or failing that, a frying-pan, the bottom of which is covered with oil and butter, half-and-half (allow about 15 g ($\frac{1}{2}$ oz) a person) – of small pieces of meat, offal, poultry, game, fish, or vegetables, which on contact crisp and brown, enclosing all the juices. The difference lies in the finishing of the dish.

Sautéing — basic recipe

Once sautéd and browned on both sides, seasoned and cooked (bleu, saignant, à point or bien cuit, as with grills, see page 46) take the pieces out of the pan and put them to keep warm on a hot dish.

Pour off all the fat into a bowl. Deglaze, that is, pour into the pan the liquid specified in the recipe – white wine, red wine, vinegar, madeira, port, sherry, vermouth, armagnac, or brandy – two tablespoons of wine per person or two teaspoons of spirits. The liquid is brought to the boil to dissolve the caramelized juices stuck to the bottom of the pan. Allow it to reduce by three-quarters of its volume.

Add three to five tablespoons of concentrated veal, chicken, game or fish stock, according to what is being cooked. Allow to reduce by half.

Remove the pan from the heat and add nuts of butter (30 g (1 oz) per person), or some cream (50 g (1¾ oz) per person) blending them into the sauce by shaking the pan with a rotary movement. The sauce should never drown the meat, it must be a 'sauce courte' which just covers whatever you have cooked and spreads delicately round it.

The meat or fish, once cooked, should be put on one side to keep hot, and should never be boiled in the deglazing liquid (spirits, wine, stock) which would transform the dish into a ragoût.

Two examples

Beef with red wine
PIÈCE DE BŒUF SAUTÉE AU BORDEAUX

For two people
Take the cooked piece of meat (500 g, about 1 lb, of entrecôte in a piece) out of the pan.

Leave a little fat in the bottom and soften a tablespoon of chopped shallots in it.

Deglaze it with four tablespoons of Bordeaux or other red wine. Allow to boil and reduce by three-quarters of its volume. Add eight tablespoons of concentrated veal stock (No 1).

Allow to boil and reduce by half. Add 60 g (2 oz) of fresh butter, and remove the shallots or leave them in, whichever you prefer.

Cover the piece of meat with the sauce and decorate with two rounds of poached marrow.

Veal escalope with cream
ESCALOPE DE VEAU SAUTÉE Â LA CRÈME

For one person
Follow the same procedure but deglaze with vermouth or port without adding the shallot.

Add two large tablespoons of double cream.

Allow to reduce by half and lightly coat the escalope.

Shortcuts and sleights of hand   The sauté method, to be absolutely perfect, should be done at the last minute.

The size of the sauté pan should correspond with the quantity of meat to be cooked. If the base of the pan is not entirely covered with the food to be sautéd, the fat will rapidly start to burn in the empty space between the pieces of meat, and give a bitter taste to the sauce.

Small pieces (tournedos, cutlets, escalopes) are cooked fast in an uncovered pan.

Larger pieces, needing longer cooking (thigh and drumstick of chicken, pieces of rabbit), are cooked covered once they have browned.

How to succeed with fish 'à la meunière'

Cooking 'à la meunière' is applied to fish (trout, young pike, turbot, red mullet, sole, John Dory, hake, etc.) or foods such as brains; it is a form of cooking similar to sautéing, but is finished without deglazing. For example, take trout.

Truite à la meunière

In a frying-pan, or oval sauté pan roughly the size of the fish, put butter and oil, half-and-half – about 20–30 g ($\frac{3}{4}$–1 oz) altogether. This mixture ensures that the butter will not brown too rapidly. If you like you can add a whole, unpeeled, clove of garlic. The flavour of the garlic stays in the background, and adds subtle undertones to the dish.

Put the pan over the heat. Wipe the fish with absorbent kitchen paper to dry it. Season with salt and pepper and then lightly dip both sides in flour. Tap to remove excess flour.

Lay the fish in the hot fat. Let it cook over a gentle heat for about four minutes on each side, until it turns an attractive pale straw colour.

Remove the fish and keep it hot on a serving dish. If it has been properly cooked, the small amount of butter remaining in the pan will still be pale gold. Increase the heat and add a further 50 g (1¾ oz) of butter to transform it into 'beurre noisette'; the butter will become a golden-brown and stop 'singing' (because the water content has evaporated). Squeeze in the juice of a lemon which will make the butter froth up, and pour it immediately over the fish, having first removed the clove of garlic.

In my opinion fish should be cooked in the minimum of fat. Fish should keep its essential flavour of river or sea when it is cooked, and not be used just to mop up quantities of butter.

Sautéing and Cuisine Minceur

Thanks to non-stick pans, sautéing can easily be applied to Cuisine Minceur, since they help to avoid the use of fats. With care, the food can be cooked 'à sec', completely dry.

Although the food to be sautéd is in fact sealed, there is no caramelization to leave a residue of delicious juices in the bottom of the cooking pan. A little time in a marinade (*see page 88*) will make up for this lack quite pleasantly. If you want to use the classical technique to produce a sauté Minceur, you must take care:

To place the food on a piece of absorbent kitchen paper, after it has been cooked, to eliminate every last vestige of fat.

To pour all the fat from the pan in which the food was cooked, leaving nothing but the residue of juices on the bottom.

To reduce, by boiling, until almost totally evaporated, the spirits and wine used in deglazing, so that the alcohol is driven off, and only the aroma remains.

To use, as should be obvious, and as I recommend in my recipes, liaisons other than butter and cream.

Frying

Frying is a method which involves 'sealing and browning' and consists of plunging a food into a bath of hot fat or 'deep fat', brought up to a maximum temperature of 170°C/325°F (arachide oil, olive oil, lard, or rendered and clarified beef or veal kidney fat), and keeping it at this temperature until the food is cooked. Butter and margarine are not used because they break down and burn at these high temperatures. To make the process easier, the food to be cooked should be very dry, and the pieces small enough for the heat to penetrate to the centre fairly rapidly. It is also important to throw in only a small quantity at a time, so that the temperature of the fat is not suddenly lowered.

Frying without coating

Potatoes: pommes frites, straw potatoes, matchstick potatoes, potato chips of various kinds, soufflé potatoes.

Choux pastry: fritters of various kinds (beignets, pets de nonne).

Shortcrust: carnival fritters.

Bread doughs: brioche fritters.

Fried eggs.

Herbs: parsley, sorrel (these must be fried at a low temperature to conserve their colour).

Small birds: small chickens, ortolans.

Frying after coating

1 In Flour
Small fish. Larger fish cut in slices (steaks).

Method: Dip the food in milk, then season with salt, and dip in flour, tapping to remove surplus flour.

2 In Breadcrumbs
Chicken, Fish, Veal Escalopes.

Method: The food is coated with beaten egg mixed with oil, and then covered with dried breadcrumbs.

3 In Fritter Batter
Fruit fritters – (apple, apricot, banana), Vegetable fritters – (cauliflower, salsify), Meat fritters – (brains,) Fish fritters – (brandade de morue or purée of salt cod).

4 In Flaky Pastry
Truffles.

Tricks and sleights of hand

How to make successful chipped potatoes The potatoes (a firm yellow variety for preference) are cut into sticks of varying thicknesses – from 1 cm ($\frac{1}{2}$ in) thick for Pont Neuf potatoes to 3 mm ($\frac{1}{8}$ in) thick for matchstick potatoes – then washed in cold water and dried in a cloth.

Heat the oil or fat in a deep-frying pan until it reaches at least 150°C/300°F. Test the temperature by throwing a chip into the oil; if it rises to the surface almost immediately (in twenty-five seconds), the oil is ready.

Plunge the chips in the frying-basket and let them cook for seven to eight minutes. To test them, take out one chip and let it cool. If it is soft enough to crush between your finger and thumb, the chip is cooked.

Take them out with a slotted spoon or straining skimmer (or simply, in the frying-basket) and turn them on to a dish covered with a cloth, or with absorbent kitchen paper.

Raise the temperature of the oil to 170°C/325°F (but do not let it start smoking) and plunge the chips back, in the frying-basket, moving it round so that the chips stay separate. Two or three minutes is enough to make them golden-brown and crisp.

Take them out of the oil again, and put them once again on their dish, on which you have put a fresh cloth or absorbent paper. Sprinkle with fine salt, mixing them around (or better still, freshly ground salt from a salt mill.

It is the second dip in hotter oil which gives the chips their impermeable crust. They become puffed-up by the volatilization of the water trapped inside (the principle also used in making pommes soufflés).

It is essential to be able to control the temperature of the oil, which should never rise above 170°C/325°F. (Use an electric deep-frying pan with a thermostat or a special thermometer.)

EDITOR'S NOTE In England, Desirée or King Edward are two good chipping varieties.

How to fry small-fry successfully A fisherman friend, whose unusual profession is the re-stocking of the lakes and ponds of France with fish, has given me all sorts of obscure information about freshwater fish, including a beautiful way of frying small-fry. He doesn't flour them before frying, but simply strings them, like pearls on a necklace, on a reed from the riverbank, leaving them in the sun for a moment to dry; then he fries them. The result is a unique lightness.

Frying and Cuisine Minceur

Food fried in oil or deep fat absorbs some of the fat in which it is cooked.

Where oil is concerned, it is important to remember that 1 tablespoon of arachide oil (peanut oil) = 1 tablespoon of olive oil = 1 tablespoon of corn oil – which if it is 20 g or $\frac{3}{4}$ oz is inevitably 20 g or $\frac{3}{4}$ oz of fats.

In other words, there is no such thing as a 'miracle' or non-fat oil. At the same time, the digestibility of fried foods is very poor because of their high absorption of cooked fats. This method of cooking is therefore risky for the purposes of Cuisine Minceur.

If you must fry, follow a few commonsense rules:

Frying fat or oil should not be used more than four to five times.

After use, leave it in the pan to allow bits and impurities to settle and then pour the fat through a fine conical sieve into another container.

Always keep the fat or oil in an airtight container.

In Cuisine Minceur, the fat should not reach a higher temperature than 140°C/275°F.

A substitute for potatoes Finally, chipped potatoes can, in Cuisine Minceur, be replaced by sliced celeriac (containing very few calories) which is cooked in exactly the same way – the result is quite surprising.

Covered cooking

Covered cooking means cooking foods by sealing or by exchange (sometimes both together) either in their own juices or in an aromatic liquid which intensifies their flavours. Aromatic steam is formed, penetrating the food, which in turn releases its juices to enrich the accompanying liquid.

Cooking in steam

This form of cooking is by sealing alone, since the enriched steam of a flavoured or plain bouillon is used to cook the food, without it giving anything back in return. It is also possible to use plain salted water as the basic liquid.

The method requires a vessel about the size and shape of the food to be cooked – a saucepan, a fish-kettle or a couscoussier are all suitable – which is quarter filled with liquid – either flavoured or not, free of fat or not, according to what is required. A wire rack or pierced metal plate is put inside the pan over the boiling liquid allowing the steam to reach the food and cook it.

There are two unique ways of steaming using the same principle.

First, the food to be cooked is placed on a bed of seaweed (for saltwater fish) or wild herbs (for freshwater fish) and covered over with another layer, and then moistened with a few tablespoons of boiling liquid to start the cooking and help induce the steam.

Second, you can follow the same procedure for a leg of lamb, or a ham, replacing the seaweed with sweet-smelling hay.

If the steam is coming from a richly flavoured bouillon with good body or substance (chicken, meat or vegetable) it can be used as the basis for a sauce. This is not possible when cooking with seaweed or hay, when the liquid must be discarded.

Cooking en vessie (in a bladder or bag)

Cooking in a bladder – a kind of cooking by exchange – is another form of steaming. The bladder is used as a cooking utensil in which the food, which may be stuffed or not, is hermetically sealed (chicken, pot-au-feu – and why not leg of lamb?). Put a few tablespoons of really good, fruity stock – either chicken or beef, to which can be added one or two tablespoons of port, madeira, the liquid from a tin of truffles, or a whole truffle, fines herbes, dried mushrooms – in with the food to be cooked. The pig's bladder should be well washed and turned inside out (any disagreeable smells which could escape or exude during cooking will then be avoided).

The food is then slipped inside and the bladder is sewn up with a needle and strong thread. It is then pricked here and there with a needle to make tiny holes which act as safety valves – otherwise the bladder would come apart under the pressure. Then, *either*: submerge it in a pan of hot water, being careful to attach the end of the sewing thread to the handle of the pan, *or*: simply put it in the top half of a double boiler over boiling water (a couscoussier or large steamer is ideal).

These methods of steaming are rather quicker than others; a 2.5 kg ($5\frac{1}{2}$ lb) chicken will be tender and succulent in three-quarters to one hour.

EDITOR'S NOTE   Instead of using a pig's bladder for cooking 'en vessie', it is much more convenient and almost as effective to use a plastic roasting bag. In this case do not prick the bag before cooking (*see recipe* No 112 Poulet en Vessie).

Cooking en papillotes (in paper cases)

Cooking en papillote is another kind of cooking by exchange. Only the wrapping is different. The food may be **pre-cooked**: sweetbreads, boiling sausage, black pudding, andouillette, pork sausages, pig's trotters (either stuffed or plain), veal chop (covered with a mushroom purée or a mirepoix of vegetables), or **raw**: all fish and shellfish, small game-birds, ortolans, young rabbits, etc., slices (escalopes) of foie gras, potatoes, fungi (truffles, ceps, etc.), apples, bananas.

The food is hermetically sealed in a sheet of greaseproof paper or aluminium foil, oiled or not, which is folded round the food in the shape of an apple turnover or Cornish pasty, pleating the edges together so that the steam isn't lost.

Two examples
1. A whole peeled and cored apple, sprinkled with caster sugar and rum together with half a vanilla pod and a nut of butter is enclosed in a little bag made of aluminium foil and pushed into the glowing embers (or into an oven) – and cooked for fifteen minutes.
2. A slice of raw salmon, seasoned, is placed on a sheet of greaseproof paper, and flavoured with a teaspoon of finely chopped shallot and a tablespoon of vegetables – carrot, celery, mushrooms cut in julienne strips (*see recipe* No 87); sprinkled with a tablespoon of fish fumet, a tablespoon of white wine and lubricated with a nut of unsalted butter.

Fold the paper over in the form of a turnover, and cook in a very hot oven on an oiled ovenproof dish for six minutes.

These two methods of cooking – en vessie and en papillote – are always very special, because they intensify and refine the flavours and aromas trapped inside.

In fact it is in these two methods – en vessie and en papillote – these 'made-to-measure' garments – that exchange during cooking is brought to perfection.

Cooking en croûte (in a crust)

The aim of this method of cooking, as in the preceding methods, is to concentrate the flavours of the food being cooked – to which can be added various other ingredients – herbs, mushroom purée etc., by covering it with a pastry crust, which may or may not be intended to be eaten, and which follows its contours exactly.

In an edible crust In certain cases the food is sealed beforehand, so that the juices stay concentrated inside, and it should be cooled before enclosing it in the pastry. Examples: fillet of beef, saddle or leg of lamb (boned), chicken, capon, game (quail, woodcock, pheasant).

The meat or game is enclosed in pâté feuilletée (flaky pastry), brioche dough, shortcrust pastry or hot-water crust and baked in the oven.

The food can also be put raw into any of the pastries mentioned above; this is the most usual way of doing a pâté en croûte. In either case the top crust should have one or two holes made in it, into which you insert little funnels made of paper, about the diameter of your little finger. These act as chimneys through which steam can escape, to prevent cracking and breaking of the pastry during cooking. The pastry is brushed with beaten egg before cooking to give it a good colour.

EDITOR'S NOTE   Edible crusts are, of course, not admissible in Cuisine Minceur.

In a non-edible crust The one used most frequently is made of a mixture of dampened coarse salt, and a little flour, You can, having first sealed it in fat in a roasting-tin, bake a rib of beef (five or six ribs) entirely enclosed in a shell of salt, a slow and tenderizing process.

Chicken baked in salt

Cover the bottom of a cast-iron casserole lined with silver paper, with a layer of coarse salt, put the chicken on top and bury it completely with another layer of salt.

Bake it, uncovered, in a hot oven; when the cooking time is complete (one hour for a chicken of 1.5 kg (3¼ lb)) ease the 'cake' of salt from its pot and take out the chicken, which will be just as crisp as if it had been roasted.

Among country people in some places, it is an old custom to use clay for cooking small birds and some poultry such as game fowl, bantams, guinea fowl and pigeon. These birds are gutted *without being plucked*, seasoned, sometimes stuffed and then covered completely with a layer of moist clay. Then they are put in the embers of a fire, or baked in the oven, just as they are. The clay, during the cooking, forms a second, hermetically sealed oven. All that needs to be done before serving is to break the crust, in which all the feathers will have stuck, and release a bird as tender as you could desire.

Braising — Ragoûts

Braising is cooking 'by exchange' par excellence. First sealed all over in fat (except in the case of fish) the browned food, together with a mirepoix of vegetables, is moistened to half its depth with a well-flavoured liquid (light stock, wine, or concentrated veal stock, *see recipe* No 1).

A heavy cast-iron casserole (or even better, a braising pan) is hermetically sealed to help the cooking, which should be *long*, *slow*, and *even*, gradually tenderizing the fibres in the food and, with the help of the juices which run out, adding an extra succulence to the cooking liquid which becomes a rich and aromatic sauce.

How to braise successfully

Take, for example, a piece of braising beef (top rump). Ask the butcher to lard the meat (this operation consists of inserting six or eight long strips of back fat – about 1 cm (just under ½ in) across, along the grain of the meat – right through the joint to 'marble' the meat thoroughly). This fat will help enhance tenderness and flavour right through to the heart of the meat.

If you decide to braise an ox-cheek (not very popular, but still a marvellous piece for braising), its own naturally gelatinous texture is enough to keep the meat succulent without larding. Marinate your chosen piece of beef (*see* marinades **Nos 12-16**) overnight to impregnate it with the aromas of the wine and the flavours of the vegetables and herbs.

Take the beef out of the marinade, wipe it dry with kitchen paper or a cloth, then heat a little oil in a heavy cast-iron casserole and brown the meat, together with a knuckle of veal, to a deep golden-brown.

Once the meat has formed an even crust on the outside, remove it from the pan and put in the vegetables from the marinade, or even better, the same quantity of mirepoix together with a bouquet garni and two unpeeled cloves of garlic, for five or six minutes, then place the piece of beef on top.

Add the liquid from the marinade, strained through a conical strainer, and boil it until reduced to half its original volume. Then pour in enough veal stock or light beef stock to come half-way up the sides of the meat.

Season very lightly, since the flavours intensify during the course of cooking. As the liquid comes to simmering point, cover the pan, and take care that the cooking remains gentle and even throughout. This can be done either in the oven or on the top of the stove, in which latter case put an asbestos disc or simmering disc under the casserole. The meat is cooked when a skewer will pierce it effortlessly.

Lift the meat on to a serving dish with the help of a skimmer. The sauce, which has become very concentrated during the course of the cooking, must be strained and skimmed to remove every trace of fat. Use a ladle to pour the juices into a conical strainer, which can be lined with absorbent paper. Finally, let the sauce reduce further to obtain the exact thickness required.

General comments Larger pieces of veal (saddle, loin, or whole leg) can be cooked in the same way, provided that the sealing is done without browning the meat at all (braisage à blanc). Veal sweetbreads (first soaked in cold water, but not necessarily blanched) can be sealed and browned or sealed 'à blanc' without being browned. Braised vegetables are usually put into an ovenproof dish, with fat or oil and herbs, and concentrated chicken stock or bouillon may be added. They are then covered with pork rind or bacon fat and cooked with the lid on.

The braising of fish is rather different – they are not cooked in a covered pot, but laid in a buttered dish and covered over with chopped shallots, then moistened to half their depth with a half-and-half mixture of white or red wine and fish fumet, and then cooked in the oven, covered either with oiled greaseproof paper or buttered aluminium foil.

As a rule, to keep it succulent, it is wise to baste the food several times with its own braising liquid during the course of cooking. Even when cooked for a very long time, braised foods always have a splendid flavour; the meat will fall to pieces and can be eaten with a spoon, 'à la cuillère'. It was in this way that the Duc de Richelieu, towards the end of his life, somewhat toothless, but still a shameless gourmand, asked for his pigeons to be cooked.

Making a ragoût uses the same method as braising, but is used for meat or poultry that has first been cut in pieces (bœuf bourguignon, navarin of lamb, veal marengo). After having been sealed and browned, the pieces of meat are sometimes sprinkled with flour (which has preferably been browned in the oven, *see page 76*) to help thicken the juices.

Enclosed cooking in Cuisine Minceur

Steaming This particular method has distinct advantages. It is a highly aromatic method of cooking, which causes the food to release its fat, whilst conserving its essential nutritious elements (mineral salts and vitamins) and its natural flavours.

Cooking en vessie (in a bladder) or en papillote (in a paper parcel) This method, thanks to the perfect blending of flavours of the different ingredients that are brought together, is a simple and very fragrant way of cooking without fat.

Cooking en croûte (in a crust) Cooking in salt and in clay can both be used.

Braising and ragoûts Contrary to what might be supposed, this way of cooking can be used in the repertoire of Cuisine Minceur; a few extra precautions are all that is necessary:

The meat must be trimmed of every trace of fat.

Once it has been browned, throw out the remaining oil from the casserole and wipe the meat with absorbent paper before returning it to the pan together with the braising liquid.

If some fat still remains, chill the dish overnight in the refrigerator, and the following day remove the fine layer of fat from the top with a spoon.

Poaching

Poaching a food means immersing it in boiling liquid (water, light stock, stock, fish fumet, court-bouillon or syrup). It can be done by putting the food into a cold liquid, into liquid that is gently simmering (shivering), or into liquid that is boiling furiously.

Starting with a cold liquid

This is cooking 'by exchange', with or without browning. Starting off with a cold liquid prevents sealing and allows the juices and flavours to be released to enhance the surrounding bouillon. Pot-au-feu is cooked in this way in order to impart the maximum flavour to the bouillon, somewhat to the detriment of the meat; so is concentrated veal stock (No 1) (although the bones are first browned in the oven) and fish fumet (No 3).

If on the other hand you want to retain the moisture and flavour of the piece of food to be cooked, you should enrich the bouillon by adding seasonings, vegetables, wine, concentrated meat or fish glazes as seem appropriate. The food will thus be compensated for any loss of flavour.

Examples Fish poached in court-bouillon or fish fumet; chicken poached in chicken stock; brains poached in a vinegary court-bouillon. If the food being cooked is going to be served cold, it is a good idea to let it cool in its own liquid, after cooking for a slightly shorter time than usual.

Pulses (haricot beans, lentils, split peas) which have first been scrupulously picked over and washed, and sometimes soaked beforehand, are started in cold water, which is then brought to the boil, skimmed, salted with coarse salt and flavoured with carrots, onions, a clove and a bouquet garni.

Starting with a hot liquid

This is cooking by sealing without browning.

Cooking in a hot liquid preserves intact practically all the flavour and nutritious value of the food.

Vegetables   must be cooked uncovered in plenty of fast-boiling salted water.

Cooking fish 'au bleu'   For this dish the fish must start not only fresh, but actually alive. The fish is killed by a quick blow on the head, cleaned and sprinkled with vinegar (to give it its beautiful blue colour) and plunged straight into simmering court-bouillon.

Cooking boiled and poached eggs

Cooking fresh or dried pasta and rice   After cooking take care to rinse the food in warm or even cold water to remove the starch, which would make it stick together.

Poaching fruit   (pears, apples, peaches, apricots, raspberries, etc.) in a syrup, which is usually flavoured with vanilla.

Shortcuts and sleights of hand

How to cook haricot verts and keep their colour   It is important to know that some vegetables, of which the French bean is one, contain certain natural acids which on contact with heat start a chain reaction which changes their colour from a beautiful tender green to khaki. These acids are volatile and must be allowed to escape, so that they do not have time to alter the colour of the beans.

The best method is as follows: boil the water in a tinned copper or a stainless-steel pan (avoid metals which react with the water) and salt it with 20 g ($\frac{3}{4}$ oz) of coarse salt per litre ($1\frac{3}{4}$ pints). Throw the French beans into the fast-boiling water, which should be cooked as fast as possible and uncovered, to prevent the build-up of volatile acids.

French beans should be eaten 'al dente', that is to say, offering a slight resistance when you bite into them. This method avoids over-cooking which destroys not only the colour, but the flavour and vitamins too.

Very young French beans, freshly picked, are cooked in four minutes; a few minutes longer if they are larger and not so fresh. Scoop them quickly out of the boiling water with a skimmer and douse them in a bowl of iced water for ten seconds; this immediately stops them from cooking any longer, and also removes some of the salt. They are deliberately oversalted to help cook them quickly and give them a fine colour.

How to cook tender asparagus   It is common knowledge that you don't eat the whole stalk when you are eating asparagus; the tips are fragile and the bottom of the stalk very stringy – so this part usually ends up left on the plate.

Here is a simple way of putting matters right: once you have washed and pared the asparagus, stand them, all tips level and pointing upwards, in a deep tin which is pierced all over with holes to make it into a sort of colander. All that is necessary is to lower the tin into boiling water in three stages, each one taking three minutes, or more according to the size of the asparagus. If it is very fresh and on the slender side, each stage will take three minutes, with first the ends, then the middles and finally the tips of the asparagus being cooked.

This means the ends, which are toughest, will have nine minutes, the middles six minutes and the tips three minutes, and the sticks of asparagus will be evenly tender from top to bottom.

Thicker or less fresh asparagus will take longer, but the principle remains the same.

Poaching and Cuisine Minceur

Poached does not necessarily mean 'boiled' in water, with all its unappetizing, even depressing associations.

A lobster cooked in salt water, in faithful imitation of seawater, will give the best possible account of its own natural flavour. Vegetables cooked in the same way, and enriched after cooking with a sliver of butter and a few finely chopped herbs are an extremely delicious dish in their own right. Get into the habit of washing them rapidly and don't leave them soaking for any length of time or their mineral salts will escape into the water. Cook them as I have described above for French beans. The water in which they have cooked becomes a bouillon itself, which can be used, for example, in the making of soups.

If anything fatty is poached in this way, the fat melts and floats to the surface, and is easily removed either with a skimming spoon or small ladle or with absorbent kitchen paper.

In addition to its other merits, poached food is extremely easy to digest.

Stocks, Liaisons and Sauces

'La renommée de la Cuisine Française est née de ses Sauces. Le Saucier en est le Magicien. Dans ce jeu alchimique, les Fonds sont les Racines qui leur permettent de fleurir et les Liaisons, l'onctuosité, Catalyse voluptueuse, qui leur permet de s'épanouir. Ils sont l'une des Pierres Angulaires de la Cuisine.'

The three essential stocks

There is no such thing as a really high quality commercial stock, or fond, whether veal, chicken or fish. To my way of thinking this is a great lack, because with this one aid the cook at home could realize his or her ideal and make all those sauces which flaunt themselves tantalizingly on the pages of the great professional cookery books.

But in the meantime, don't despair. It is not as difficult as it looks. In just the same way as you lightly undertake the annual ritual of making jam for the family, I urge you to give up a couple of afternoons to making up these three recipes for fonds. Once you have mastered the somewhat mysterious art of sauce-making, you will be very pleased with yourself, and your friends will be faint with envy.

1. *Golden veal stock*
FOND BLOND DE VEAU

Ingredients

2 litres (3½ pints) cold water
1 kg (2¼ lb) broken veal bones (shin and knuckle bones)
500 g (1 lb) beef trimmings ⎫
50 g (1¾ oz) uncooked ham ⎪ (all cut
100 g (3½ oz) carrots ⎬ into little cubes as
100 g (3½ oz) mushrooms ⎪ for a
50 g (1¾ oz) onions ⎪ mirepoix)
15 g (½ oz) celery ⎭

½ teaspoon chervil
½ teaspoon tarragon
1 whole clove garlic, crushed
1 chopped shallot
1 bouquet garni
1 tablespoon tomato purée
2 fresh tomatoes, deseeded
7 tablespoons dry white wine

1 Brown the bones in a roasting dish in a very hot oven for fifteen minutes, without fat ('à sec'). Turn them several times whilst they are browning with a metal spoon.

2 Add the ham, trimmings, carrots, mushrooms, onions, celery, herbs, garlic and shallot, return the dish to the oven and allow the vegetables to sweat (cook without browning) for five minutes.

3 Put the bones and vegetables into a saucepan or small deep pot, pour on the white wine and let it boil until it has almost evaporated. Add the cold water, fresh tomatoes and tomato purée and the bouquet garni.

4 Let it cook slowly, uncovered, for three or four hours. During this time, take great care to keep the surface perfectly clear of fat and scum by skimming regularly. Then strain the liquid, about a litre ($1\frac{3}{4}$ pints), through a conical strainer into a bowl in which it can be kept until it is needed. To ensure that it is completely free of fat, put the cooled stock in the refrigerator for an hour or more. Any remaining fat will rise and solidify and can easily be removed.

Demi-glace To give the stock made as described above a more substantial consistency, it can be very lightly thickened in the following way.

5 Dilute a tablespoon of cornflour or arrowroot in three tablespoons of water or white wine. Gradually pour this mixture into the boiling veal stock, stirring with a wire whisk to obtain a smooth liaison.

6 Let it come gently back to the boil, and simmer until the stock has reduced by half. The stock will once again froth up at this stage, throwing up any remaining impurities which will rise and form a greyish-brown scum on top; this can be lifted off with a perforated spoon.

Glace de viande The same unctuous quality can be achieved without a thickening agent; it is simply a matter of simmering the basic veal stock gently on a very low heat, and skimming it regularly all the time. The glaze is perfect when it will cover a spoon dipped into it with a smooth and glistening coat, by which time it will have reduced to about one-tenth of its original volume.

Uses for basic stock In many dishes served in their own sauce; either as the liquid used in the recipe, or as an extra ingredient in the cooking liquid: ragoûts, coq-au-vin, matelotes, fricassées, etc.

Uses for demi-glace As a base for sauces in which either spirits or wine, heated and reduced, are used to dissolve, or deglaze, the caramelized juices which have stuck to the bottom of the pan in which meat was cooked, for instance, top rump of beef cooked in red wine.

Uses for glace de viande   Its light touch can improve a characterless sauce and make it succulent and generous.

NOTE   This stock can be made ahead of time and kept in a glass or plastic container to be used as needed. It will keep in the refrigerator for eight days, or in the freezer, or in small glass preserving jars (sterilize for sixty minutes) which will keep some months in a cool place. Game stock and glace de gibier are made in exactly the same way as golden veal stock and glace de viande, but with bones and trimmings of game. In addition to the usual ingredients, five juniper berries and a sprig of sage are added.

2. *Pale chicken stock*
FOND BLANC DE VOLAILLE

For one litre (1¾ pints) of stock

Ingredients

2 litres (3½ pints) cold water
1 kg (2¼ lb) of crushed chicken carcases and giblets (roasting or boiling chickens)
100 g (3½ oz) of mushrooms, thinly sliced
100 g (3½ oz) of carrots, thinly sliced
50 g (2 oz) onion, whole

1 chopped shallot
1 leek, sliced
1 small stick celery
1 whole clove of garlic, crushed
1 bouquet garni
1 clove
7 tablespoons dry white wine

1   Put the crushed carcases in a pan with the vegetables and garlic. Add the white wine, bring it to the boil and boil until it has almost totally evaporated.

2   Add the cold water, bouquet garni and the onion stuck with the clove. Allow to simmer gently, uncovered, for three hours, skimming frequently.

3   Strain the remaining stock through a conical strainer and put in a cool place until it is needed.

Uses   As the liquid element in dishes cooked in pale sauces (blanquettes, fricassées, poules au blanc, etc.), in some soups and in the cooking of some vegetables (rice, lettuce, etc.).

NOTE   White veal stock is made in exactly the same way, replacing the chicken carcases with the same weight of veal bones (blanched by boiling one minute). Personally, I prefer the subtlety of chicken stock.

2a. *Golden Poultry stock*
FOND BLOND DE VOLAILLE

This is made like golden veal stock (**No 1**) replacing the veal bones with browned poultry carcases (preferably duck). Do not forget to add one tablespoon of tomato purée.

Uses For the moistening of certain chicken or other poultry dishes (poulet au vinaigre, etc.).

3. *Fish stock, or fish fumet*
FOND OU FUMET DE POISSON

For one litre (1¾ pints) of stock

Ingredients

1½ litres (2½ pints) cold water
1 kg (2¼ lb) fish heads and bones (sole gives the best flavour, turbot, brill, whiting. Avoid oily fish)
1 chopped shallot
100 g (3½ oz) onions, finely sliced
50 g (2 oz) mushrooms, finely sliced

1 bouquet garni containing plenty of parsley
25 g (1 oz) butter
1½ tablespoons arachide oil (peanut oil)
7 tablespoons dry white wine
salt

1 Soak the fish bones in cold water to remove blood, unless they are extremely fresh. If you use fish heads, remove the gills.

2 Sweat the vegetables and roughly crushed fishbones in the oil and butter for five minutes without browning them.

3 Moisten with the dry white wine and boil until it has almost totally evaporated.

4 Pour in the cold water, and add salt and the bouquet garni. Bring it back to the boil, and allow to simmer, uncovered, for twenty minutes. Skim the surface every time a layer of scum forms on the top of the liquid.

5 Strain the fumet (there should be about 1 litre (1¾ pints) remaining) through a conical strainer, or a fine sieve into a bowl, pressing the bones gently with a spoon. Cover and put in a cool place until it is needed.

Jellied fish stock – Glace de Poisson To obtain a concentrated fish glaze proceed in the same way as you did for glace de viande. That is:

6 Simmer the fumet gently to reduce it, skimming frequently.

7 Remove from the heat when about seven tablespoons of the syrupy, glossy liquid remains. Put in a cool place.

Uses Fumet is used to moisten fish dishes cooked with a small quantity of liquid, and braised fish. Jellied fish stock can be used in the same way as glace de viande, but in this case of course, with fish dishes.

Simple methods of making the basic stocks

Chicken stock cubes can not only be used effectively to replace classical chicken fonds, but they can also be used as a base for two other traditional stocks.

---

4. *Simple veal stock*
FOND DE VEAU

Ingredients

1 tablespoon oil
1 large carrot
1 large onion
100 g (3½ oz) button mushrooms
1 calf's foot
bouquet garni, with plenty of parsley
  stalks
1 clove

1 large tomato
15 g (½ oz) dried fungi
1 teaspoon tomato purée
1 teaspoon arôme Patrelle (*optional*)
2 litres (3½ pints) cold water
3 chicken stock cubes
1 level teaspoon cornflour

1 Heat the oil in a saucepan and brown the carrot, onion and button mushrooms, all cleaned and cut into 1 cm (½ in) cubes.

2 Add the calf's foot cut into eight pieces, the bouquet garni, clove, tomato, cut in half, dried fungi (ceps, morels, etc.), one teaspoon of tomato purée and a teaspoon of arôme Patrelle. Add the cold water and the chicken stock cubes. Simmer, uncovered, for two-and-a-half hours.

Skim five or six times during cooking to remove the scum which rises to the surface.

3   At the end of this time, strain the remaining half litre (scant 1 pint) of bouillon through a conical sieve into a clean saucepan. Bring it back to the boil, whisking into the liquid a level teaspoon of cornflour dissolved in a little water.

The veal stock is ready and it is almost demi-glace de viande. It is excellent! Put it in a covered bowl in the refrigerator and remove the layer of fat from the top on the following day.

EDITOR'S NOTE   Like the classic veal stock (No 1) this stock can be frozen, refrigerated for a limited period or stored in sterilized jars. Arôme Patrelle is a form of gravy browning only occasionally available outside France, and its purpose is mainly to colour the stock, so don't worry if you can't obtain it.

---

5. *Simple fish fumet*

Ingredients

1 tablespoon olive oil	1 calf's foot
1 large carrot	bouquet garni
1 large onion	5 peppercorns
100 g (3½ oz) button mushrooms	1 clove
Broken-up bones of 6 sole or other firm white fish	2 litres (3½ pints) cold water
	3 chicken stock cubes

1   Heat the olive oil in a saucepan and add the carrot, onion and button mushrooms, all peeled and cut into 1 cm (½ in) cubes. Sweat the vegetables without letting them brown.

2   Add the broken-up fish bones, the calf's foot cut into eight pieces, the small bouquet garni, peppercorns and clove. Add the cold water and stock cubes.

3   Allow to simmer, uncovered, for two hours. Skim five or six times during cooking to remove the scum which rises to the surface. At the end of the cooking, strain the remaining 500 ml (scant 1 pint) of stock through a conical strainer.

This stock is astonishingly richly flavoured, and it can be diluted with 250 ml (½ pint) of water before use.

Liaisons and sauces

Liaisons using cereals and other starches   The required thickening of the basic liquid is obtained by addition of the starch found in various flours, which include wheat, maize (cornflour), barley, potato, rice and arrow-root. On contact with heat, in the presence of moisture, the starch will bring about the necessary thickening and create the liaison. This method of thickening sauces is disappearing, although, strictly speaking it is, when subtly made, far more easily digested than any sauce thickened exclusively with butter and reduced cream. In any case, my personal opinions prevent me from using either of these methods in ordinary gourmet cooking, and very rarely in Cuisine Minceur, so I am describing them mainly to show the basic principles involved.

Liaison with a cooked roux   Whether it is brown, light brown or white, a roux is a mixture of equal quantities of melted butter and flour, the combination of which will enable them to bind or thicken the chosen liquid. (If only half the quantity of butter is used, it will produce a sauce lighter in cholesterol.)

The change from white to brown roux is brought about by stirring it with a whisk over a moderate heat until it has reached the required colour. (The simultaneous heating of butter and flour together causes the browning of the roux.)

This can be achieved in another, better way which is both lighter and healthier – because it contains butter which has not been heated to high temperatures.

It is done quite simply, by melting the butter, as in the making of a white roux, and adding the same weight of torrefied flour (farine tor-réfiée) – that is, flour which has previously been spread out on a dish and cooked in a slow oven (150°C/300°F/Mark 2) to a chestnut-brown.

Making a White Roux

To make one litre (1¾ pints) of sauce

Ingredients

75 g (2½ oz) butter **or** 35 g (1¼ oz) for the lighter version of the sauce

75 g (2½ oz) flour

1 litre (1¾ pints) of liquid (milk, light chicken stock, light beef stock, fish fumet, etc., according to the dish)

1   Melt the butter in a saucepan (do not let it brown). Add the flour and whisk them together rapidly, to obtain a homogenous paste.

2   Allow the roux to cool a little, then gradually add the boiling liquid, whisking all the time to prevent lumps.

3   Bring the mixture slowly back to the boil and let it simmer for twenty minutes; the sauce, rather heavy at the start, becomes lighter during cooking.

Uses Béchamel Sauce, Chicken Velouté, Fish Velouté, Sauce for Civets, etc.

The process of 'crusting' – sprinkling with white flour and 'singeing' in the oven – pieces of meat which have already been sealed and browned, which is used in the making of ragoûts, stews (estouffades), and brown fricassées, works on more or less the same principle as the making of a roux.

Liaison with an uncooked starch   If a sauce seems too thin, it can be slightly thickened by adding a little potato flour dissolved in cold water or white wine; gradually add the mixture to the boiling liquid to be thickened, stirring rapidly all the time. Allow between two and eight tablespoons of potato flour to every litre ($1\frac{3}{4}$ pints) of liquid. Allow to boil for about fifteen minutes.

Liaison with a mixture of uncooked flour and butter or cream (beurre manié, crème manié)   To obtain the same result as in the above method, but giving extra velvetiness and flavour, a sauce can be thickened with beurre manié or crème manié. This is the equivalent of an 'uncooked roux'. Take either butter or cream, cold, mix it well with flour – one-third flour, two-thirds butter or cream – and add it to the simmering liquid in little bits, stirring all the time with a whisk, until it has reached the required texture. It thickens almost immediately.

Liaison with egg yolks   This is done by beating egg yolks and mixing them with some of the liquid to be thickened. Return this mixture to the hot liquid and whisk over a moderate heat. On no account must it boil. Heating to more than 70°C (160°F) will coagulate the egg and cause it to separate.

Uses Velouté Soups, Sauce Poulette, Blanquettes, etc.

A Cuisine Minceur egg-yolk liaison or Light Sabayon Whisk together four egg yolks and six tablespoons of cold water. As the whisk

77

leavens the sauce with air, the mixture greatly increases in volume. Now, simply whisk the mixture into the boiling sauce or soup to be thickened: the aerated egg yolk coagulates on contact with the heat, and gives the whole thing a great feeling of lightness and volume. (*See* No 91 – John Dory with Sabayon Sauce.)

Liaison with blood or coral   Use the same method as before, replacing the egg yolks with blood from pork, game, fish (lampreys), etc., or the coral from lobster, etc. (sometimes mixed beforehand with crème fraîche or butter). Do not allow to boil. (*See* Sauce Américaine No 10.)

Uses   Coq-au-Vin, Civets of game, Civets of fish, matelotes, Homard à l'Américaine.

Liaisons using butter or crème fraîche   The liaison using butter is intended to thicken and, more important, to enrich the sauce and to make it more unctuous. It is simply a matter of slipping little dabs of butter into the sauce to be thickened, over a very gentle heat, whilst swirling the whole pan – a sauté pan in this case – round in a rapid circular movement.

Another equally effective method is to boil the two elements to be united (sauce and butter) over a fierce heat; this method will give a less creamy, but at the same time, a glossier sauce. To make a liaison with crème fraîche, all that is necessary is to bring the mixture (cream and the sauce) to the boil and let it reduce.

A liaison using foie gras   Like the liaison using butter, this is a mixture of two-thirds tinned or freshly cooked foie gras to one-third double cream, which is incorporated into the sauce, away from the heat, with a whisk.

The cream/foie gras mixture is made in a few seconds in a liquidizer, or simply by working them together with a fork.

Liaison by emulsion   A liaison by emulsion is a successful and homogenous combination of two products that are naturally incompatible, for example: water and fat – oil, butter, cream, etc.

A third element – unrelated to either of the original products, but sympathetic to them – takes on the role of go-between, or catalyst and brings the two together. This element can be egg yolk, mustard, etc.

Cold emulsified sauces (mayonnaise and its derivatives) and hot emulsified sauces (béarnaise, hollandaise and their derivatives) are sometimes a bit risky for the cook at home; to make them less capricious, I have developed the detailed recipes you will find at the end of this chapter.

Liaisons using vegetable purées This liaison, useful in Cuisine Minceur, is made by adding a certain quantity of finely puréed cooked vegetables to the liquid to be thickened. The vegetables are cooked, either with the meat or fish whose sauce they are to thicken, or separately.

These purée-liaisons are rich in vitamins and are extremely digestible since the cellulose in the vegetables is broken down after they have been cooked. The subtle and specific mixtures of vegetables which make these liaisons are based on completely new combinations of flavours. They form, in fact, one of the fundamental principles of Cuisine Minceur and you will find them used in many of my recipes.

It is also possible to experiment with new flavours based on selective combinations of fruits and vegetables.

Liaisons using yoghurt or fromage blanc You will see later on in the book that this is another liaison crucial to the art of Cuisine Minceur, but not used to excess, since yoghurt can leave a tart taste and non-fat fromage blanc can leave a slight sensation of dryness on the palate – which can to some extent be compensated for.

Other forms of liaison Some liaisons are made with products made expressly for the purpose – such as alginates, made from seaweeds, or edible gums such as gum arabic, etc.

Some star sauces from traditional French cuisine

Here are a few timeless recipes deeply loved in my country. First of all there is the ubiquitous Mayonnaise, then lightest of sauces, Béarnaise, and next their strongly flavoured country cousin Beurre Blanc. L'Américaine with its primitive taste, comes straight from the sea, and last, sensual and earthy, is Sauce Périgueux.

EDITOR'S NOTE With the exception of Sauce Américaine (No 10) these sauces are not used in Cuisine Minceur. But the underlying principles are the same and apply to the delicate Cuisine Minceur versions which will be found in the chapter dealing with sauces – pages 102–16.

6. *Mayonnaise*
(*For Minceur version see No 26*)

Basic ingredients

1 egg
1 teaspoon dry mustard
salt
freshly-milled pepper (cayenne or
white pepper)

200 ml ($\frac{1}{3}$ pint) oil (arachide, olive or
whichever you prefer)
a few drops of vinegar (preferably
wine vinegar or, if using olive oil,
fresh lemon juice is better)

1   Separate the egg yolk from the white. Put the yolk into a bowl and add the mustard, salt and pepper – perferably white as it will not show up as black specks in the mayonnaise.

2   Beat, with a whisk or stir with a wooden spoon. When the ingredients are well blended, pour in the oil in a thin stream, stirring energetically and flexibly all the time. As the sauce thickens progressively, gradually stir in the vinegar or lemon juice to thin it.

3   Beat in the remaining oil and taste for seasoning.

Shortcuts and sleights of hand
Use egg yolks and oil at the same temperature (preferably room temperature).
    Do not add the oil too quickly.
    If the mayonnaise has curdled, mix it, a little at a time, into some French mustard.
    Keep the sauce in a cool place, but not in the refrigerator – the oil will seize up and the other ingredients will separate.
    Mayonnaise makes a succulent binding for macedoines of vegetables or meat. Made 'piquant', it is good with cold meat or fish. But it really becomes more interesting when other elements are added to give it character. Here are a few variations.
Sauce Aïoli   Mayonnaise made with olive oil, puréed raw garlic, and a little cooked mashed potato.
Sauce Antiboise   Mayonnaise made with olive oil, garlic, coriander, chervil and parsley.
Sauce Andalouse   Mayonnaise with puréed tomatoes and little cubes of red or green pimento.
Sauce Tartare   Mayonnaise with capers, gherkins, onions, parsley, chervil and tarragon.

Sauce Vendangeur Mayonnaise with red wine and chopped shallots.
Sauce Vincent Mayonnaise with sorrel purée, parsley, chervil, watercress, chives and chopped hard-boiled eggs.

---

7. *Béarnaise sauce*
(*For Minceur versions see Nos 36 and 37*)

For eight people

Ingredients for the reduction
7 tablespoons red wine vinegar
2 tablespoons chopped tarragon (out
of season, use either tarragon
preserved in vinegar (make your
own) or frozen tarragon)
1 teaspoon chopped chervil
salt
1 heaped teaspoon peppercorns,
coarsely crushed

*Ingredients for the liaison and for
finishing the sauce*
5 egg yolks

300 g (10½ oz) butter (plain unsalted
or clarified) **or** double cream **or**
whipping cream

Equipment
1 stainless-steel bain-marie
1 heavy saucepan or sauté pan of a
suitable size
1 conical strainer

Depending on whether you have chosen to make the sauce with clarified butter, plain butter or cream, there are three different methods of procedure.

a To obtain clarified butter, melt the butter slowly in a pan, it will become transparent, like olive oil, and form a deposit of whitish milk solids on the bottom of the pan.

b When using plain butter, all that is necessary is to bring it to room temperature (20°C/68°F) without letting it get too soft, and to drop it in hazelnut-sized pieces into the 'reduction' ingredients. I like the second method better, because the presence of the milk solids gives the sauce a 'fruitier' butter flavour.

c The third recipe uses double cream or whipping cream – the latter gives a wonderfully light sauce.

In methods **b** and **c**, because the butter or cream is used at a lower temperature, the pan should be left over the heat rather longer.

1   Put the ingredients for the reduction (vinegar, shallots, pepper, and herbs) in a heavy saucepan and bring them to the boil.

2   Reduce rapidly for five minutes (you should now have two or three tablespoons of liquid).

3   Allow it to cool, and in the meantime separate the egg yolks from the whites.

4   Add the egg yolks to the reduction, place the pan in a bain-marie over a gentle heat, and start beating the mixture vigorously with a whisk. Gradually raise the temperature to 65°C/150°F (the temperature at which egg yolks start to coagulate – the back of your finger when lightly dipped into the mixture, can easily stand the heat). The function of the whisk in this essential part of the operation is to keep the egg yolks at a uniform temperature as they coagulate, and to incorporate air to aerate the sauce and make it lighter.

5   The mixture now thickens and becomes creamy; when the strokes of the whisk leave clear traces on the bottom of the pan, start to incorporate, a little at a time – either the tepid clarified butter, the cold butter cut in little pieces, or the cream, whisking continuously.

Keep the pan, covered, over a gentle heat (60°C/140°F) on one side of the hotplate – take care not to let it stand in too hot a bain-marie. The sauce can either be served just as it is, or strained through a conical sieve, and freshly chopped tarragon and chervil added.

Shortcuts and sleights of hand
What can go wrong during the making of this recipe?
    If the egg yolks become too thick, the temperature has risen too high; add a few drops of cold water.
    If the egg yolks froth up but do not become thick and creamy, the temperature is too low, increase the heat a little.
    Sauce béarnaise is a succulent accompaniment for: poached eggs, poached or grilled fish, grilled meat, and asparagus. It can also be varied almost infinitely by the addition of various complementary ingredients:

Sauce Choron is béarnaise enriched, during or after whisking, with roughly-chopped tomato pulp (*see page 220*) – (two tablespoons of tomato to 300 g (10½ oz) of butter).
Sauce Arlésienne has the same ingredients as Choron, plus anchovy essence.
Sauce Foyot is béarnaise enriched with two teaspoons of glace de viande (meat glaze).

Sauce Paloise, a béarnaise in which, in the reduction ingredients, the tarragon is replaced by fresh mint.

Sauce Tyrolienne is béarnaise in which the butter in the ingredients for the liaison is replaced by oil and a small amount of tomato purée to colour the sauce.

Sauce Hollandaise is a béarnaise in which the reduction is replaced by plain cold water – one teaspoon – and the sauce is finished by adding lemon juice – half a lemon for every 300 g (10½ oz) of butter.

Sauce Mousseline is a hollandaise sauce to which whipped cream is added at the end.

Sauce Maltaise is a hollandaise sauce to which the juice and blanched, shredded peel of an orange are added.

Sauce Moutarde is a hollandaise sauce to which mustard is added.

---

8. *Beurre blanc I*
(*For the Cuisine Minceur version see No 35*)

For four people

Ingredients
½ glass water
½ glass wine vinegar
2 tablespoons chopped shallots
250 g (9 oz) unsalted or slightly
  salted butter
salt, pepper

Equipment
1 small saucepan or sauté pan with a
  heavy base
1 small whisk

1   Put the water, vinegar and finely chopped shallots into the pan over a moderate heat. Reduce the mixture until it is the consistency of a moist purée. Allow to cool a little, letting the temperature fall to about 60°C/140°F.

2   Gradually whisk in the cold butter, straight from the refrigerator, dropping it in, a little bit at a time. The mixture will become creamy. Finish incorporating the butter, whisking more vigorously and slightly increasing the heat under the pan to make up for the drop in temperature caused by adding the chilled butter.

3   Season with salt and pepper before serving. You can strain this sauce through a conical strainer to remove the shallots, but personally I leave them to preserve the authentic rustic quality of the beurre blanc.

9. *Beurre blanc II*

This shorter method shows exactly how the intense boiling of the liquid is enough to make a spontaneous liaison between water and butter, without the help of a whisk.

1 Use the same ingredients as before, but only evaporate two-thirds of the water and vinegar.

2 Allow to boil over a fierce heat and put a 250 g (9 oz) block of cold butter in the middle of the liquid.

3 This will gradually melt and be carried off into the seething liquid, thickening it as it does so.

4 The beurre blanc is now made, but to make it lighter still, add four tablespoons of cold water, at the last moment, whisking the mixture vigorously to a froth.

NOTE We shall see, later on, how useful the next sauce is in Cuisine Minceur. Like the three great stocks (*see pages 70–74*), it can be made in advance and preserved (either by freezing or in sterilized preserving jars).

When made with lobster, the cost is high; to lower the price it is possible to use crab instead of that noble crustacean, the lobster, in which case it should be accompanied by bones of sole, heads of Dublin Bay prawns, freshwater crayfish, etc.

10. *Sauce Américaine*

For six people

Main ingredients
1 raw lobster of 800 g (1¾ lb)
1 tablespoon olive oil
1 tablespoon arachide oil
1 tablespoon cold butter
2 diced shallots
1 diced carrot
half an onion, diced
1 unpeeled clove of garlic, crushed
   whole
1 bouquet garni containing a sprig of
   tarragon
3 fresh tomatoes, skinned, deseeded
   and coarsely chopped
1 tablespoon tomato purée
3 tablespoons armagnac, **or** cognac
250 ml (just under ½ pint) white wine

250 ml (just under ½ pint) fish fumet
   (No 3) **or** water
salt, pepper, a pinch of cayenne pepper

Ingredients for the liaison
50 g (1¾ oz) unsalted butter, crushed
   with the coral and intestines of the
   lobster **and** 1 level teaspoon flour
   (*optional*)

Equipment
1 large knife
1 bowl
1 large saucepan with low sides
   (sauté pan)
1 heavy-based saucepan
1 skimmer
1 whisk

1   Remove the tail and claws from the raw lobster. Crack the latter with a blow from the back of a heavy knife to make it easier to remove the flesh after cooking. Cut the front part of the creature in half lengthwise. Discard the little gravelly pouch which lies inside the head. Remove the greenish part (intestines and coral) with a teaspoon and put it on one side in a small bowl.

2   Cut the tail into several slices.

3   Heat the oils and butter in a shallow saucepan (sauté pan). Sweat (allow to cook gently, without allowing to brown) the shallots, carrot, onion, garlic and bouquet garni.

4   Remove them with a slotted spoon, draining them against the side of the pan to allow the oil to run back into it. Put in the pieces of lobster, sprinkled with salt and pepper and allow the shells to redden.

5   Add the armagnac or the cognac and cover the casserole: the alcohol should be boiled to reduce it by three-quarters and to impregnate the lobster with its flavour, without flaming it. (In my opinion, flambéing is pointless, and it also runs the risk of burning the delicate legs of the lobster, giving the sauce an unpleasant bitter taste).

6   Cover the pieces of lobster with the mirepoix of vegetables, the fresh tomatoes, and tomato purée and season with salt, pepper and a pinch of

cayenne. Moisten with the white wine and fish fumet. Allow to cook briskly, uncovered, for ten minutes.

7   Remove the pieces of lobster (reserving the flesh for, perhaps, a lobster salad). Allow the sauce to boil, uncovered, and reduce to two-thirds of its volume.

8   Pour the sauce through a conical strainer into another saucepan. Incorporate the ingredients of the liaison – butter, coral, intestines, and flour (if used) mixing them in vigorously with a whisk. Allow to boil for two minutes longer.

see note on page 84.

---

11. *Truffle sauce*
SAUCE PÉRIGUEUX

For eight people

Basic ingredients
250 ml (½ pint) port
8 tablespoons armagnac or cognac
50 g (1¾ oz) chopped truffles from a
   tin
4 tablespoons of the truffle liquid
   from the tin

500 ml (scant 1 pint) demi-glace
   (concentrated meat stock) (No 1)
50 g (1¾ oz) fresh butter (*optional*)
salt, pepper

1   Heat a saucepan, pour in the port and armagnac, bring them to the boil and reduce by three-quarters of their original volume.

2   Add the juice from the truffles, the chopped truffles, and the demi-glace. Season with salt and pepper and allow to cook over a low heat, simmering gently for fifteen minutes. You can, if you like, incorporate the butter just before serving, adding it in little bits and swirling the pan round to mix it in.

   In Cuisine Minceur you can use the same sauce, without incorporating the butter, or you can replace it with a sauce of dried wood mushrooms (No 44).

Sauce au Vin Rouge de Bordeaux is made in the same way, but replacing the port and armagnac with the equivalent quantity of claret, replacing the truffle juice with a tablespoon of tomato purée and adding two finely chopped shallots to the red wine.

Some ways of improving your sauces
For a sauce which should be well-flavoured, but seems rather flat. Add a squeeze of lemon juice or a few drops of vinegar – something sharp to liven it up.

For a sauce which has become tart or bitter, during cooking. Add a sprinkling of sugar, or a few drops of a fortified wine such as port, and, if necessary, a little cream.

For a sauce which seems to lack character and is not a good colour. Add a little glace de viande (**No 1**) or glace de poisson, jellied fish stock (**No 3**), according to the dish, a turn or two of the peppermill and sometimes a few drops of armagnac or cognac.

It is sometimes better, when using wine in the making of a sauce, to reduce it by boiling, both to decrease the volume and evaporate the alcohol. With white wine, it also eliminates any acidity, with red wine it concentrates the bouquet. Spirits need the same treatment, but on the other hand fortified wines, which have a more fugitive flavour, are often better if added at the last moment.

Points to Remember
In sauces based on a roux, lemon juice should be added after the thickening and cooking – added at the beginning it will prevent the liaison from working by slackening the mixture.

In emulsified sauces, on the other hand, the lemon juice actually encourages the coagulation of the egg yolks.

The acids naturally present in most vegetables (with the exception of spinach, cabbage and cauliflower) make milk unsuitable as a cooking medium, as they sour and curdle it.

Marinades

In the past, the use of marinades in cooking was an ingenious way of preserving meat, making it tender and improving its flavour. Today these 'spiced baths' are still used to flavour such things as venison and other game and some meats, tenderizing the flesh in the first case (with game animals, wild boar, venison, etc.) and in the second case (beef, mutton, etc.) imparting a hearty venison flavour to the meat.

The meat, whilst it is slowly soaking up the flavours of the marinade, should be kept cool, and turned over from time to time. The marinade is often used later, as the liquid for the sauce which will accompany the food which has been soaked in it.

12. *Classic uncooked marinade*

Ingredients
1 onion
2 shallots
half a carrot
a stick of celery, the length of your
  little finger
thyme, a bayleaf
parsley stalks
1 clove garlic

2 cloves
6 peppercorns
6 coriander seeds
a pinch of salt
500 ml (scant 1 pint) white **or** red
  wine
10 tablespoons wine vinegar
6 tablespoons oil

Slice the vegetables thinly and make a bed of half the vegetables and garlic, herbs and spices in the bottom of a suitable dish.

Put the meat on top and cover it with the rest of the vegetables, etc. Moisten it with red or white wine (depending on the recipe), vinegar and oil.

13. *Classic cooked marinade*

The cooked marinade speeds up the process of tenderizing the meat. It is made with the same ingredients as the uncooked marinade. But the vegetables (onions, shallots, carrot, celery) must first be sweated in the oil, then add the wine, vinegar, herbs and spices and allow to simmer for half an hour.

14. *Tahitian marinade*

Raw fish prepared in the Tahitian manner are macerated in a little lemon juice and pepper which has the effect of partly 'cooking' them. Fish can also be marinaded before grilling in a mixture of oil, thin slices of peeled lemon, thyme, bayleaf, fennel, parsley stalks, basil, finely sliced onion, chopped shallot, salt, pepper, saffron, etc.

15. *Scandinavian marinade*

The Scandinavian way of marinating fish is equally fascinating – it consists of putting a layer of fresh dill between two boned, but not skinned, fillets of fish (salmon for example) and burying them in a mixture of salt, sugar and black pepper, and pressing beneath weights for twenty-four hours.

The exact ingredients are as follows: 225 g (8 oz) coarse salt, 300 g (10 oz) granulated sugar, 1 bunch of dill, 25 g (scant 1 oz) coarsely crushed black peppercorns.

Marinades in Cuisine Minceur

Because they make little or no use of fats, marinades are most useful in Cuisine Minceur. Their spicy and succulent nature allows them to make up for the noticeable lack of certain rich ingredients in the making of these light dishes.

I will enlarge on the subject in the recipes, but the following principles should be observed in Cuisine Minceur:

If the marinade contains oil, wipe away every trace with a cloth, before cooking.

If the marinade is to be used as a basis for making a sauce, skim off the oil, and then reduce it by boiling to evaporate the alcohol, retaining only its flavour.

EDITOR'S NOTE   If you are feeling economical you can save on the amount of liquid needed to marinate a piece of meat or fish by putting both liquid and meat in a polythene bag in a bowl.

---

16. *The perfect Minceur marinade – the infusion*

For an uncompromisingly Minceur marinade use an infusion. Wine as the basis for a marinade can be cleverly replaced by an infusion of herbs in boiling water: rosemary, thyme, marjoram, basil, etc. In the same way an aromatic infusion can be used to cook certain fish and delicate meats in its fragrant steam.

A Note on Herbs and Seasonings

Pepper   Milled, whole, crushed, white or black (with the skin still on), pepper is found in almost every dish. Ideally it should be added towards the end of cooking in order to keep its flavour. Fresh or green pepper is soft and subtle, imposing its personality on every dish it touches. In its freeze-dried form it can be used generously as a spice; ground, it functions in the same way as ordinary pepper.

EDITOR'S NOTE   Green pepper is now freely available in tins. The liquid the peppercorns are packed in can also be used, with discretion, as a flavouring.

Parsley   For flavouring purposes I prefer flat (Continental) parsley which has a better taste and aroma. Curly parsley, used all too often for decoration, is especially delicious deep-fried and served with fried fish, rissoles, etc. Both types can be chopped or pounded and are used in bouquet garni.

Bouquet Garni   I use bouquet garni, the symbol of French cooking, often in my recipes. I use parsley stalks, thyme and bay (these last sparingly). You can add a small piece of celery or other herbs such as basil, tarragon and chervil as the fancy takes you. The herbs are tied in a bundle with a thread and removed when the cooking is complete.

Remember . . .
All flavourings must be treated with tact and judgement.

Excessive use of herbs and spices unbalances a dish – usually irreparably.

Flavours must not be allowed to swamp the taste of the main ingredient whether it be fish, flesh or vegetable, but must enhance it.

Heat intensifies flavour.

Some herbs which are originally mainly medicinal are also used in cooking, especially in Cuisine Minceur. For instance, lime-blossom, hyssop, rosemary, thyme, mint, marjoram, etc.

In pâtisserie, cocoa, coffee, vanilla, cinnamon, orange and lemon peel are the basic flavourings.

Part Two
Cuisine Minceur Recipes

Soups

17. *Light consommé with fresh garden vegetables*
BOUILLON DE LÉGUMES D'EUGÉNIE

For four people

Main ingredients
50 g (2 oz) carrots
50 g (2 oz) button mushrooms
25 g (1 oz) white part of leek
25 g (1 oz) celery (or celeriac)
1 teaspoon parsley, chopped
1 teaspoon chervil, chopped
80 g (3 oz) coarsely chopped tomato
  pulp

1 sprig tarragon
1¼ litres (2¼ pints) chicken stock
  (No 2) **or** stock made with stock
  cubes

Equipment
1 mouli-julienne
1 saucepan with a lid
4 white porcelain soup bowls

1   Cut the vegetables – carrots, mushrooms, the white part of leek and celery – into julienne strips, 2 mm ($\frac{1}{16}$ in) wide by 4 cm (1½ in) long. In the case of carrots and celeriac, it is quicker and easier to use a mouli-julienne. Mushrooms have more pliable flesh and should be sliced with a small knife.

2   Bring the chicken stock to the boil and season with salt and pepper.

3   Throw in the sliced vegetables and allow them to cook with a tilted lid on the pan, for fifteen minutes. The vegetables should remain whole and still have a slightly firm texture between the teeth.

4   Add the fresh tomato pulp.

5   Serve the soup hot or chilled in the four soup bowls, sprinkled with the freshly chopped parsley, chervil and tarragon.

It is the careful balance of vegetables which gives this clear soup its fresh 'vegetable garden' flavour.

18. *Fresh tomato soup with pounded basil*
SOUPE DE TOMATES FRAÎCHES AU PISTOU

For four people

Main ingredients
300 g (11 oz) ripe tomatoes
1 tablespoon tomato purée
1 small carrot
half a leek
1 shallot
1 clove garlic
1¼ litres (2¼ pints) chicken stock
   (No 2) or water
1 sprig thyme
half a bayleaf

1 teaspoon salt, a pinch of pepper
1 teaspoon oil

Ingredients for the pistou
2 teaspoons basil, pounded to a paste
   with 1 teaspoon olive oil

Equipment
1 heavy-based saucepan
1 conical strainer
4 white porcelain soup bowls

1   Skin the tomatoes, cut them in half and press the halves lightly in the palm of your hand to squeeze out excess liquid and seeds.

2   Peel the carrot, leek, shallot and garlic, and chop them coarsely.

3   Brown them lightly in the saucepan in which you have first heated the olive oil; add the sprig of thyme and the half bayleaf. Cover them with the fresh tomatoes and the tomato purée. Moisten with the chicken stock or water.

4   Cook gently, uncovered, for twenty minutes.

5   Remove the thyme and bayleaf, put the mixture into the liquidizer, purée it and strain back into the saucepan, and reheat.

6   Serve in separate soup bowls, adding the pistou (the paste made from basil and oil) at the last moment.

Delicious hot, this soup is also good when served iced; in which case, do not reheat it after puréeing in the liquidizer. Simply chill the mixture in the refrigerator after straining, do not add the pistou until you serve the soup, and decorate it with a little sprig of fresh basil.

19. *Foamy cream of sorrel soup*
CRÈME D'OSEILLE MOUSSEUSE

For four people

Main ingredients	*Equipment*
120 g (4¼ oz) fresh sorrel	1 saucepan
2 cloves garlic	1 bowl
1 litre (1¾ pints) chicken stock (**No 2**)	1 whisk
or stock made with stock cubes	1 liquidizer
2 teaspoons olive oil	4 white porcelain soup bowls
1½ teaspoons salt, pepper	

Ingredients for the liaison
2 eggs

1   Heat the oil in the saucepan.

2   Peel the cloves of garlic, crush them whole with the blade of a knife, and brown them lightly in the olive oil. Add the chopped sorrel, the salt and pepper, and stir.

3   Moisten with the chicken stock and cook for fifteen minutes.

4   Pour the mixture into the liquidizer and blend for two minutes, to obtain a smooth liquid.

5   Return the soup to the saucepan and heat to the point where it is just starting to shiver.

6   Just before serving, whisk the two eggs in a bowl until they are light and frothy, then quickly incorporate the hot, but not boiling, soup, whisking all the time. The eggs, aerated by the whisking, will set on contact with the hot liquid, and make the soup light, airy and velvety.

20. *Frogs' legs soup*
SOUPE DE GRENOUILLES

For four people

Main ingredients
24 frogs' legs
800 ml (1½ pints) fish fumet (No 3)
7 tablespoons dry white wine
1 bunch watercress
1 chopped shallot
1 sprig tarragon
1½ teaspoons salt, pepper

Ingredients for the liaison
1 tablespoon fromage blanc
1 tablespoon crème fraîche

Equipment
2 saucepans
1 liquidizer
1 small whisk
4 white porcelain soup bowls

1   Bring the fish fumet to the boil in the first saucepan.

2   Drop in the frogs' legs and as soon as the liquid comes back to the boil take them out. Put them on one side wrapped in a napkin.

3   Put the white wine, chopped shallot, tarragon, salt and pepper in the second saucepan. Bring to the boil and reduce, uncovered, until the white wine has all but evaporated (to drive off the alcohol, preserving only the flavour).

4   Add the fish fumet in which the frogs' legs were poached, and the watercress, washed, and with the larger stalks removed. Allow to cook for seven minutes. This short cooking keeps the watercress a tender shade of green.

5   Purée the mixture in the liquidizer. Keep it hot.

6   Meanwhile, bone the frogs' legs.

7   Whip the cream and the fromage blanc lightly together. Stir it into the soup. Taste for seasoning and do not allow to boil.

8   Arrange the boned frogs' legs in the soup bowls, and cover them with the very hot soup. Decorate each bowl with a few watercress leaves floating on the top like lily pads.

EDITOR'S NOTE Frogs' legs, although not commonly eaten outside France, can now be obtained frozen from high-class grocers and delicatessens.

21. *Soup of vineyard thrushes*
SOUPE À LA GRIVE DE VIGNE

For four people

Main ingredients
4 thrushes

Ingredients for making the stock
1 carrot, peeled and coarsely chopped
1 onion, peeled and coarsely chopped
1 bouquet garni
1 teaspoon olive oil
4 juniper berries
2 litres (3½ pints) cold water

Ingredients for finishing the soup
  (*optional*)
1 teaspoon truffle juice
2 tablespoons sauce Périgueux
  (No 11)

Other ingredients
20 g (¾ oz) dried mushrooms

60 g (2 oz) carrot
60 g (2 oz) onion
60 g (2 oz) button mushrooms
10 g (⅓ oz) celery
all peeled and finely chopped
  separately to make tiny mirepoix
  dice
1 teaspoon olive oil
1 teaspoon chopped chervil
salt, pepper, a pinch of thyme

Equipment
2 saucepans, one with a heavy base
1 wooden spatula
1 wire sieve
4 white porcelain soup bowls
4 round pieces of aluminium foil
  about 15 cm (6 in) across

1   Pluck and clean the birds – keep the livers. Remove the wings and breasts – the white meat of the bird as it were – and put them on a plate. Chop up the remaining parts of the birds coarsely – legs, carcasses and livers.

2   Lightly coat the bottom of a saucepan with oil, heat it and brown the chopped birds and all the ingredients for making the stock. Cook for five minutes, stirring, then add the cold water.

3   Bring the liquid to the boil, skim carefully, lower the heat so that the liquid is just simmering, and allow to reduce to half the quantity. (About 1¼ hours.)

4   Meanwhile, wash the dried mushrooms and soak them in cold water. When they have reconstituted, drain them dry and put them on one side.

5   In the heavy-bottomed pan, heated and coated with the second teaspoon of olive oil, sauté the ingredients of the mirepoix, adding the vegetables at three-minute intervals in the following order: carrots first, then celery and onion, and finally the button mushrooms – in this way the carrots will cook for nine minutes, the celery and onion six minutes and

the mushrooms only three minutes. Season with salt and pepper and sprinkle with thyme.

Add the truffle-juice and the sauce Périgueux if wanted, bring to the boil and take the pan off the heat.

6   Strain the stock through the wire sieve and pour it on to the vegetable mixture. Return to the heat, add the soaked mushrooms and cook over a gentle heat for five minutes. Season.

7   Just before serving the soup, poach the breasts of the birds for $1\frac{1}{2}$ minutes in the bouillon. Put one breast in each bowl, add the bouillon and vegetables, and decorate with the chopped chervil and cover each bowl with a piece of aluminium foil tied in place with string.

EDITOR'S NOTE   In France, where thrushes are considered pests, this soup would cause no tears. Elsewhere it would be as well to substitute young pigeons (squabs).

---

22. *Velouté of wood mushrooms*
VELOUTÉ AUX CHAMPIGNONS DES BOIS

For four people

Main ingredients
50 g (2 oz) dried morilles (morel, *morchella esculenta*)
50 g (2 oz) dried mousseron mushrooms (miller, *clitopilus prunulus*)
80 g (3 oz) dried cèpes (cep, *boletus edulis*)
100 g (3½ oz) fresh button mushrooms
1 litre (1¾ pints) chicken stock (No 2) or stock made with chicken stock cube

Other ingredients
1 tablespoon olive oil
50 g (2 oz) onions, finely sliced

50 g (2 oz) chopped leek
1 clove garlic, cut in half
2 tomatoes, peeled and deseeded

Ingredients for decorating the soup
1 teaspoon freshly chopped parsley
1 tablespoon tomato, peeled and cut into little cubes
40 g (1½ oz) dried mousserons (millers)

Equipment
1 liquidizer
1 heavy-based saucepan
4 white porcelain soup bowls

1   Wash the dried mushrooms from the main ingredients carefully in several waters, soak them in warm water for one hour.

2   Drain them and spread them out on a dry cloth.

3   Heat the olive oil in the saucepan, sauté the onions, leeks and garlic, and then add the main ingredients – the drained dried mushrooms, cleaned button mushrooms and, lastly, the two tomatoes which give the soup a sweet flavour and a fresh taste.

4   Allow to cook for five minutes, stirring.

5   Add the chicken stock, and season.

6   Cover the saucepan with a tilted lid, and allow to simmer for half an hour.

7   At the end of this time, pour the contents of the saucepan into the liquidizer and purée very finely. Keep hot.

8   To serve the soup, poach the mousserons, kept for the garnish, in a little chicken stock.

Fill the four soup bowls with the soup, arrange the poached and drained mousserons on top and sprinkle with freshly chopped parsley and tomato cut in tiny cubes.

EDITOR'S NOTE   The different kinds of mushrooms and fungi, and possible substitutes for them, are discussed on pages 28–9.

23. *Truffle soup*
SOUPE DE TRUFFES

For two people

Main ingredients
2 truffles (fresh or tinned) of 25 g (approximately 1 oz) each, cut into paper thin slices
50 g (scant 1 oz) uncooked chicken breast
60 g (2 oz) uncooked veal sweetbreads
40 g (1½ oz) carrot
40 g (1½ oz) button mushrooms
15 g (½ oz) celery
½ teaspoon olive oil
thyme

Other ingredients
240 ml (scant ½ pint) chicken stock (No 2) or stock made with chicken stock cube (No 4)
1 teaspoon juice from a tin of truffles
1 tablespoon sauce Périgueux (No. 11) (*optional*)
salt, pepper

Equipment
2 white porcelain soup bowls
1 small saucepan
2 round pieces of aluminium foil, 15 cm (6 in) diameter

1   Prepare the vegetable mirepoix: Cut the carrots, button mushrooms

and celery each into tiny dice. Heat the saucepan, just cover the bottom with the olive oil and start adding the vegetables every three minutes in succession, sweating them with the lid on to extract their juices. First add the diced carrots, then the diced celery, and lastly the diced mushrooms. In this way the carrots will cook for nine minutes, the celery six minutes and the mushrooms for three minutes. Season with salt and pepper, and sprinkle with thyme.

2 Braise the sweetbreads (*see* the recipe for Ragoût fin d'Eugénie, No 109).

The chicken breast can be cooked in the same braising liquid, for the same length of time as the sweetbreads. To save time it is also possible to poach each for ten minutes in a good chicken stock, and then cut them into dice $\frac{1}{2}$ cm ($\frac{1}{4}$ in) across.

3 Put a tablespoon of the vegetable mirepoix into each soup bowl, then half a teaspoon of sauce Périgueux (if used) and half a teaspoon of truffle juice. Add the diced veal sweetbreads, chicken breast and sliced truffles. Cover with the chicken stock. Cover each soup bowl with a disc of aluminium foil, tied in place with thread, like the top of a pot of home-made jam.

4 Bake in a hot oven for ten minutes 240°C/475°F/Mark 9. Let your guest remove the lid for himself, and enjoy the aromas that waft out of the soup.

This is the Cuisine Minceur version of Paul Bocuse's celebrated soup.

Sauces

24. *Sauce vinaigrette 1*

For four people

Main ingredients
1 tablespoon olive oil
3 tablespoons sunflower oil

1 tablespoon wine vinegar
1 tablespoon lemon juice
salt, pepper

Uses   Marine Salad (No 69)

25. *Sauce vinaigrette 2*

For four people

Main ingredients
4 tablespoons sunflower oil, in which
   the following ingredients are steeped
   for 2 hours:
1 peeled clove garlic
½ teaspoon tarragon leaves

½ teaspoon sprigs of chervil
2 chopped basil leaves
1 tablespoon sherry vinegar
1 tablespoon lemon juice
salt, pepper

Uses   Freshwater crayfish salad (No 73)
           Truffle salad with parsley (No 68)

26. *Mayonnaise*

For six to eight people

Main ingredients
1 egg
1 teaspoon Dijon mustard
1 teaspoon lemon juice

1 tablespoon olive oil
4 tablespoons sunflower oil
2 tablespoons fromage blanc

This sauce is made in the usual way (*see* recipe No 6) using only the yolk of the egg. The fromage blanc is added at the end. The left-over white of egg can be beaten into a soft snow, and folded delicately into the mayonnaise with a wooden spatula. It is also equally possible to make the sauce in a liquidizer following the same procedure.

Uses   Artichokes Mélanie (No 52)
         Lambs' brain salad (No 75)

For an even more Minceur version, I suggest replacing the sunflower oil with the following:
    2 level tablespoons arachide oil
    1 level tablespoon onion purée (No 134)
    $\frac{1}{2}$ level tablespoon carrot purée (No 130)

---

27. *Sweet-sour onion sauce*
SAUCE AIGRE-DOUCE À L'OIGNON

For five people

Main ingredients
2 eggs
2 tablespoons onion purée (No 134)
1 tablespoon fromage blanc

1 tablespoon olive oil
1 tablespoon sunflower oil
1 tablespoon tomato ketchup
1 teaspoon Dijon mustard

Uses   Pigeon salad with chervil (No 76)

---

28. *Orange sauce*

For five people

Main ingredients
1 tablespoon carrot mousse (No 130)
1 tablespoon orange juice
2 tablespoons fromage blanc
1 tablespoon wine vinegar

1 tablespoon sunflower oil
1 tablespoon olive oil
1 teaspoon Dijon mustard
1 teaspoon freshly-chopped herbs
    (chervil, tarragon, parsley)

Uses   Salad of lambs' brains (No 75)

29. *Rose sauce*

For five people

Main ingredients
2 egg yolks
2 tablespoons tomato ketchup
1 teaspoon Dijon mustard

1 tablespoon sunflower oil
1 tablespoon olive oil
4 tablespoons fromage blanc
salt, pepper

Uses   Salad of freshwater crayfish (No 73)
Geisha salad (No 66)

30. *Favourite sauce*
SAUCE PRÉFÉRÉE

For five people

Main ingredients
5 tablespoons fromage blanc
2 tablespoons wine vinegar
1 tablespoon soy sauce

1 teaspoon Dijon mustard
1 teaspoon freshly chopped herbs
   (chervil, tarragon, parsley)
salt, pepper

Uses   Garden salad with chives (No 67)

31. *Sauce créosat*

For five people

Main ingredients
50 g (2 oz) cucumber
25 g (1 oz) green pimento
75 g (2½ oz) onion
20 g (¾ oz) fresh tomato
10 g (⅓ oz) gherkins
10 g (⅓ oz) capers

Seasoning ingredients
½ teaspoon Worcestershire sauce
½ teaspoon mustard

3 tablespoons wine vinegar
1 teaspoon olive oil
1 whole peeled clove of garlic
1 sprig thyme
half a bayleaf
salt, pepper

Equipment
1 small salad bowl
1 fork, 1 bowl

1 Cut the prepared vegetables – cucumber, pimento, onion, fresh tomato, gherkin – into $\frac{1}{2}$ cm ($\frac{1}{4}$ in) dice.

2 Mix them together in the salad bowl with a fork.

3 Mix all the seasoning ingredients together in a small bowl, to make a dressing. Pour this mixture into the bowl of diced vegetables and let it soak in, stirring with a fork.

4 Put the bowl in the refrigerator and let it steep for at least three days. Use as needed having first removed the clove of garlic.

Serve with all kinds of grilled steak.

32. *Sauce grelette*

For ten people

Main ingredients
600 g (1¼ lb) whole tomatoes
½ teaspoon chopped tarragon
½ teaspoon chopped parsley
1 tablespoon tomato ketchup
the juice of 1 lemon
6 tablespoons fromage blanc
1 tablespoon crème fraîche

1½ teaspoons salt, a generous pinch of white pepper
2 teaspoons Armagnac (*optional*)

Equipment
1 saucepan
1 salad bowl
1 small whisk

1 Skin the tomatoes, cut them in half and press them gently in the palm of your hand to squeeze out the excess juice, and seeds. Then cut them into little dice (*see* No 138).

2 Whisk the fromage blanc in the salad bowl together with the cream. Add the chopped herbs, tomato ketchup, lemon juice, Armagnac (if used) and finally the chopped tomato. Season.

3 Chill in the refrigerator or on cracked ice until the moment it is needed.

Uses Potted salmon with lemon and green peppercorns (No 61)
       Fish Terrine with fresh herbs (No 62)

33. *Cold lobster sauce*
SAUCE 'HOMARDIÈRE' FROIDE

For four people

Main ingredients
2 tablespoons arachide oil
1 tablespoon olive oil
2 tablespoons fromage blanc
1 egg, separated
½ teaspoon mustard
a few drops of lemon juice
salt, pepper

Other ingredients
½ teaspoon chopped chervil
½ teaspoon fresh tarragon

1 tablespoon chopped vegetables
  from a court-bouillon in which
  shellfish have been cooked (*see*
  USES)
4 tablespoons sauce Américaine
  (No 10)

Equipment
1 small saucepan
1 salad bowl
1 small whisk

1 Bring the sauce Américaine to the boil in a small saucepan, over a
gentle heat, and let it reduce by half, stirring it frequently. Let it cool.

2 Make a mayonnaise with the main ingredients, incorporating the
fromage blanc at the end.

3 Add the cooled sauce Américaine, the chopped vegetables from a court-
bouillon, the chervil and tarragon. Taste the sauce for seasoning and fold
in the whisked egg-white just before serving.

Uses   Lobster salad with caviar (No 74)
       Crab salad with grapefruit (No 72)
       Salad of freshwater crayfish (No 73)

34. *Tomato sauce*
SAUCE VIERGE

For six to eight people

Main ingredients
3 fresh tomatoes
1 whole unpeeled clove of garlic
2 tablespoons chopped chervil
2 tablespoons chopped parsley
1 tablespoon chopped tarragon
8 crushed coriander seeds
4 level tablespoons fromage blanc

2 level tablespoons water
1 level tablespoon mustard
1 level teaspoon Worcestershire sauce
3 tablespoons olive oil
salt, pepper

Equipment
1 small saucepan

1   Skin the tomatoes, cut them in half and press them in the palm of your hand to squeeze out the seeds and excess juice. Cut them into tiny dice.

2   Simply put all the ingredients together in the pan, stand it in a bain-marie and let the sauce heat through gently.

Uses   Bass cooked in seaweed (No 92)

35. *Butter sauce*
SAUCE BEURRE BLANC

For four people

Main ingredients
4 tablespoons water
4 tablespoons wine vinegar
2 tablespoons chopped shallots
60 g (2 oz) chilled unsalted butter
1 tablespoon crème fraîche

200 g (7 oz) fromage blanc
salt

Equipment
1 small heavy-based saucepan
1 small whisk

1   Combine the water, vinegar and chopped shallots in the saucepan and place it over a gentle heat.

2   Reduce the mixture by two-thirds of its volume.

3   Increase the heat and bring the reduction to a fast boil. Put the butter, straight out of the refrigerator, into the centre of the boiling liquid. The

butter will gradually melt and be caught up in the seething liquid, thickening it as it does so. The crème fraîche is added at this point to help the process.

4 Remove the pan from the heat and allow to cool a little. Whisk in the fromage blanc. Taste for seasoning.

Uses Hot Terrine of sea-bass with asparagus tips (No 64)

---

36. *Eugénie Béarnaise sauce 1*

For four people

Main ingredients
2 egg yolks
1 tablespoon cold water
2 tablespoons olive oil
8 tablespoons hot chicken stock
(No 2, or stock made with chicken stock cubes)
salt

Ingredients for the reduction
50 g (2 oz) chopped shallots
1 tablespoon chopped tarragon

1 heaped teaspoon crushed peppercorns
4 tablespoons wine vinegar

Other ingredients
200 g (7 oz) fresh coarsely chopped tomato pulp (No 138)
1 teaspoon tomato purée
1 teaspoon chopped chervil

Equipment
2 small stainless-steel saucepans
1 small whisk

1 Put the shallots, tarragon, crushed pepper and vinegar into one of the small saucepans. Bring the mixture to the boil and let it reduce to a moist purée. Allow it to cool.

2 In the other saucepan, cook the tomato pulp until the liquid has completely evaporated.

3 To the first saucepan, add the tablespoon of cold water and the two egg yolks. Put it back over the heat and start beating it with a small whisk (*see* method in No 7).

4 When the mixture has the consistency of a creamy mousse, and each stroke of the whisk leaves its traces on the bottom of the pan, remove it from the heat. Then, gradually add the olive oil, in a thin stream, then the chicken stock. Season with fine salt, add the cooked tomatoes, tomato purée and chopped chervil. Keep warm until needed.

Uses   Pot-au-feu served like a fondue (No 100)
        Chicken cooked in coarse salt (page 64)
        All kinds of grilled steak, chicken and fish

37. *Eugénie Béarnaise sauce 2*

For eight people

Main ingredients
2 egg yolks
5 tablespoons cold water
2 tablespoons olive oil

Ingredients for the reduction
50 g (2 oz) chopped shallots
1 tablespoon chopped tarragon
1 heaped teaspoon crushed
  peppercorns
4 tablespoons wine vinegar

Other ingredients
200 g (7 oz) coarsely chopped tomato
  pulp (No 139)
1 tablespoon light mushroom purée
  (No. 132)
salt
1 teaspoon finely-chopped chervil

Equipment
2 small stainless-steel saucepans
1 small whisk

1   Put the shallots, tarragon, crushed peppercorns and vinegar in one of
the two small pans. Bring them to the boil and reduce until you have a
moist purée. Allow to cool.

2   In the second small pan, cook the tomatoes until all their liquid has
evaporated (*see* No 139).

3   Add the cold water and the two egg yolks to the reduction in the first
saucepan. Put it back over the heat and start beating the sauce with a wire
whisk (*see* method in No 7).

4   When the mixture has reached the consistency of a creamy mousse,
and each stroke of the whisk leaves its trace on the bottom of the saucepan,
remove the pan from the heat. Then gradually stir in olive oil, adding it in
a thin stream. Season with fine salt, add the fresh tomatoes, the mushroom purée and the teaspoon of freshly chopped chervil. Keep warm until
needed.

Uses   Pot-au-feu served like a fondue (No 100)
        Chicken cooked in coarse salt, *see* page 64
        All kinds of grilled steak, chicken and fish

38. *Fresh tomato sauce*
SAUCE COULIS DE TOMATES FRAÎCHES

For four people

Main ingredients
300 g (10½ oz) fresh tomatoes
1 teaspoon tomato purée
1 chopped shallot
1 clove garlic
1 bouquet garni
1 teaspoon olive oil

180 ml (generous ¼ pint) chicken stock

Equipment
1 heavy-based saucepan
1 colander, 1 liquidizer

1   Skin the tomatoes, cut them in half and press each half gently in the palm of your hand to squeeze out pips and excess juice.

2   Heat the olive oil in the saucepan, and cook the clove of garlic and chopped shallot gently without browning. Add the fresh tomato and the tomato purée, the bouquet garni and the chicken stock. Cook over a low heat for twenty minutes.

3   At the end of the cooking remove the bouquet garni and purée the sauce in the liquidizer. Check the seasoning. If the coulis is too thin, return it to the pan and reduce it further.

Uses   Sweet onion tart (No 57)
       Chicken liver mousse (No 65)
       Carrot gâteau with chervil (No 55)
       Grilled veal chop with a salad (No 102)
       Onions Tante Louise (No 137)
       Pot-au-feu served like fondue (No 100)

39. *Asparagus sauce*
SAUCE COULIS D'ASPERGES

For four people

Main ingredients
350 g (¾ lb) fresh asparagus, **or**
180 g (6 oz) tinned asparagus
8 tablespoons chicken stock (No 2) **or**
  stock made with stock cubes
¾ teaspoon salt

a pinch of pepper
1 teaspoon crème fraîche (*optional*)

Equipment
1 liquidizer

1   If you are using fresh asparagus, prepare it according to the recipe on page 68.

2   Slice the asparagus and purée it in the liquidizer with the chicken stock, salt, pepper and crème fraîche. Taste for seasoning and keep hot in a bain-marie until needed.

Uses   Asparagus gâteau (No 56)
         Mousseline of frogs' legs with watercress (No 63)
         Sweet onion tart (No 57)
         Carrot gâteau with chervil (No 55)

---

40. *Artichoke sauce*
SAUCE COULIS D'ARTICHAUTS

For four people

Main ingredients
3 globe artichokes each weighing
   about 250 g (9 oz)
2 litres (3½ pints) water
30 g (a generous ounce) coarse salt
juice of 1 squeezed lemon
1 teaspoon crème fraîche

8 tablespoons chicken stock (No 2) or
   stock made with stock cubes

Equipment
1 large stainless-steel saucepan
1 liquidizer

1   Wash the artichokes and cut off their stalks. Cook them for forty-five minutes, covered, in two litres of boiling salted water to which you have added the lemon juice.

2   At the end of the cooking, refresh the artichokes in cold water, pull off their leaves, remove the chokes and take out the hearts, which are then puréed in the liquidizer with the crème fraîche and chicken stock. Taste for seasoning and keep hot in a bain-marie until needed.

Uses   Asparagus gâteau (No 56)
         Mousseline of frogs' legs with watercress (No 63)
         Sweet onion tart (No 57)
         Carrot gâteau with chervil (No 55)
         Grilled veal escalope with artichoke sauce (No 103)

41. *Parsley sauce*
SAUCE AU PERSIL

For two people

Main ingredients
30 g (1 oz) very fresh parsley
  (preferably the flat variety)
1 chopped shallot
1 teaspoon mushroom purée (No 132)
1 tablespoon fromage blanc
8 tablespoons fish fumet (No 3) or
  veal stock (No 1)

a few drops of lemon juice
salt, pepper

Equipment
1 stainless-steel saucepan
1 wire sieve
1 liquidizer

1   Wash the parsley and remove the stalks.

2   Heat the saucepan and cook the parsley and chopped shallot in the fish fumet seasoned with salt and pepper, for fifteen minutes.

3   Strain the parsley and shallots keeping the liquid and purée in the liquidizer with the mushroom purée, lemon juice and fromage blanc. Moisten the mixture with the liquid in which the parsley was cooked. Taste for seasoning. Keep hot in a bain-marie.

Uses   Seafood pot-au-feu (No 95)
        Pot-au-feu served like fondue (No 100)

42. *Creamy garlic sauce*
SAUCE À LA CRÈME D'AIL

For four people

Main ingredients
12 peeled cloves garlic
70 g (2½ oz) button mushrooms cut in
  half
250 ml (scant ½ pint) water
25 g (1 oz) skimmed milk powder
1 teaspoon glace de veau (No 1) or
  veal stock made with stock cubes
  (No 4)

1 teaspoon freshly chopped parsley
salt, pepper
a small pinch of nutmeg

Equipment
1 small heavy-based saucepan
1 small whisk
1 liquidizer

1   Bring the garlic to the boil three times in unsalted water, using fresh water each time – to weaken the strong flavour and remove any bitterness.

2   Mix the milk powder and water in the saucepan with a whisk. Add the garlic, mushrooms, parsley, salt, pepper and nutmeg.

3   Cook over a gentle heat for twenty minutes.

4   Pour this mixture into the liquidizer, add the glace de veau (or veal stock skimmed and considerably reduced) and purée until you have a completely homogenous sauce.

5   Keep hot in a bain-marie until needed.

Uses   Grilled pigeon with creamy garlic sauce (No 120)

---

43. *Apple sauce*
SAUCE À LA POMME

For four people

Main ingredients
350 g (¾ lb) apples (about 3 medium sweet apples)
4 tablespoons lemon juice
2½ tablespoons chicken stock (No 2) or chicken stock made with stock cubes

30 g (1 oz) lemon zest
salt, sugar

Equipment
1 heavy-based saucepan with a lid
1 liquidizer
1 bowl

1   Blanch the lemon zest in boiling water for seven or eight minutes. Drain and chop finely.

2   Peel and core the apples (you will have about 250 g (9 oz)).

3   Cut them in quarters and cook them for twenty minutes in the covered saucepan with the lemon juice.

4   When they are tender, put them into the liquidizer and reduce them to a fine purée with the chicken stock.

5   Put the sauce into a bowl and stir in the chopped lemon rind. Taste for seasoning. According to taste you can add a pinch of sugar and a tiny pinch of cinnamon.

Uses   Grilled pigeon, in place of creamy garlic sauce (No 120)

44. *Wild mushroom sauce*
SAUCE AUX CHAMPIGNONS DES BOIS

For six people

Main ingredients
15 g (½ oz) dried morilles (morels)
15 g (½ oz) dried mousserons (millers)
15 g (½ oz) dried cèpes (ceps) or
  Chinese mushrooms
500 ml (scant 1 pint) veal stock
  (No 1)
2 tablespoons port
salt, pepper

Ingredients for the liaison
1 tablespoon fromage blanc

1 tablespoon mushroom purée (No
  132)
juice of half a lemon

Equipment
2 saucepans
1 wooden spatula
1 conical strainer
1 liquidizer

1   Soak the mushrooms in cold water for quarter of an hour, changing the water several times, and rubbing the mushrooms between your hands to eliminate every trace of sand and grit. Drain them.

2   Heat the saucepan and cook the mushrooms in the dry pan 'à sec', until all their liquid has evaporated. Stir from time to time with the wooden spatula.

3   Add the port, then the veal stock. Cook at a bare simmer over a very low heat; allow to reduce for twenty minutes.

4   At the end of the cooking strain the liquid through the conical strainer. Remove the mushrooms and chop them finely with a sharp knife. Put them on one side.

5   Mix the mushroom purée and fromage blanc in the liquidizer having first added the mushroom cooking liquid and a few drops of lemon juice to heighten the flavour.

6   Heat the sauce, season and add the chopped mushrooms.

Uses   Sweetbread gâteau with morilles (No 108)
       Grilled veal chop with a salad (No 102)

EDITOR'S NOTE   For a discussion of wild mushrooms and fungi, see pages 28–9.

45. *Hot lobster sauce*
SAUCE 'HOMARDIÈRE' CHAUD

For five people

Main ingredients
3 tablespoons dry white wine
1½ tablespoons Armagnac
8 tablespoons sauce Américaine
  (No 10)
250 ml (scant ½ pint) fish fumet
  (No 3)

Ingredients for flavouring the sauce
70 g (2½ oz) carrots
20 g (¾ oz) onions
salt, pinch of pepper
a pinch thyme

1 teaspoon olive oil

Ingredients for the liaison
2 tablespoons mushroom purée
  (No 132)
1 teaspoon crème fraîche (*optional*)
½ teaspoon chopped tarragon
30 g (1 oz) fromage blanc

Equipment
2 small saucepans
1 small whisk
1 liquidizer

1 Bring the white wine and Armagnac to the boil in the first saucepan and reduce their volume by three-quarters.

2 Add the fish fumet and again reduce, this time by half.

3 Stir in the sauce Américaine, keep hot.

4 Chop the flavouring vegetables (carrots and onions) into tiny dice.

5 Cook them 'al dente' (ten minutes) in the second pan, having first coated the bottom with the olive oil. Season to taste with salt and pepper.

6 Liquidize the mushroom purée, tarragon, crème fraîche (if used) and fromage blanc. Pour this mixture into the reduction in the first saucepan. Beat them together thoroughly with a wire whisk.

7 Add the mirepoix of vegetables, and a pinch of thyme. Heat the sauce but do not allow to boil.

Uses   Chicken served in a soup bowl with crayfish (No 114)

46. *Red wine sabayon sauce*
SAUCE SABAYON AU VIN ROUGE

For four people

Main ingredients
4 tablespoons red wine
4 tablespoons fish fumet (No 3)
4 turns of the peppermill

Ingredients for the sabayon
2 egg yolks
6 tablespoons cold water

Equipment
1 heavy-based saucepan
1 small bowl
1 small whisk

1 Heat the red wine in the saucepan together with the fish fumet and pepper, and let it reduce by half.

2 Whisk the egg yolks and water together vigorously in a bowl until they have become the consistency of a creamy mousse.

3 Away from the heat, incorporate the egg yolks into the red wine, whisking continuously; the sabayon (egg yolks and water) will coagulate and give the sauce added volume and a feeling of tremendous lightness.

Uses   Seafood pot-au-feu (No 95)

First courses

47. *Eggs baked in water*
OEUF AU PLAT À L'EAU

For one person

Main ingredients
2 fresh eggs
1 tablespoon of water
salt, pepper

Equipment
2 identical shallow earthenware
cocottes

1   Preheat the oven to 220°C/425°F/Mark 7. Heat one of the cocottes, in which you have put a tablespoon of water. Let it come to the boil and remove from the heat.

2   Break the eggs into a saucer and slide them into the cocotte in which the water is just simmering.

3   Put the second cocotte on top so that the eggs heat evenly. Leave for three minutes.

4   Put the cocottes into the oven. Remove them just as the whites are beginning to set. Season with salt and pepper when cooked.

48. *Glazed eggs with ratatouille*
OEUF GLACÉ À LA RATATOUILLE

For four people

Main ingredients
1 litre (1¾ pints) water
3 tablespoons vinegar
4 very fresh eggs
8 tablespoons ratatouille (No 144)
7 tablespoons jellied stock or aspic
sprigs of chervil

Equipment
4 cups
1 saucepan
1 wire sieve
1 cloth
4 large plates

1   Make the ratatouille and allow it to cool.

2   Poach four eggs in the traditional way: Break each egg into a cup. Bring 1 litre (1¾ pints) of water in which you have put three tablespoons of vinegar to a gentle simmer (on no account add salt – it liquefies the egg whites). Carefully slide in the eggs one at a time and allow to poach gently for three minutes. Remove them with a perforated spoon or skimmer and plunge them into a bowl of iced water for a few seconds. Lift them out and lay them on a cloth to drain. Trim them to a nice oval shape with a small knife, removing all the little filaments of egg white from round the edge. Place in the refrigerator to chill thoroughly.

3   Bring the jelly to an oily coating consistency: to do this, melt the jelly without boiling, and then cool it on crushed ice or in the refrigerator, stirring gently just as it starts to set.

4   Coat the four eggs with jelly, using a spoon. Repeat three or four times until each egg has a lustrous coating.

5   Decorate each one by arranging a few sprigs of chervil on top.

6   Divide the ratatouille between the four dishes and place the eggs on top.

49. *Watercress with poached eggs*
CRESSON À L'OEUF POCHÉ

For four people

Main ingredients
320 g (11½ oz) watercress purée
  (No 135)
4 fresh eggs

Other ingredients
8 asparagus tips
4 slices of truffle (*optional*)

Equipment
2 stainless-steel saucepans
1 slotted spoon or skimmer
4 hot plates

1   Poach the four eggs in the traditional way (No 48)

2   Heat the watercress purée in a stainless-steel saucepan.

3   When the eggs are cooked, drain them on a cloth. Trim them to a nice oval shape with a small knife, removing all the little filaments of white from round the edge.

4   Arrange the watercress purée on the four plates and place the eggs on top, decorated with the slices of truffle, if used. Arrange the asparagus tips all round like a crown.

Note for Australia See recipes 125–134 for alternative purées where watercress is difficult to obtain.

50. *Caviar with creamed eggs*
OEUF POULE AU CAVIAR

For four people

Main ingredients
4 very fresh eggs
2 × 30 g (1 oz) pots of Iranian Sevruga caviar
1 tablespoon finely-chopped onion
1 teaspoon chopped chives
2 teaspoons fromage blanc
1 teaspoon salt, a pinch of pepper

Equipment
1 small heavy-based saucepan
1 whisk
4 egg cups

See colour illustrations between pages 128 and 129

1   Slice the tops off the eggs with a fine saw-edged knife, sawing the shell delicately about 1 cm ($\frac{1}{2}$ in) above the widest part of the egg; empty the shells, keeping both parts to serve the eggs in. Carefully wash the shells in hot water and put them to dry on a cloth.

2   Beat three of the four eggs. Strain them through a wire sieve to remove pieces of shell and the strings in the egg whites.

3   Pour the beaten eggs into a small heavy-based saucepan, and put them over a low heat. Beat them vigorously with a small whisk, until the eggs start to form a light cream.

4   Take the pan off the heat. Season with salt and pepper. Still stirring add the fromage blanc and the chopped onion and chives. Taste for seasoning.

5   Put the washed and dried egg shells into the egg cups. Fill them three-quarters full with the creamed egg. Finish by filling each one to the top with 15 g ($\frac{1}{2}$ oz) of caviar and cover the top with the tops of the egg shells. You can just see the caviar under these little bonnets.

These creamed eggs are accompanied by the ritual flavours used with caviar – onion and chives – which add an enjoyable Eastern European flavour to the dish.

Note for Australia Russian caviar or lump fish roe can be used in this recipe, though Monsieur Guérard specifies Sevruga caviar.

---

51. *Oysters with poached eggs*
HUÎTRES À LA POULE

For four people

Main ingredients
4 large oysters
4 fresh eggs

Accompanying sauce
4 tablespoons lobster and basil sauce
  (*see* No 81)

Other ingredients
4 large cooked prawns
1 teaspoon caviar (*optional*)

1 Take the oysters out of their shells and poach them for one minute at a very low temperature – the back of your finger should be able to tolerate the heat – in their own juice.

2 Poach the four eggs in the traditional way (No 48). When they are cooked and cooled, put them on a clean cloth to drain. Remove the little filaments of egg white from round the edge, giving the eggs a nice round shape.

3 Put the eggs into the oyster-shells, which you have previously washed, cover them with the poached oysters, and coat them delicately with the sauce.

4 Plant a prawn in the middle of each oyster, and sprinkle a little caviar round it.

Note for Australia If you cannot find oysters with shells large enough to support an egg, use small scallop shells, available from fishmongers.

52. *Artichokes Mélanie*
ARTICHAUTS MÉLANIE

For four people

Main ingredients
3 globe artichokes **or** 3 tinned
  artichoke hearts
12 asparagus tips, fresh or tinned
100 g (3½ oz) grated carrot
40 g (1½ oz) lettuce
1 teaspoon chopped parsley

Other ingredients
40 g (1½ oz) button mushrooms
30 g (1 oz) cooked asparagus stalks
50 g (2 oz) apples
50 g (2 oz) coarsely chopped tomato
  pulp (No 138)
all cut in little mirepoix dice 5 mm
  (¼ in) across

Accompanying sauces
2 tablespoons mayonnaise (No 26)
2 tablespoons vinaigrette No 1 (No 24)

Equipment
1 saucepan
1 bowl
4 plates

1   If they are fresh, cook the asparagus tips, preferably the green variety, for three to five minutes, according to size (*see page 68*). Cook the whole artichokes in boiling water acidulated with lemon juice (No 40). Remove the leaves and choke, and keep the hearts, which should be cut in quarters.

2   Delicately mix the mirepoix ingredients with two tablespoons of mayonnaise. Season with salt and pepper.

3   Arrange the lettuce, washed, dried, and cut in ribbons on the middle of each plate. Arrange three pieces of artichoke in a circle in the middle and sprinkle them with vinaigrette. Cover them with the nicely seasoned vegetables in mayonnaise, divided equally, and decorate with the asparagus tips.

4   Scatter the grated carrot moistened with vinaigrette, over the top, and sprinkle with freshly chopped parsley.

53. *Aubergine caviar*
CAVIAR D'AUBERGINES

For four people

Main ingredients
2 aubergines about 220 g (8 oz) each
3 tablespoons water

Other ingredients
half a clove garlic, crushed
50 g (2 oz) coarsely chopped tomato
   pulp (No 138)
25 g (1 oz) red pimentoes cut in little
   dice
80 g (3 oz) button mushrooms
15 g (½ oz) chopped chervil
1 chopped shallot

Ingredients for the liaison
1 egg yolk
a few drops of lemon juice

1½ tablespoons olive oil
4 tablespoons arachide oil
4 teaspoons fromage blanc
1 heaped teaspoon salt
a pinch of pepper

Ingredients for finishing the dish
10 chervil leaves
8 lettuce leaves

Equipment
1 ovenproof dish
1 non-stick frying-pan
1 bowl
1 small whisk
1 serving dish

1   Preheat the oven to 180°C/350°F/Mark 4. Cut the stalks off the aubergines, bring them (the stalks) to the boil and put them on one side.

2   Wash the aubergines and bake them for thirty minutes in the oven in a dish containing three tablespoons of water. Turn them several times whilst they are cooking.

3   Let them cool, then cut them in half lengthwise and remove the flesh with a teaspoon. Be careful not to make holes in the black skins.

4   Sauté the seasoned mushrooms, cut in little cubes 5 mm (¼ in) across, in the non-stick frying-pan. Let them cool.

5   Put the egg yolk, lemon juice, salt and pepper in the bowl, and start stirring them with a whisk, and slowly adding the olive oil, the arachide oil and the fromage blanc, as if you were making mayonnaise. When the mayonnaise is ready, stir in all the 'other ingredients', not forgetting the mushrooms.

6   Fill the skins of the aubergines with this mixture (5) pushing them back to their original shape.

7   Cover the serving dish with fresh lettuce, arrange the aubergines on top, and decorate them with their own stalks, arranging the little line of chervil leaves down the middle like a backbone.

54. *Gâteau of green vegetables*
GÂTEAU D'HERBAGE À L'ANCIENNE

For four people

Main ingredients
4 green cabbage leaves
150 g (5 oz) spinach
60 g (2 oz) sorrel
150 g (5 oz) leeks
60 g (2 oz) blette (spinach beet)
1 bouquet garni

Ingredients for the liaison
1 whole egg
1 egg white
200 ml (⅓ pint) water
20 g (¾ oz) skimmed milk powder

⅛ teaspoon of chopped tarragon
⅓ teaspoon of chopped chives
½ teaspoon of chopped parsley
½ onion, chopped

Equipment
1 large saucepan
1 bowl
1 whisk
1 cake tin 5 cm (2 in) high and 15 cm (6 in) across
1 bain-marie
1 round serving dish

1   Preheat the oven to 220°C/425°F/Mark 7. Remove the cabbage stalks and the thick parts of the ribs. Wash the spinach, sorrel and blette and remove the stalks. Wash the leeks and cut them into fine rounds.

2   Bring a large pan of salted water to the boil with the bouquet garni, and in it blanch the cabbage leaves, sorrel, blette and spinach for four minutes, and the sliced leeks for nine minutes.

3   Beat the whole egg and the egg white with a fork, just enough to mix them together. Add the skimmed milk, the salt, pepper and chopped herbs and onion.

4   Line the inside of the cake tin with the cabbage leaves, leaving enough hanging over the sides to cover up the contents completely, once the stuffing has been added.

5   Arrange the cake in layers, first the leeks, then spinach, sorrel and blette and then the liasion (3). Fold the cabbage leaves over the top.

6   Bake the gâteau, covered with aluminium foil, and standing in a bain-marie, in the oven for 1 hour 15 mins.

7   Take it out of the oven and allow to rest for fifteen minutes before turning it out of the cake tin, so that it can settle a bit and will keep its shape when sliced.

55. *Carrot gâteau with chervil*
GÂTEAU DE CAROTTES FONDANTES AU CERFEUIL

For four people

Main ingredients
460 g (1 lb) carrots
35 g (1¼ oz) unsalted butter
sugar substitute equivalent to 1½
  teaspoons sugar
1 teaspoon salt
a pinch of pepper
250 ml (scant ½ pint) of chicken stock
  (No 2) or stock made with stock
  cubes

Other ingredients
1 teaspoon olive oil
100 g (3½ oz) button mushrooms
half a chopped shallot

Ingredients for the liaison
2 whole eggs
20 g (¾ oz) grated Gruyère cheese

20 g (¾ oz) coarsely chopped chervil

Accompanying sauces
Asparagus sauce (No 39) or
Artichoke sauce (No 40)

Equipment
1 heavy-based saucepan with a lid
1 non-stick frying-pan
1 ring-shaped decorated mould (of
  the kind used to make savarins or
  kügelhopf)
1 pastry brush
1 small bowl
1 round serving dish

*See colour illustrations between pages
  128 and 129*

1   Wash the carrots and peel thinly with a potato-peeler.

2   Cut them into rounds 5 mm (¼ in) thick.

3   Heat 25 g (1 oz) of the butter in the saucepan and cook the carrots in it until they are lightly browned.

4   Add the sugar substitute, stock, salt and pepper. Cover the pan and cook over a moderate heat for twenty minutes. By the end of this time, the liquid should have evaporated.

5   Cut the mushrooms into little dice 5 mm (¼ in) across. Sauté them in the frying-pan, coated with the teaspoon of olive oil, adding the chopped shallot.

6   Preheat the oven to 220°C/425°F/Mark 7. Remove the carrots from the pan in which they were cooked, and chop them coarsely, either with a knife or through the coarsest disc of the moulin-légumes.

7   Beat the eggs in a bowl with a fork, add the chopped carrots, grated Gruyère and chervil. Mix them together lightly.

8   Brush the inside of the mould with the remaining butter. Fill it with the mixture.

9 Cook the gâteau, covered with aluminium foil, and standing in a bain-marie in the oven (220°C/425°F/Mark 7) for twenty minutes.

10 Turn the gâteau out carefully on to the serving dish and surround it with the asparagus or artichoke sauce.

---

56. *Asparagus gâteau*
GÂTEAU MOELLEUX D'ASPERGES

For four people

Main ingredient
1 kg (2¼ lb) asparagus

Ingredients for the liaison
2 whole eggs
1 egg yolk
1½ teaspoons salt
a pinch of pepper
a hint of grated nutmeg

Other ingredients
12 asparagus tips
1 teaspoon tomato sauce (No 38)
½ teaspoon chopped parsley

Accompanying sauces
Asparagus sauce (No 39) **or**
Artichoke sauce (No 40)

Equipment
1 saucepan
1 liquidizer
4 small earthenware or glass dishes,
   9 cm (3½ in) across and 4 cm (1½ in)
   deep
4 hot plates

1 Trim the asparagus with a potato-peeler – peeling away from the heads. Wash them and cook them in plenty of salted water.

2 Drain them and purée them in the liquidizer. If there are any coarse fibres in the purée, sieve it.

3 Put the mixture in a saucepan and let it reduce by one-third of its volume over a gentle heat, stirring frequently.

4 Take it off the heat and whisk in the two whole eggs, egg yolk, salt, pepper and nutmeg.

5 Preheat the oven to 220°C/425°F/Mark 7. Brush the inside of the little dishes with butter – it will disappear during the course of the cooking – and fill them with the purée.

6 Cook them in a bain-marie in the oven for one hour. Half-way through the cooking, cover the pots with a sheet of aluminium foil.

7 Heat the asparagus tips in salted water. Turn out the little gâteaux on to the plates which have previously been coated with your chosen sauce,

and decorate each with three asparagus tips arranged to look like a little bunch tied together with a thread of fresh tomato sauce. Sprinkle the sauce with freshly chopped parsley.

---

57. *Sweet onion tart*
TOURTE AUX OIGNONS DOUX

For six people

Main ingredients for the filling
1 kg (2¼ lb) onions, peeled and very thinly sliced
200 g (7 oz) button mushrooms, 150 g (5½ oz) peeled carrots (cut into small cubes)
6 green cabbage leaves
a pinch of thyme
1 teaspoon olive oil (*optional*)
salt, pepper

Ingredients for the liaison
2 eggs
20 g (¾ oz) skimmed milk powder
200 ml (⅓ pint) water

Accompanying sauces
200 ml (⅓ pint) Tomato sauce (No 38) or
200 ml (⅓ pint) Artichoke sauce (No 40), or
200 ml (⅓ pint) Asparagus sauce (No 39)

Equipment
1 heavy-based saucepan with a lid
1 other saucepan
1 cake tin, 16 cm (6 in) across and 4 cm (1½ in) deep

1   Sweat the diced carrots 'à sec' in the heavy saucepan so that they exude their juice. This operation is easier with a teaspoon of olive oil in the pan. Stir constantly with a spatula to prevent the carrots from sticking. Cook them for five minutes, then add the sliced onions seasoned with salt and pepper. Cover the pan and leave it over a moderate heat for fifteen minutes.

2   At the end of this time, add the mushrooms and stir them in with a fork. Cook for a further ten minutes.

3   Cut away the ribs of the cabbage leaves and blanch them in boiling salted water for four minutes, drain and pat them dry on a cloth.

4   Prepare the liaison by beating the eggs lightly with a fork to mix them together. Add the skimmed milk, salt and pepper.

5   Preheat the oven to 220°C/425°F/Mark 7. Line the cake tin with the cabbage leaves. Leave enough hanging over the sides to fold over the top and completely enclose the filling (1 and 2).

6   Mix the filling with the liaison (4). Fill the mould, enclose the filling with the cabbage leaves and cook covered with aluminium foil, in a bain-marie, in the oven for fifty minutes.

7   Take the tart out of the oven and leave ten minutes before turning out to allow it to set and keep its shape. Turn it out on to a round serving dish and pour the chosen sauce around it.

---

58. *Fresh tomato tarts with thyme*
TARTE DE TOMATES FRAÎCHES AU THYM

For five people

Main ingredients	*Equipment*
500 g (1 lb 2 oz) cooked, coarsely-chopped tomato pulp (No 139) You will need 1.5 kg (3½ lb) tomatoes to start with salt, pepper 300 g (11 oz) leaf spinach 5 small sprigs of thyme	1 saucepan 5 individual oven dishes, 12 cm (4½ in) across, **or** 5 small flan tins, 12 cm (4½ in) across

See colour illustrations between pages 128 and 129

1   Prepare the cooked tomatoes following the method given in recipe No 139.

2   Preheat the oven to 220°C/425°F/Mark 7. Remove the stalks from the spinach. Blanch for two minutes in a large pan of boiling water. Spread them out carefully on a cloth, then line the oven dishes or tartlet tins with the leaves in layers, leaving enough falling over the edges to cover the top.

3   Fill each dish or tart tin with tomato pulp, reserving five teaspoons for decoration. Fold the spinach 'jacket' over the top so that the tomato is no longer visible. Decorate each dish with a sprig of thyme.

4   Cook in the oven for fifteen minutes.

5   Serve the tarts in their dishes, pouring a teaspoon of cooked tomato on to each one, beneath the sprig of thyme, to give a pretty effect of contrasting red and green.

59. *Fresh tomato soufflé*
SOUFFLÉ AUX TOMATES FRAÎCHES

For four people

Main ingredients	*Equipment*
1 litre (1¾ pints) fresh tomato sauce (No 38)	1 saucepan
	2 bowls
2 sheets of gelatine or 2 level teaspoons of powdered gelatine	4 little earthenware dishes, 9 cm (3½ in) across and 4 cm (1½ in) deep
6 egg whites	1 balloon whisk
½ teaspoon chopped tarragon	1 small whisk
	1 wooden spatula

1 Soak the gelatine for quarter of an hour in cold water to soften.

2 Bring the tomato sauce, together with the tarragon, to the boil and reduce it by two-thirds of its volume. Stir in the gelatine and allow to cool.

3 Whisk the egg whites to a soft snow in a bowl beating them, gently at first, with the balloon whisk to break them down. Gradually increase the rhythm as the eggs whiten. Do not allow them to become too firm.

4 Stir some of the beaten egg whites into the cold tomato sauce (2) with a small whisk. Then add the remaining egg whites, folding them in delicately with a wooden spatula.

5 Preheat the oven to 220°C/425°F/Mark 7. Lightly brush the insides of the small pots with butter and fill them right to the top with the egg and tomato mixture. Smooth the surface with a metal palette knife or with the back of a knife. Push the mixture inwards 5 mm (¼ in) away from the edge of the dishes with your thumb, to help the soufflés to rise.

6 Cook for eight to ten minutes and serve immediately.

This recipe can be given an element of surprise by slipping a poached egg into the middle of each soufflé before putting it in the oven. Also, the gelatine can be replaced by two egg yolks, at the cost of adding extra calories.

Other vegetable soufflés are made in the same way, replacing the reduced tomato sauce with the equivalent amount of a purée made from the chosen vegetable.

No 50 Creamed eggs with caviar *(Oeuf poule au caviar)*

No 58 Fresh tomato and spinach tarts with thyme *and* No 55 Carrot gâteau with chervil
(*Tarte de tomates fraîches au thym, Gâteau de carottes fondantes au cerfeuil*)
No 61 Potted salmon with lemon and green peppercorns
(*La hure de saumon au citron et poivre vert*)

No 64 Terrine of sea-bass with asparagus tips
(*La terrine de loup chaude aux pointes d'asperges*)
No 70 Mussel, saffron and lettuce-heart salad
(*Salade de moules au safran et aux coeurs de laitue*)

No 106 Veal kidney 'in a green waistcoat' braised in spinach and lettuce leaves
(Rognon de veau 'en habit vert')

No 107 Steamed calf's liver with sweet-sour leeks
(Foie de veau à la vapeur aux blancs de poireaux en aigre-doux)

No 161 Bananas 'en papillote ,
No 169 Little pear soufflés *and*
No 159 Light apple tart
(*Bananes en papillote, Soufflé léger aux poires,
Tarte fine aux pommes chaudes*)

60. *Truffles cooked in salt*
TRUFFES SOUS LE SEL

For three people

Main ingredients
3 truffles 40 g (1½ oz) each, fresh **or** tinned
1 raw chicken breast, from a bird weighing approximately 1.5 kg (3½ lb)
600 g (1¼ lb) coarse salt
2 egg whites
1 teaspoon flour

Ingredients for the marinade
1 teaspoon olive oil
the juice of half a lemon
pinch of pepper
salt

Equipment
1 potato-peeler
3 sheets of aluminium foil, 20 cm by 20 cm (8 in by 8 in)
3 hot plates

1   Slice the raw chicken breast into three thin escalopes. Marinate for one hour with the oil, lemon juice, pepper and salt.

2   Pare the truffles with a potato-peeler, keep the peelings for another time.

3   Prepare the jacket of salt. Beat the egg whites lightly with a fork, then mix them with the salt and the flour to make a smooth paste.

4   Preheat the oven to 230°C/450°F/Mark 8. Armour each truffle by rolling it up in a chicken escalope and encasing each with the salt paste, and shaping it into a ball.

5   Enclose each ball hermetically in its sheet of aluminium foil and cook on a baking sheet in a hot oven for thirty minutes.

6   To serve the truffles, open the aluminium foil envelopes, break the salt crusts, lay the chicken breasts on the plates and arrange the truffles, cut in slices and seasoned with salt and pepper, on top.

61. *Potted salmon with lemon and green peppercorns*
'HURE' DE SAUMON AU CITRON ET POIVRE VERT

For ten people

Main ingredients
500g (just over 1 lb) of salmon, off the
  bone
3 whole eggs
5 lemons
80 g (3 oz) red pimento (tinned) cut
  into little dice
4 heaped teaspoons green peppercorns
2 tablespoons freshly chopped parsley
1 tablespoon freshy chopped tarragon
  and chervil
2 chopped shallots
2 teaspoons salt, ½ teaspoon pepper
250 ml (scant ½ pint) dry white wine
250 ml (scant ½ pint) of fish fumet
  (No 3)

Ingredients for the jelly
1 litre (1¾ pints) fish fumet (No 3)
120g (4 oz) tomatoes
70 g (2½ oz) onions

70 g (2½ oz) cleaned and trimmed leek
quarter celery stalk
20 g (¾ oz) button mushrooms
2 tablespoons freshly chopped chervil
  and tarragon
200 g (7 oz) minced beef
8 sheets leaf gelatine **or** 8 level
  teaspoons of powdered gelatine
1½ tablespoons lemon juice
2 teaspoons salt, 1 teaspoon pepper
2 egg whites

Accompanying sauce
Sauce Grelette (No 32)

Equipment
1 heavy-based saucepan
1 conical strainer
1 porcelain terrine, 15 cm (6 in) long,
  9 cm (3½ in) wide and 10 cm (4 in)
  deep

See colour illustrations between pages 128 and 129

1   Put the terrine in the refrigerator.

Preparing the jelly
2   Chop coarsely the vegetables from the ingredients for the jelly (onions,
whites of leek, celery, tomatoes, mushrooms).

3   Put them into the saucepan with the minced beef, lemon juice, tarragon, chervil, salt, pepper and the two egg whites broken up with a fork.

4   Pour in 1 litre (1¾ pints) of fish fumet, and bring to a slow boil, stirring
with a wooden spoon. Allow to simmer gently for twenty minutes.

5   If using leaf gelatine, soak it in cold water for ten minutes to swell and
soften, then drain and add to the fish fumet. Powdered gelatine can be
softened in a spoonful of the fish fumet.

6   Moisten a cloth and use it to line a conical strainer. Slowly pour the

jelly through into a bowl, and put in the refrigerator, stirring from time to time to prevent it from setting.

Preparing the salmon

7   Cut the salmon into strips 2 cm (¾ in) across. Put these in a flame-proof oval dish with the white wine, 250 ml (scant ½ pint) of fish fumet, parsley, salt and pepper and leave to marinate for one hour.

8   Hard-boil the three eggs in boiling water (eight minutes). Run them under cold water, peel, and separate the yolks and whites, chopping each separately.

9   Poach the salmon in its marinade for two or three minutes (not more) after bringing to the boil and then remove from the heat. Drain the fillets on a cloth.

10   Peel the lemons, removing both peel and pith with a well-sharpened knife. Cut the flesh into small cubes.

Filling the terrine

While this is going on, the jelly should have been kept cool and at the consistency of oil – which means it is all but set.

11   Pour a small ladleful of jelly in the bottom of the terrine and sprinkle it with the filling ingredients – chopped whites and yolks of eggs, cubes of lemon and red pimento, green peppercorns, shallots, chopped chervil and tarragon. Lay some of the strips of salmon lengthwise on top and put to set in the refrigerator.

12   Repeat the process until all the ingredients are used up and the terrine is filled. Chill for twenty-four hours.

Serving the dish

13   To serve the terrine, turn it out, having first dipped it into hot water for a few seconds. Cut in slices 1 cm (½ in) thick. Accompany with Sauce Grelette.

Clarification   Added to the vegetables, the egg whites (albumen) coagulate on contact with the heat and form a thick skin on the surface which traps all the impurities that arise from the liquid to be cleared – hence 'clarification'. It does, it is true, somewhat mute the flavours of the bouillon or fumet being treated and for this reason minced beef is added – to make up for the loss of essential flavours.

Note for Australia The salmon trout available in Australia is a good substitute for salmon in this recipe.

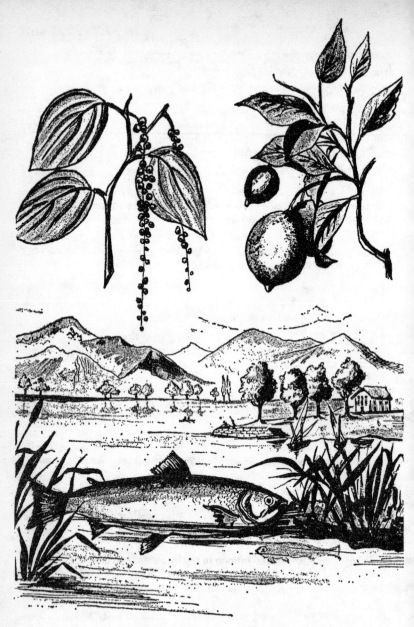

La hure de saumon au citron et poivre vert

62. *Fish terrine with fresh herbs*
TERRINE DE POISSONS AUX HERBES FRAÎCHES

For ten people

Main ingredients for the filling
320 g (11½ oz) boned fish, (80 g (3 oz) angler fish or monk fish and 240 g (8½ oz) salmon)
1 tablespoon beaten egg
half an egg white
25 g (1 oz) spinach
15 g (½ oz) sorrel
30 g (1 oz) watercress
15 g (½ oz) tarragon
15 g (½ oz) chervil
1 teaspoon salt, pinch of pepper
a hint of chopped garlic

Other ingredients
3 tablespoons dry white wine
200 g (7 oz) button mushrooms
200 g (7 oz) fish fillets (salmon, John Dory, or pike, or whiting, in equal quantities)
1 tablespoon parsley
half chopped shallot
15 g (½ oz) jellied fish stock (No 3) (*optional*)
½ teaspoon salt, pinch of pepper.

Accompanying sauce
Sauce Grelette (No 32)

Equipment
1 dish suitable for marinating the fish
1 saucepan, 1 non-stick frying-pan
1 bowl, 1 liquidizer
1 porcelain terrine, 15 cm (6 in) long, 9 cm (3½ in) wide and 10 cm (4 in) deep

1   Cut the fish fillets, with bones and skin removed, into strips 1 cm (½ in) wide.

2   Marinate them for one hour in the white wine. Season with salt, pepper and a tablespoon of freshly-chopped parsley.

3   Cut the button mushrooms into little dice.

4   Sauté them with the chopped shallot, either in the non-stick pan, or in a frying-pan coated with a teaspoon of olive oil.

5   Blanch the watercress, sorrel and spinach one after the other in a pan of boiling salted water.

6   Purée the angler fish and salmon in the liquidizer for two minutes with the salt, pepper and garlic. Add the blanched green vegetables, and the herbs, and blend for one minute. Add the beaten egg and half egg white and blend for two minutes more.

7   Preheat the oven to 200°C/400°F/Mark 6. Coat the interior of the terrine with a layer of forcemeat (6) 5 mm (¼ in) thick. Lay a layer of the drained, marinated fish fillets and mushroom mixture on top. Cover with

133

another layer of the forcemeat and repeat the process until the terrine is completely filled, ending with a layer of forcemeat.

8   Cover with a sheet of aluminium foil. Stand the terrine in a bain-marie and cook in the oven for fifty minutes.

9   Allow the terrine to cool. When it has cooled, cover the top with the jellied fish stock melted and mixed with chopped parsley (if used). Then keep it in the refrigerator until it is needed.

10   It can then be either turned out and cut into slices 1 cm (½ in) thick, or cut in the terrine, as and when required. The slices will cut more cleanly if the knife is first dipped in hot water.

11   The terrine should be served with a Sauce Grelette (No 32).

See the **Note for users in Australia**, pp. 31–5, for suggested equivalents to European fish.

---

63. *Mousseline of frogs' legs with watercress*
MOUSSELINE DE GRENOUILLES AU CRESSON DE FONTAINE

For four people

Main ingredients
80 g (3 oz) uncooked boned frogs' legs
16 uncooked whole frogs' legs
2 uncooked scallops (about 35 g)
250 ml (scant ½ pint) fish fumet (No 3) or 8 tablespoons water and 8 tablespoons dry white wine
half an egg
½ teaspoon salt, a pinch of pepper
1½ teaspoons skimmed milk powder, dissolved in 4 tablespoons water
2 tablespoons watercress purée (No 135)
16 tiny bunches of fresh parsley
butter for coating the oven dishes

Accompanying sauce
200 ml (scant ½ pint) Tomato sauce (No 38) or
Artichoke sauce (No 40) or
Asparagus sauce (No 39)

Equipment
1 bowl
1 small saucepan
1 small pastry brush
1 liquidizer
4 little earthenware or porcelain oven dishes, 9 cm (3½ in) across, 4 cm (1½ in) deep
1 sheet of aluminium foil
1 serving dish

1   Preheat the oven to 220°C/425°F/Mark 7. In the liquidizer, purée the boned frogs' legs, scallops, half an egg, beaten, the skimmed milk powder dissolved in water, and the watercress purée, all seasoned with salt and pepper.

2 Lightly brush the insides of the small oven dishes with butter – this butter will disappear when the mousselines are turned out. Or, to prevent sticking, the dishes can simply be brushed all over, bottom and sides, with water. When this is done fill the little dishes with the mixture made in **1** and cook them in a bain-marie, in a moderate oven for ten minutes. Cover the pots with a sheet of aluminium foil during cooking.

3 Poach the sixteen whole frogs' legs for two minutes in the fish fumet, or water and white wine, flavoured with a little bunch of parsley and half a chopped shallot, salt and pepper.

4 When the mousselines are cooked, turn them out on to a serving dish and pour the chosen sauce around them. Arrange the sixteen frogs' legs around the outside, putting the miniature bunches of parsley in between.

For a note on frogs' legs see No **20**.

---

64. *Hot terrine of sea-bass with asparagus tips*
TERRINE DE LOUP CHAUDE AUX POINTES D'ASPERGES
    (*schnapper, teraglin or perch*)

For four people

Main ingredients
1 sea-bass of 700 g (1½ lb) or
350 g (¾ lb) sea-bass fillets
2 egg whites
30 g (1 oz) skimmed milk powder
  dissolved in
300 ml (generous ½ pint) water
salt, pepper
12 asparagus tips, fresh or tinned
1 teaspoon chopped shallot
1 teaspoon chopped tarragon
4 tablespoons dry white wine
20 g (¾ oz) butter

Ingredients for the sauce
250 ml (scant ½ pint) fish fumet
  (No 3)

1 teaspoon chopped shallot
60 g (2 oz) button mushrooms
15 g (½ oz) skimmed milk powder
1 teaspoon crème fraîche
1 teaspoon olive oil

Equipment
1 dish suitable for marinating the fish
1 heavy-based saucepan
1 liquidizer
1 pastry-brush
4 small oval earthenware terrines with
  lids, 10 cm (4 in) long by 4 cm (1½
  in) high
1 oval serving dish
4 hot plates

See colour illustrations between pages 128 and 129

Preparing the fish

1 Scale and clean the fish and cut off the fins with a pair of kitchen scissors. Fillet it by making an incision along one side of the backbone with a pliable knife. Remove the fillets whole and skin them by sliding the same knife between skin and flesh, keeping the fillet flat on the board.

2 Marinate the fillets for two hours in the dry white wine, with the chopped shallots and tarragon.

Preparing the forcemeat (farce)

3 Purée 220 g (scant 8 oz) of the sea-bass fillet, seasoned with salt and pepper, in the liquidizer for two minutes. Add the egg whites and blend for a further minute. Now add the milk powder dissolved in water and blend for a further two minutes.

4 If the asparagus is fresh, cook it for three to four minutes in boiling salted water. Drain.
   Cut the remaining bass into little cubes 5 mm ($\frac{1}{4}$ in) across.

Filling the terrines

5 Preheat the oven to 220°C/425°F/Mark 7. Soften the butter to a cream and lightly brush the insides of the little terrines with it.

6 Half fill the terrines with the forcemeat, place a layer of the cubes of sea-bass on top and put three asparagus tips in each. Fill to the top with the remaining forcemeat, put on the lids and cook in a bain-marie, in the oven for fifteen minutes.

Preparing the sauce

7 Whilst the terrines are cooking, put the olive oil in the heavy-based saucepan, and soften the chopped shallots and button mushrooms, washed and cut in quarters, without browning.

8 Pour in the white wine from the marinade, and reduce it by half to eliminate the alcohol, then add the fish fumet in which you have dissolved the skimmed milk powder.

9 Cook over a gentle heat – at a slow simmer – for fifteen minutes, and reduce to a fine purée in the liquidizer, having first added the crème fraîche. Keep the sauce hot.

To serve the dish

10 Serve the terrines, straight from the oven, on an oval dish. Turn them out at the table, and coat them lightly with the white-wine and mushroom sauce.

Note for Australia Schnapper may prove to be the best Australian equivalent of sea bass in this recipe, but if fillets are used, most white fish that are not too oily will give good results.

La terrine de loup chaude aux pointes d'asperges

65. *Chicken liver mousse*
GÂTEAU DE FOIES BLONDS DE VOLAILLE

For four people

Main ingredients
110 g (4 oz) of the palest chicken livers
1 small egg
25 g (1 oz) skimmed milk powder dissolved in 250 ml (scant ½ pint) water
scant teaspoon of salt, a pinch of ground nutmeg
half clove of garlic
½ teaspoon freshly chopped parsley
½ teaspoon truffle juice (*optional*)

Accompanying sauce
150 ml (¼ pint) fresh tomato sauce (No 38)
3 tablespoons of reduced sauce Américaine (No 10)

For decoration
4 whole freshwater crayfish **or** Dublin Bay prawns
4 black olives

Equipment
1 pastry-brush
1 liquidizer
1 bowl
1 small saucepan
4 small earthenware or porcelain oven dishes, 9 cm (3½ in) across by 4 cm (1½ in) deep
1 sheet of aluminium foil
1 serving dish

1 Clean the livers, removing any strings or greenish parts.

2 Blend them in the liquidizer together with salt, pepper, nutmeg, garlic, beaten egg, the truffle juice (if used), and the skimmed milk powder dissolved in water, then add the chopped parsley.

3 Preheat the oven to 220°C/425°F/Mark 7. To prevent the mousse from sticking, lightly brush the insides of the four little pots with butter – the butter will stay behind when the pots are turned out. Alternatively, the pots can be brushed with water.

4 Fill the pots with the chicken liver mixture and cook in a bain-marie in the oven for thirty minutes. Protect them with a sheet of aluminium foil whilst they are cooking.

5 Meanwhile poach the freshwater crayfish or Dublin Bay prawns in boiling salted water (or even better, in 120 ml (scant ¼ pint) of water, plus 120 ml (scant ¼ pint) of dry white wine flavoured with a miniature bouquet garni, salt, pepper and half a shallot, chopped).

6 When the mousses are cooked, turn them out on to a dish and cover them with the tomato sauce mixed with the reduced sauce Américaine.

Arrange the freshwater crayfish or Dublin Bay prawns around the dish and decorate with halved black olives. Serve hot.

Either look for very pale super-fine livers, or put ordinary chicken livers to soak in milk for two to three hours, or overnight in the refrigerator.

Salads

66. *Geisha salad*
SALADE À LA GEISHA

For two people

Main ingredients
2 medium-sized tomatoes
80 g (3 oz) crab meat
1 grapefruit
40 g (1½ oz) scraped carrots
50 g (2 oz) bean sprouts
6 fresh prawns
½ teaspoon chopped chervil
30 g (1 oz) curly endive

Dressing
Sauce rose (No 29) or
Vinaigrette 2 (No 24)

Equipment
1 saucepan
1 small salad bowl
2 plates

1   Skin the tomatoes, then decapitate them with a saw-bladed knife and keep the tops. Using the handle of a teaspoon, remove the pips and core from each tomato. Press them lightly in the palm of your hand to extract the excess liquid. Season the insides with salt and pepper.

2   Peel the grapefruit, and skin the segments over a plate, so that you collect all the juice. Cut half of the segments into little cubes. Keep the rest for some other purpose.

3   Grate the carrots.

4   Plunge the bean sprouts in boiling water for five seconds and refresh in cold water.

5   Fill the tomatoes with crab meat mixed with the grapefruit cubes and put one in the centre of each plate, on a layer of curly endive.

6   Toss the bean sprouts and grated carrots in the chosen dressing and arrange them round the tomatoes.

7   Stand the pink prawns against the sides of the tomatoes with their antennae in the air.

8   Crown the tops of the tomatoes with their little hats, and lightly cloak them with the chosen dressing.

67. *Garden salad with chives*
SALADE DES PRÉS À LA CIBOULETTE

For four people

Main ingredients
120 g (4 oz) very small French beans
150 g (5½ oz) ceps, fresh or tinned
  'au naturel'. (Button mushrooms can
  be substituted for the ceps.)
1 grapefruit
1 apple
80 g (3 oz) grated carrot
20 g (¾ oz) cooked sweetcorn, frozen
  or tinned

20 g (¾ oz) chopped chives
1 lettuce

Dressing
Favourite sauce (No 30) or
Vinaigrette 1 (No 24)

Equipment
1 stainless-steel saucepan
5 bowls
4 plates

1   Peel the grapefruit, and skin the segments, over a bowl to collect the juice that drips out.

2   Peel and quarter the apple and cut it into thin slices. Macerate them in a bowl with the grapefruit segments and juice.

3   Cook the French beans 'al dente' (*see page 68*).

4   If they are fresh, clean the earth from the ceps, wash them and blanch for one minute in boiling salted water. Cut into fine slices. If they are tinned, rinse and slice them.

5   Put all the vegetables (French beans, ceps, grated carrots, sweetcorn) in separate bowls and coat them with the chosen dressing.

6   Arrange the lettuce, washed and shaken dry, on the four plates.

7   Mound the green beans on top in little pyramids. Arrange a coronet of carrot all round, and overlay with the grapefruit segments and apple, placed to make a palette of pretty colours.

8   Complete the dish by sprinkling the whole salad with sweetcorn and chopped chives.

68. *Truffle salad with parsley*
SALADE DE TRUFFES AU PERSIL

For two people

Main ingredients
20 g (¾ oz) parsley, preferably the flat variety (*see page 91*)
40 g (1½ oz) truffles
1 artichoke heart, freshly cooked or tinned
80g (3 oz) raw coarsely-chopped tomato pulp (No 138)
8 lettuce leaves

Dressing
Vinaigrette 1 (No 24)

To decorate the dish
2 slices of truffle

Equipment
2 small earthenware or glass dishes, 9 cm (3½ in) across, 4 cm (1½ in) deep
2 plates

1   Wash and dry the parsley and remove the stalks. Prepare the tomatoes according to the method in No 138. Cut the truffles into fine julienne strips, 3 cm by 2 mm (1¼ in by 1/16 in). Slice the lettuce leaves into a chiffonade (strips the width of your little finger). Cut the artichoke heart into fine slices. Dress each of these vegetables separately.

2   Fill the little dishes with vegetables in the following order: flat parsley leaves, julienne of truffles, tomato pulp, lettuce chiffonade, and pack all down tightly in the dishes.

3   Turn out the dishes on to the two plates, and arrange the slices of artichoke around the edge. Decorate the top of each mould with a slice of truffle.

69. *Marine salad*
SALADE PLEINE MER

For two people

Main ingredients
200 g (7 oz) very small French beans
80 g (3 oz) fillets of sole
4 whole Dublin Bay prawns
2 scallops
400 ml (generous ½ pint) fish fumet (No 3)
4 lettuce leaves

Dressing
Vinaigrette 1 (No 24) or
Cold Lobster sauce (No 33)

To decorate the dish
2 whole freshwater crayfish **or** Dublin Bay prawns
1 teaspoon chervil

Equipment
1 saucepan
1 small salad bowl
2 plates

1   Slice the fillets of sole into 'goujonettes', strips cut diagonally across the width of the fillet. Remove the tails from the Dublin Bay prawns and shell them. Open the scallops and remove them from their shells.

2   Top and tail the French beans and cook them 'al dente' (*see page 68*). When they are cool put them into a small bowl and coat with the chosen dressing.

3   Put the saucepan over the heat, pour in the fish fumet and bring to the boil. Poach the different sorts of fish and shellfish including the freshwater crayfish in it one at a time. One to two minutes simmering is enough for each item. Remove each with a slotted spoon, drain on a cloth and allow to cool.

4   Put a layer of lettuce leaves on the plates and arrange the French beans in a pyramid on top. Slice the scallops into the finest possible rounds and arrange them in a coronet around the beans. Stud this coronet with the goujonettes of sole and the Dublin Bay prawns, and coat the fish with the chosen sauce. Decorate the French beans with little fans of chervil – the leaves only, delicately plucked off the stalks. Plant the freshwater crayfish in the pyramid of French beans.

You can improve this recipe by adding oysters and clams poached for an instant in their own juices.

70. *Mussel, saffron and lettuce-heart salad*
SALADE DE MOULES AU SAFRAN ET AUX CŒURS DE LAITUE

For four people

Main ingredients
1½ litres (2½ pints) mussels, washed
 and scraped
1 chopped shallot
the white part of half a leek
4 tablespoons fish fumet (No 3)
2 tablespoons dry white wine

*Other ingredients for preparing the
 salad*
2 fresh lettuce hearts
2 celery stalks
8 tarragon leaves
juice of 1 lemon
1 tablespoon raw diced tomato
 pulp (No 138)

Ingredients for the sauce
1 pinch saffron
1 teaspoon crème fraîche
half chopped shallot
1 teaspoon olive oil

Equipment
1 large stainless-steel saucepan with a
 lid
1 small saucepan
1 bowl
4 unheated plates

See colour illustrations between pages 128 and 129

1   With a sharp knife, cut the white part of the leek, and the celery into
fine julienne strips and chop the tarragon coarsely.

2   Put the white wine, chopped shallots, strips of leek and fish fumet in
the large saucepan and bring it to the boil. When it boils, throw in the
mussels, cover the pan and cook until they have all opened.

3   Take the mussels out of their shells, put them in a bowl and keep their
cooking liquid on one side.

4   Heat the olive oil in the small saucepan, add the chopped shallot,
cream, saffron and the cooking liquid from the mussels. Allow to boil for
one minute, then throw in the shelled mussels, stir them round and allow
to cool in their sauce.

5   On each plate arrange half a lettuce heart sprinkled with fresh lemon
juice, and spoon the mussels, bathed in their sauce, over the top. Decorate
each salad with little strips of celery, chopped tarragon and diced tomato,
arranged prettily on top.

71. *Marinated raw fish salad*
SALADE DE POISSONS CRUS MARINÉS

For four people

Main ingredients
160 g (6 oz) filleted fish (John Dory, salmon, daurade, sea-bream, or bass)
3 teaspoons olive oil
half a shallot
1 heaped teaspoon green peppercorns
40 g (1½ oz) ginger preserved in vinegar

1 tablespoon fresh bilberries or tinned bilberries
1 lemon
1 lettuce
salt, pepper

Equipment
1 deep dish
4 plates

1   With an extremely sharp and fine-bladed knife, cut the fillets of fish into slices so thin that they are almost transparent.

2   Put them into the dish and sprinkle them with salt, pepper, chopped shallot, green peppercorns and oil. Allow to marinate for fifteen minutes.

3   Cut the ginger into julienne strips 3 cm long by 1 mm wide (1 in by $\frac{1}{16}$ in), peel the lemon and cut the peel into fine julienne strips the size of a pine-needle. Plunge them into boiling water, then refresh in iced water.

4   Shred the lettuce into a chiffonade (ribbons about the width of your little finger). Season with salt, pepper and the juice of half a lemon and arrange on the four plates. Scatter the strips of ginger and lemon peel over the lettuce, together with the bilberries. Arrange the fine slices of fish around the outside like the petals of a flower. Put the salads into the refrigerator for fifteen minutes before serving.

EDITOR'S NOTE   Ginger preserved in vinegar can be found in Oriental delicatessens.

See the **Note for Users in Australia** for suggested equivalents to European fish.

72. *Crab salad with grapefruit*
SALADE DE CRABE AU PAMPLEMOUSSE

For four people

Main ingredients
1 cooked crab of 800 g (1¾ lb)
200 g (7 oz) very small French beans
12 asparagus tips, fresh or tinned
1 grapefruit
8 leaves red (radicchio di Treviso) or
    white chicory or red mignonette
1 tablespoon freshly chopped chervil

Sauce
Cold Lobster sauce (No 33)

Equipment
1 saucepan
1 bowl
4 plates

1   Cook the vegetables in boiling salted water – the French beans 'al dente' (*see page 68*) and the asparagus tips, if fresh, cut 4 cm (1½ in) long, for three to five minutes (*for technique, see page 68*).

2   Peel the grapefruit, skin and pith together (*for technique, see* No 66), taking out the skinned segments and cutting them into ½ cm (¼ in) cubes.

3   Arrange the washed and dried chicory on the plates, mound the French beans tossed with the lobster sauce, in a little pyramid in the centre, and stick the asparagus in the top.

4   Scatter the crab, dressed with the same sauce, over the top and sprinkle with the diced grapefruit and freshly chopped chervil.

EDITOR'S NOTE   If you start with a live crab, wash it well, then boil it fast in court-bouillon (No 77) for ten minutes. Cool and open the shell and claws to obtain the crab meat, discarding the inedible parts.

73. *Freshwater crayfish salad*
SALADE D'ÉCREVISSES DE RIVIÈRE
   (*yabbies or king prawns*)

For four people

Main ingredients
400 g (14 oz) very small French beans
12 fresh, or tinned, asparagus tips
1 chopped shallot
50 g (2 oz) red chicory (radicchio di
  Treviso)
32 crayfish or Dublin Bay prawns
1 litre (1¾ pints) nage or
  court-bouillon (No 77)

Ingredients for finishing the dish
1 tablespoon vegetables from the
  court-bouillon

1 tablespoon chopped chervil
4 whole crayfish

Dressings
6 tablespoons Cold Lobster sauce
  (No 33) or
Sauce rose (No 29)
6 tablespoons Vinaigrette 2 (No 25)

Equipment
1 stainless-steel saucepan
1 bowl
4 plates

1 Cook all the crayfish for four minutes in the fast-boiling court-bouillon or plain salted water. Keep four whole crayfish for decoration and shell the rest.

2 Top and tail the French beans, wash them and cook them 'al dente' (*for technique see page 68*). If using fresh asparagus, cook the asparagus tips – cut to a length of 4 cm (1½ in) – for three to five minutes (*see page 68*).

3 Toss the beans and asparagus in the bowl with the chopped shallot and the vinaigrette sauce.

4 Arrange the salad, washed and dried, on the plates. Pile the green beans on top in a pyramid and stick the asparagus tips in here and there.

5 Scatter on the crayfish tails, which have been coated, using a teaspoon, with lobster sauce or sauce rose.

6 Decorate with the vegetables from the court-bouillon and with chopped chervil, and arrange a whole crayfish 'rampant' on top.

74. *Lobster salad with caviar*
SALADE DE HOMARD AU CAVIAR

For two people

Main ingredients
1½ litres (2½ pints) nage or court-
   bouillon (No 77)
1 live lobster of 400 g (14 oz)
180 g (6½ oz) French beans
12 fresh, or tinned, asparagus tips
half a chopped shallot
20 g (¾ oz) caviar
30 g (1 oz) red chicory (radicchio di
   Treviso) **or** Batavian endive (red
   mignonette)

Ingredients for finishing the dish
1 tablespoon vegetables from the
   court-bouillon
Cold Lobster sauce (No 33)
1 tablespoon chervil leaves

Equipment
2 stainless-steel saucepans
1 bowl
2 small plates

1   Wash the lobster in cold running water and plunge it into the fast boiling court-bouillon for ten minutes.

2   Remove the shell, keeping the flesh from the claws in one piece. Cut the tail into eight thick slices.

3   Top and tail the beans and cook them 'al dente' (*for technique see page 68*). Drain them. If using fresh asparagus, prepare and cook it carefully. When tender, drain and trim to 4 cm (1½ in) long with a sharp knife. Toss the beans and the asparagus, separately, in the lobster sauce, which you have flavoured with the chopped shallot.

4   Pick over, wash and dry the red chicory or endive, and arrange it on two small plates. Mound up the beans in a pyramid in the middle. Stud the pyramid with the asparagus tips and the vegetables from the court-bouillon.

5   Arrange the pieces of lobster round the outside in a coronet, coat them with the lobster sauce and cover with beads of caviar. Stick the claws of the crustacean into the top.

75. *Salad of lambs' brains*
SALADE DE CERVELLES D'AGNEAU

For four people

Main ingredients
2 lambs' brains
200 g (7 oz) cucumbers
2 teaspoons gherkins, chopped
2 teaspoons capers, chopped
60 g (2 oz) button mushrooms cut in julienne strips 3 cm long by 2 mm wide ($1\frac{1}{4}$ in by $\frac{1}{16}$ in)
60 g (2 oz) raw coarsely chopped tomato pulp (No 138)
half a bunch watercress, 20 g ($\frac{3}{4}$ oz) sorrel, 20 g ($\frac{3}{4}$ oz) lettuce, all sorted and washed
2 teaspoons freshly chopped parsley

Ingredients for cooking the brains
250 ml (scant $\frac{1}{2}$ pint) water
$2\frac{1}{2}$ tablespoons wine vinegar
1 bouquet garni
salt, pepper

Appropriate dressing
Mayonnaise (No 26) and
Vinaigrette 1 (No 24) **or**
Sauce orange (No 28)
Equipment
1 saucepan
4 plates

1   Leave the brains under cold running water for fifteen minutes to remove every last trace of blood.

2   Bring the ingredients for cooking the brains to the boil in a saucepan.

3   Plunge the brains in, bring once more to the boil, then allow to cool in the liquid.

4   Peel the cucumber thinly with a potato-peeler, cut it in half lengthwise and remove the pips with a teaspoon. Cut into thin crescents and leave to drain, sprinkled with the salt, to extract excess water.

5   Slice the salads into a chiffonade – that is, cut them delicately into ribbons the width of a finger. Remove the watercress stalks.

6   Put the chiffonade and watercress on the plates, and sprinkle with capers, gherkins and cucumber dressed either with sauce orange or vinaigrette. Slice the brains and spread them on top in a fan; coat them lightly with mayonnaise. Lastly, sprinkle with the mushrooms, the coarsely chopped tomato and freshly chopped parsley.

76. *Pigeon salad with chervil*
SALADE DE CERFEUIL À L'AILE DE PIGEON
  (*spatchcock*)

For four people

Main ingredients
2 small pigeons
60 g (2 oz) coarsely chopped tomato
  pulp (No 138)
1 artichoke heart, fresh **or** tinned
12 asparagus tips, fresh **or** tinned
30 g (1 oz) sweetcorn, tinned **or**
  frozen
50 g (2 oz) large fresh mushrooms
zest of 1 lemon
40 g (1½ oz) chervil

half a lettuce
half a curly endive
1 litre (1¾ pints) chicken stock **(No 2)**
  or stock made with stock cubes

Accompanying sauce
Vinaigrette 1 (No 24) **or**
Sweet-sour onion sauce (No 27)

Equipment
2 saucepans
2 plates

1   Ask the butcher or poulterer to clean and truss the pigeons, or do it
yourself in the normal way.

2   Bring the chicken stock to the boil in a saucepan. Gently simmer the
pigeons in it for eight to ten minutes. The breasts should be a rosy-pink
when they are taken out.

3   Allow them to cool and cut off wings and breasts together in one piece.
Take off the drumstick; skin the breasts and slice them finely. Leave the
legs whole and do not skin them.

4   If the asparagus and artichokes are fresh, cook them in the usual
manner. Cut the artichoke heart into thin slices.

5   Carefully cut up the lettuce to make a chiffonade (ribbons the width
of your finger) and coarsely chop the endive.

6   Cut the mushrooms into julienne strips – little strips 3 cm long by
2 mm wide (1¼ in by 1/16 in).

7   Pare the lemon rind with a potato-peeler and cut into very fine
julienne strips the size of a pine-needle.

8   Dress the chiffonade, endive, asparagus tips and sliced artichoke heart
with the chosen sauce.

9   Pile the salad in a mound on each plate, arrange the slices of artichoke
heart round the edge like a crown. Stick the asparagus tips in here and
there.

10 Plant the drumstick in the top, the bone pointing upwards, and overlap the slices of pigeon breast, well seasoned with salt and pepper, all round. It should look rather like a turban.

11 Sprinkle the salad with the juliennes of mushroom and lemon peel, the sweetcorn, little sprigs of chervil and chopped tomato.

Note for Australia Spatchcock is a good substitute for pigeon in this recipe.

Fish, Shellfish and Crustaceans

77. *Nage or court-bouillon*

To serve four

Main ingredients
500 ml (scant 1 pint) dry white wine
1 litre (1¾ pints) water
35 g (1¼ oz) coarse salt
2 medium-sized carrots
the white part of 1 leek
30 g (1 oz) celery stalk
60 g (2 oz) pickling onions
2 shallots
2 whole unpeeled cloves garlic

5 strips of lemon peel
25 green peppercorns
1 clove
bouquet garni made with 6 parsley
    stalks, half bayleaf, 1 small sprig of
    fresh fennel and 1 sprig of thyme

Equipment
1 large stainless-steel saucepan

1   Wash and peel all the vegetables.

2   Cut channels all round the carrots with a special channelling knife (*optional*).

3   Cut all the vegetables – carrots, white of leek, celery, small onions, shallots – into tiny slices.

4   Sauté them without fat in the covered saucepan for ten minutes to extract their juices.

5   Add the white wine, water, salt and the seasoning ingredients: unpeeled cloves of garlic, lemon zest, green peppercorns, clove and bouquet garni.

6   Cook gently for forty minutes. The vegetables should still be *just* firm.

Uses   Lobster, crawfish or crayfish à la nage (No 80)
         Lobster with fresh tomatoes and basil (No 81)
         Seafood pot-au-feu (No 95)
         Roast Lobster (No 83)

78. *Oysters in champagne sauce*
HUÎTRES AU CHAMPAGNE

For two people

Main ingredients
12 oysters
8 tablespoons champagne
2 egg yolks
1 teaspoon crème fraîche
1 teaspoon water
pepper

Equipment
2 small stainless-steel saucepans
1 small whisk
1 oval dish packed with sea-salt or
    other salt-crystals

1   Open the oysters and loosen them from the hollow shell with a knife or a tablespoon. Put on one side and strain their juice through a fine cloth. Wash the hollow shells and arrange them on the dish of salt-crystals. Keep them hot in the bottom of the oven.

2   Pour the champagne into a small saucepan, bring it to the boil and reduce it to a quarter of its original volume. Let it cool. Add the egg yolks, cream and water, and proceed as if it were a Béarnaise (No 36), beating vigorously with the whisk. The mixture gradually thickens and becomes creamy. Remove the sauce from the heat.

3   Poach the oysters for thirty seconds in their own filtered liquid, drain them and put them back into their shells. Whisk the poaching liquid into the sauce.

4   Cover each oyster with a tablespoon of champagne sauce and slip them into a very hot oven for thirty seconds until they are a pretty golden colour.

Note for Australia Small scallop shells can be used for serving this recipe if the oyster shells are not large enough.

79. *Scallops and oysters with truffles*
SAINT-JACQUES ET BELONS AUX TRUFFES

For two people

Main ingredients
6 oysters
6 scallops
30 g (1 oz) truffles, cut in julienne
strips 3 cm long and 3 mm wide
(1¼ in by ⅛ in)
1 teaspoon arachide oil

Ingredients for the sauce
½ teaspoon truffle juice (*see page 22*)
1 teaspoon mushroom purée (No 132)
1 teaspoon crème fraîche
2 teaspoons skimmed milk powder
dissolved in 4 tablespoons water
pepper

Vegetables for decorating the dish
20 g (¾ oz) carrots
20 g (¾ oz) the white part of leek
20 g (¾ oz) button mushrooms
10 g (⅓ oz) celery
(all cut in julienne strips)

Equipment
2 saucepans
a fine muslin cloth for straining
a small perforated spoon or skimmer
a small non-stick frying-pan
2 deep plates

1   Open the oysters carefully, detach them from their shells and keep the juice, which should be strained through a piece of fine muslin.

2   Open the scallops by running the blade of a knife flat against the surface of the flat shell. Remove the scallops (white part and coral) with a tablespoon. Wash them well under cold running water.

3   Heat the arachide oil in the small saucepan and lightly sauté the strips of truffle, seasoned with pepper; add the cream, skimmed milk powder mixed with water, and the truffle juice. Bring to the boil, simmer for two minutes and put on one side.

4   Poach the scallops in the strained liquid from the oysters. Give them two minutes on each side, remove them and keep them hot. Put in the oysters and let them poach for twenty seconds on each side.

5   Stir the mushroom purée and the poaching liquor into the truffle sauce. This liquor will provide the necessary salt. The sauce should be very light.

6   Cut the vegetables into very fine julienne strips, season with salt and pepper, and sauté them lightly 'à sec' (without fat or oil) for two minutes in the non-stick frying-pan.

7   Put the oysters and scallops higgledy-piggledy in the two deep plates.

8   Cover them lightly with the truffle sauce and scatter the julienne of vegetables over the top.

---

80. *Lobster, crawfish or freshwater crayfish à la nage*
HOMARD, LANGOUSTE OU ÉCREVISSES 'À LA NAGE'

For two people

Main ingredients
1 live lobster of 700 g (1½ lb) **or**
1 live crawfish of 700 g (1½ lb) **or**
20 freshwater crayfish, each weighing
    60 g (2 oz)
1 tablespoon freshly chopped parsley
Court-bouillon for cooking the
    crustaceans (No 77)

Accompanying sauce
Sauce grelette (No 32) **or**
Cold lobster sauce (No 33)

Equipment
1 large stainless-steel saucepan
1 oval dish or serving dish

1   *Cooking the crustaceans*
Plunge the crustaceans into the boiling court-bouillon, taking great pains over the timing. Give a lobster or a crawfish of 700 g (1½ lb) twelve minutes and crayfish two minutes.

2   *Preparing the dish*
a. **Lobster or crawfish.** Cleave it in half lengthwise. Remove the claws and the shell. Remove the little gravelly pouch found in the head (*see* Roast Lobster, No 83). Arrange on an oval dish, with the vegetables from the court-bouillon on top. Moisten with 240 ml (scant ½ pint) of the court-bouillon, and sprinkle with chopped parsley.

b. **Freshwater crayfish.** Pile them up, whole, in a pyramid, on a serving dish. Sprinkle them with chopped parsley.
   Serve with the chosen sauce.
   If, when eating crayfish, you are worried by the idea of the dark thread-like alimentary canal which runs through the body, put the live crayfish into a solution of water and skimmed milk powder for twelve hours, to clean out the alimentary tract.
   When you wish to use just the shelled tails of the crayfish, it is easy, once you have removed their shells, to pull out the alimentary canal by pinching it between finger and thumb and drawing it out from head to tail.
   It is very important to remember: that overcooking crustaceans makes

the flesh disagreeably chewy; that slightly undercooking them makes them more succulent; that a pause between cooking and serving will give the flesh a moment to relax, and become more tender.

EDITOR'S NOTE Dealing with a live lobster at home is a problem – if possible ask your fishmonger to kill it for you and then hurry home and cook it. On a hot day take a cold insulated bag to carry it in. Remember that raw shellfish should be kept for a minimum of time as it deteriorates very rapidly. If you *are* stuck with doing the job yourself, however, the following method is probably the kindest: Take a cleaver or heavy knife and bang it down sharply where the shell of the head meets that of the body. This will kill the creature instantly.

---

81. *Lobster with fresh tomatoes and basil*
HOMARD À LA TOMATE FRAÎCHE ET AU PISTOU

For four people

Main ingredients
4 live lobsters of 350 g (¾ lb) each
Nage or court-bouillon (No 77)

Ingredients for the accompanying sauce
25 g (1 oz) skimmed milk powder dissolved in
250 ml (scant ½ pint) fish fumet (No ?) or white wine
40 g (1½ oz) carrots, peeled and coarsely chopped
40 g (1½ oz) onions, peeled and coarsely chopped

1 teaspoon tomato purée
1 tablespoon fromage blanc
1 tablespoon crème fraîche
4 tablespoons raw chopped tomato (No 138)
¼ teaspoon basil pounded with a few drops of olive oil

Equipment
2 stainless-steel saucepans, 1 large, 1 small
1 pair of kitchen scissors
4 hot plates

1 Plunge the lobsters whole into the boiling nage for five minutes. Allow to cool somewhat in the liquid while you prepare the sauce.

2 Stir the skimmed milk powder into the fish fumet. Cook the vegetables (carrots and onions) in this liquid for twenty minutes, covered. After cooking, purée them in the liquidizer, having first added the cream, the fromage blanc, and the tomato purée. Heat this mixture, stirring in the raw chopped tomato and the basil. Adjust the seasoning, if need be, and keep the sauce hot.

3 Remove the four lobster tails and take off the shells by cutting

through the underparts with scissors. Remove and shell the claws. Having removed the rather pulpy flesh from the shells of the heads (the flesh will come in useful for making Sauce Américaine (No 10)) make two slits in them and insert two shelled claws, pointing upwards, in each.

4   Serve on four hot dishes, arranging the heads and their claws carefully on one side, followed by the tails, sliced into 'medaillons' or rounds, 5 mm ($\frac{1}{4}$ in) thick; these rounds are then coated with the sauce.

82. *Lobster with watercress*
HOMARD AU CRESSON

For two people

Main ingredients
2 live lobsters of 350 g ($\frac{3}{4}$ lb) (or 1 of 800 g ($1\frac{3}{4}$ lb)) preferably females which contain eggs

Other ingredients for the lobster
250 g (9 oz) light watercress purée (No 132)

Ingredients for the court-bouillon
$1\frac{1}{2}$ litres ($2\frac{1}{2}$ pints) water
500 ml (scant pint) dry white wine
50 g (2 oz) coarse salt
1 bouquet garni
half a carrot and half an onion sliced into rounds
20 peppercorns

Ingredients for the sauce
2 tablespoons dry white wine
80 g (3 oz) button mushrooms, sliced
1 chopped shallot
salt, pepper
5 tablespoons fish fumet (No 3)
$\frac{1}{2}$ teaspoon chopped tarragon
$1\frac{1}{2}$ teaspoons fromage blanc
$1\frac{1}{2}$ teaspoons crème fraîche (*optional*)
25 g (1 oz) skimmed milk powder

Equipment
2 small stainless-steel pans
1 non-stick frying-pan
1 serving dish

1   Make the court-bouillon by boiling the water, wine, salt, carrot, onion and bouquet garni together for twenty minutes, adding the peppercorns five minutes before the end.

2   Remove the claws of the lobsters, and cook them in the court-bouillon (*see* Roast Lobster, No 83), together with the eggs taken from underneath the bodies if they are females.

3   Reduce the two tablespoons of dry white wine to three-quarters of its volume and throw in the chopped shallot, mushrooms, and tarragon; season with salt and pepper. Allow it to cook, covered, for two minutes,

then add the skimmed milk powder, dissolved in the fish fumet, bring back to the boil, and add the fromage blanc and the cream, if used.

4   Shell the raw lobster tails, season them and sauté them on each side, for two minutes only, either in a frying-pan in which you have put two teaspoons of olive oil, or dry ('à sec'), in a non-stick pan.

5   Pour the light watercress purée into the bottom of a hot serving dish, arrange the two lobster tails on top, covered with the sauce, and decorate with the shelled claws and a sprinkling of the poached lobster eggs, now a bright red.

The shells, which still contain the coral and intestines, can be used to make a sauce Américaine (No 10) for another dish.

---

83. *Lobster roasted in oven*
HOMARD RÔTI AU FOUR

For two people

Main ingredients
1 live lobster of 700 g (1½ lb)
1½ litres (2½ pints) nage or court-
  bouillon (No 77)

Reduction for the sauces
5 tablespoons dry white wine
60 g (2 oz) chopped shallot
2 teaspoons chopped tarragon
2 teaspoons chopped chervil
1 teaspoon lemon juice
150 ml (¼ pint) sauce Amèricaine
  (No 10)
1 egg yolk
salt, pepper

*The sauces to accompany the lobster
  and to coat it during cooking*
A
three-quarters of the above reduction
half the lobster's coral
160 g (5¾ oz) fromage blanc
B
quarter of the above reduction
half the lobster's coral
1 tablespoon fromage blanc
1 teaspoon crème fraîche

Equipment
1 medium saucepan
2 small heavy-based saucepans
1 oval ovenproof gratin dish
1 slotted spoon or skimmer
1 whisk
1 liquidizer
1 sauceboat

1   Cook the lobster for four minutes in the boiling nage. Remove it from the heat and let it cool in the liquid for five minutes.

2 Reduce the sauce Américaine to half its volume in a heavy saucepan. In a separate saucepan boil the white wine, shallots, lemon juice, tarragon, chervil, salt and pepper, until it is reduced to a moist purée (there should be about two tablespoons left). Remove from the heat, and whisk in the egg yolk and the reduced sauce Américaine. Keep it hot.

3 Take the lobster out of its cooking liquid, cleave it down the middle, discard the small stony pouch found in the top of the head, and remove the coral and intestines, the greenish part, with a spoon, keeping it on one side. Remove the claws and break them, extract the flesh of each in one piece, and place one on each head part, now clean and empty.

4 Liquidize the coral and intestines.

Sauce A. For coating the lobster Take three-quarters of the reduction made in step 2 and stir in half the puréed coral and intestines, together with 160 g (5¾ oz) fromage blanc with a fork.

Sauce B. Accompanying sauce Take the remaining quarter of the reduction and stir in the second half of the puréed coral and intestines, together with a tablespoon fromage blanc and one teaspoon crème fraîche.

5 Preheat the oven to 240°C/475°F/Mark 9. Arrange the two lobster halves on the oval oven dish in which you have put four or five tablespoons of water, to prevent the lobster from drying up. Coat each half with **Sauce A** and roast in a very hot oven until really hot right through.

6 To serve the dish, take it straight from the oven to the table and accompany it with **Sauce B**, lightly whisked at the last moment, in a separate sauceboat.

84. *Lobster-cakes with glazed carrots*
GÂTEAU DE HOMARD AUX CAROTTES FONDANTES

For six people

Ingredients for the farce (forcemeat)
160 g (6 oz) raw lobster or salmon
1 egg
1 teaspoon salt, a pinch of pepper
8 tablespoons water
2 teaspoons skimmed milk powder

Other ingredients for the filling
6 scallops
150 g (5 oz) lobster
30 g (1 oz) truffles cut in strips
2 tablespoons sauce Américaine
  (No 10)

Ingredients for the sauce
1 tablespoon carrot purée (No 130)
6 tablespoons sauce Américaine
  (No 10)
24 g (1 oz) skimmed milk powder
  dissolved in
240 ml (scant ½ pint) water

1 teaspoon port
½ teaspoon chopped tarragon
450 g (1 lb) carrots
500 ml (generous ¾ pint) water
sugar substitute equivalent to 1
  teaspoon sugar
1 teaspoon butter (*optional*)
6 thin slices of truffle

Cooking liquid
200 ml (⅓ pint) nage or court-bouillon
  (No 77)

Equipment
1 medium saucepan with a lid
1 large steamer or fish-kettle
1 wooden spatula
1 liquidizer
12 sheets of aluminium foil, 10 cm by
  10 cm (4 in by 4 in)
6 hot plates

Preparing the farce (forcemeat) and the rest of the filling

1 Purée the 160 g (6 oz) lobster or salmon in the liquidizer for two minutes. Add the salt, pepper and egg. Blend again for one minute, then stir in the skimmed milk, dissolved in the water. Put in a cool place.

2 Poach the scallops for thirty seconds in the simmering nage, and the 150 g (5 oz) of lobster for two minutes. Drain and cut both in 1 cm (½ in) dice, then allow to cool.

3 Bring the sauce Américaine to the boil and let it reduce by half. Allow to cool.

4 Mix all the ingredients for the lobster-cakes together, with a wooden spatula or spoon – the cubed scallops and lobster, the forcemeat, the sauce Américaine and the strips of truffle.

5 Use this mixture to make six flat cakes, 10 cm (4 in) across by 1.5 cm (⅝ in) deep, place each one on a piece of aluminium foil and cover with another.

Making the sauce

6   Scrape the carrots and cut them into the finest rounds. Cook them for twenty minutes, covered, in a saucepan in which you have put the water, sugar substitute and the teaspoon of butter (*optional*). By the end of the cooking time the water should have completely evaporated.

7   Purée together in the liquidizer the carrot purée, tarragon, port and six tablespoons of sauce Américaine. Moisten with the skimmed milk and pour over the carrots. Taste for seasoning.

Steaming the lobster-cakes

8   In a steamer or fish-kettle large enough to take all six cakes, first put the nage, then the rack. Arrange the six cakes in their foil overcoats on the strainer of the fish-kettle or on the rack placed inside the saucepan above the level of the nage.

9   Steam, with the lid on the pan, for three minutes on each side. The lobster-cakes will rise and become very moist and succulent.

Serving the dish

10   Spoon some of the carrots in their sauce over the bottom of each plate. Unwrap the lobster-cakes and place them lightly on the sauce. Decorate each with a slice of truffle.

---

85. *Escalopes of salmon with sorrel*
ESCALOPE DE SAUMON À L'OSEILLE
   (*salmon trout*)

For four people

Main ingredient
1 piece salmon weighing 250 g (9 oz) cut in a fillet along one side of the backbone

Ingredients for the accompanying sauce
1 tablespoon dry vermouth
2 tablespoons concentrated veal stock (demi-glace) (No 1)
8 tablespoons fish fumet (No 3)
half a shallot, chopped
50 g (2 oz) button mushrooms, cut in quarters
180 ml (⅓ pint) fish fumet (No 3)

1 tablespoon skimmed milk powder
1 tablespoon mushroom purée (No 132)
1 teaspoon crème fraîche
30 g (1 oz) fresh sorrel
salt, pepper

Equipment
8 sheets aluminium foil, 12 cm by 12 cm (4½ in by 4½ in)
1 steak-beater
1 stainless-steel saucepan
1 liquidizer
1 non-stick frying-pan
4 hot plates

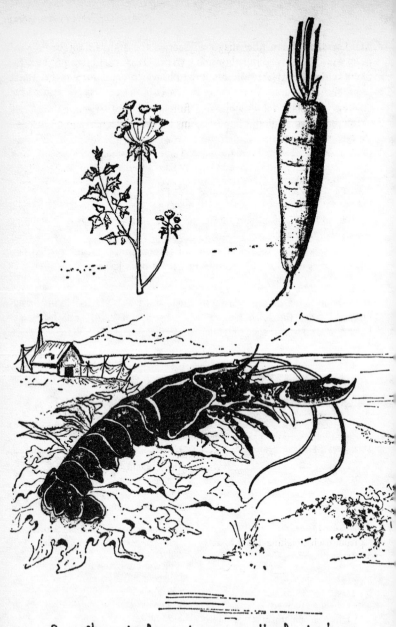

Le gâteau de homard aux carottes fondantes

1 Cut the salmon fillet diagonally across the grain to obtain four thin escalopes, each weighing about 60 g (2 oz). To flatten them put each one between two sheets of aluminium foil and bang them with the steak-beater.

2 Put the eight tablespoons fish fumet, the dry vermouth, the demi-glace, chopped shallot and mushrooms into the saucepan and let it reduce very slowly to half its volume.

Having made this reduction, add the tablespoon of skimmed milk powder, dissolved in the 180 ml (⅓ pint) of fish fumet and bring back to the boil. Let it simmer for three minutes. Meanwhile, pick over the sorrel, wash it well and remove the stalks. Shred it up into thin ribbons.

Put the warm reduction into the liquidizer together with the crème fraîche and mushroom purée and blend to a thin purée. Pour it into a saucepan, add the strips of raw sorrel and let it simmer gently for five minutes (this should be done at the last minute, just before serving the dish). Taste the sauce for seasoning.

3 Season the salmon escalopes with salt and pepper. Heat the non-stick frying-pan and place the escalopes in it, allowing them ten seconds contact with the heat on each side.

4 Coat the bottom of each serving plate with the sauce, which must be very hot, and arrange the salmon escalopes on top. Serve immediately.

Note for Australia Escalopes of salmon trout would be a delicious substitute for salmon in this recipe. Tinned Pacific salmon is not recommended.

---

86. *Trout en papillote with dill and lemon*
TRUITE EN PAPILLOTE À L'ANETH ET AU CITRON

For four people

Main ingredients
4 trout each weighing 180 g to 200 g
(about 7 oz)

Other ingredients
2 teaspoons olive oil
1 chopped shallot
1 tablespoon dry vermouth
4 tablespoons fish fumet (No 3)
1 lemon

4 branches of dill or fresh fennel
salt, pepper

Equipment
1 pair of kitchen scissors
4 sheets of aluminium foil cut into
   rounds with a diameter of 30 cm
   (12 in)
4 hot plates

1   Scale and clean the trout, cut off their fins and wipe them thoroughly with kitchen paper.

2   Season the inside with salt and pepper and stuff them with the dill **or** fennel branches.

3   Preheat the oven to 230°C/450°F/Mark 8. Fold each piece of aluminium foil into an oval, like a boat, with raised sides; lay a trout in each, sprinkle it with chopped shallot, vermouth, fish fumet, and olive oil, and cover it with slices of lemon with all the peel and pith removed.

4   Pleat the foil over at the top to enclose the fish, pinching it together carefully and shaping it rather like a Cornish pasty.

5   Put these papillotes (little parcels) on an oval ovenproof gratin dish and cook them in a hot oven for eight minutes.

6   Serve just as they are, first cutting gently through the top pleat of the papillote to make them easier for your guests to open.

---

87. *Whiting with Julienne vegetables*
MERLAN À LA JULIENNE DE LÉGUMES

For two people

Main ingredients
2 whiting, weighing 220 g (8 oz) each

Ingredients for the forcemeat (farce)
1 teaspoon olive oil
50 g (2 oz) carrots
50 g (2 oz) large mushrooms
25 g (1 oz) celeriac
¾ teaspoon salt
a pinch of pepper
chopped tarragon

Ingredients for the sauce
25 g (1 oz) carrots
25 g (1 oz) mushrooms
10 g (⅓ oz) celery

2 heaped teaspoons skimmed milk
    powder dissolved in
    150 ml (¼ pint) fish fumet (No 3)
¾ teaspoon salt, a pinch of pepper
1 teaspoon crème fraîche (*optional*)
½ teaspoon port
½ teaspoon of chopped parsley

Cooking liquid for the fish
4 tablespoons fish fumet (No 3)
half a shallot, chopped

Equipment
1 pair of scissors
1 oval enamelled cast-iron gratin dish
1 mouli-julienne
2 saucepans
2 hot plates

1   Cut off the fins and clean the whiting, removing their guts through the gills.

2   Bone them whole; make two incisions along the spine, and ease the fillets on either side away from the bone. Cut through the now free backbone with scissors, just by the tail and remove it. The whiting can now be opened and shut like a book.

3   Peel and slice the carrot and celeriac into julienne strips 2 mm ($\frac{1}{16}$ in) wide and 4 cm ($1\frac{1}{2}$ in) long either with the appropriate blade of a mouli-julienne or on a mandoline. The mushrooms, with their resilient flesh, must be cut into strips the same size with a small knife.

4   In the first saucepan, coated with oil, sauté the vegetables, adding them every three minutes in the following sequence: carrots, celeriac, mushrooms (the carrots will cook, altogether, for nine minutes, the celeriac for six and the mushrooms for three minutes). Season them with salt and pepper, cover the pan and let them stew for a further ten minutes. Cooked in this way, the vegetables will still be 'al dente', slightly firm between the teeth, and will retain their own individuality. Stir in the chopped tarragon and allow to cool.

5   In the other saucepan, put the skimmed milk powder dissolved in the fish fumet, and the carrots, celery and mushrooms, all coarsely chopped, and allow to cook for twenty minutes. When cooked put the mixture into the liquidizer with a teaspoon of cream, if used, and blend. Reheat the mixture together with a third of the julienne of vegetables and the half teaspoon of port.

6   Preheat the oven to 240°C/475°F/Mark 9. Season the whiting inside with salt and pepper, and stuff them with the remaining two-thirds of the julienne of vegetables. Lay the whiting on the oval gratin dish which you have sprinkled with the chopped shallot, add the 4 tablespoons of fish fumet and cook in a very hot oven for eight minutes, basting them frequently.

7   Drain the whiting and put on hot plates. Coat generously with the sauce and sprinkle with freshly chopped parsley.

88. *Plaice cooked in cider*
CARRELET AU CIDRE
(*flounder*)

For three people

Main ingredient
1 plaice **or** other flat fish weighing
600 g (1¼ lb)

Ingredients for the cooking liquid
1 teaspoon chopped tarragon
1 teaspoon chopped shallot
8 tablespoons fish fumet (No 3)
8 tablespoons cider
1 tablespoon mushroom purée
(No 132)
salt, pepper

Other ingredients
1 tablespoon coarsely chopped tomato
pulp (No 138)
1 apple
2 tablespoons lemon juice

Equipment
1 oval ovenproof dish
1 spatula

1   Wash and clean the fish and cut off the fins.

2   Preheat the oven to 240°C/475°F/Mark 9. Sprinkle the chopped tarragon and shallot over the bottom of the ovenproof dish and put the fish, seasoned with salt and pepper, on top. Pour on the mushroom purée mixed with the cider and fish fumet.

3   Put the dish, covered with a sheet of aluminium foil, into a very hot oven for fifteen minutes. Baste during cooking.

4   Meanwhile peel and core the apple and cut it into little sticks. Squeeze the lemon juice over them and sprinkle them round the plaice seven minutes before the end of the cooking.

5   Lift the fish from its dish with a spatula, peel off the skin and then carefully remove the fillets. Put these back into the dish, season them with salt and pepper and sprinkle the whole thing with the chopped tomato before serving.

Note for Australia Flounder is the perfect substitute for plaice in this recipe.

89. *Sea bream cooked on a bed of vegetables*
DAURADE CUITE SUR LITIÈRE
   (*black bream or John Dory*)

For two people

Main ingredient
1 bream, bass **or** John Dory weighing
   500 g (just over 1 lb) scaled and
   cleaned

Other ingredients
70 g (2½ oz) coarsely chopped tomato
   pulp (No 138)
the white part of half a leek
half an onion
quarter clove of garlic, chopped
40 g (1½ oz) carrots
30 g (1 oz) button mushrooms
1 teaspoon shallot, chopped

1 branch thyme
half a bayleaf
salt, pepper
1 teaspoon olive oil
7 tablespoons fish fumet (No 3) **or**
   3½ tablespoons white wine, 3½
   tablespoons water
1 teaspoon crème fraîche (*optional*)
½ teaspoon freshly chopped parsley

Equipment
1 oval flameproof dish
1 small wire sieve
1 liquidizer

1 Preheat the oven to 230°C/450°F/Mark 8. Coat the bottom of the oval oven dish with a teaspoon of olive oil and sauté the carrots, onions, mushrooms and leeks, all cut into dice 5 mm (¼ in) across, together with the chopped shallot, garlic, thyme and bayleaf. Let them sweat gently over a moderate heat, stirring them with a fork from time to time. They should remain slightly firm, 'al dente'.

2 Pour in the fish fumet, add the fresh tomato pulp and place the bream on top of the bed of vegetables.

3 Allow to cook in a hot oven for twenty minutes. Baste the fish three or four times with its juices as it cooks.

4 Take the dish out of the oven and keep the fish hot. Meanwhile collect the cooking liquid by straining the vegetables through a sieve and reduce it by fast boiling to a quarter of its original volume. Blend in the liquidizer with the cream, if used.

5 Lift the skin off the fish. Season and put it back into its original cooking dish. Scatter the vegetables, reserved in the sieve, higgledy-piggledy over the top to keep the simple country character of the dish. Pour the sauce around the fish and put back into the hot oven for a few moments.

EDITOR'S NOTE Daurade, one of the complicated and numerous bream family, is, in fact, gilt-head bream and is regarded as the best eating of all the breams. It is not easily obtained away from the Mediterranean, but this recipe is delicious with any firm-fleshed salt-water fish.

Note for Australia The black bream found in Australian waters is very similar to the Atlantic bream.

---

90. *Stuffed rascasse*
CHAPON DE MER FARCI
   (*schnapper*)

For four people

Main ingredient
1 rascasse weighing 1 kg (2¼ lb) or
   other firm-fleshed fish

Ingredients for the stuffing
1 tablespoon chopped onion
3 tablespoons finely diced button
   mushrooms
1 teaspoon chopped chervil
1 teaspoon chopped tarragon
1 teaspoon olive oil
the liver of the rascasse

Ingredients for cooking the fish
250 ml (scant ½ pint) fish fumet
   (No 3)
8 tablespoons dry white wine
1 tablespoon chopped shallot
1 teaspoon chopped chervil

Ingredients of the liaison for the sauce
2 tablespoons raw coarsely chopped
   tomato pulp (No 138)
1 tablespoon mushroom purée (No
   132)
4 tablespoons water and 2 level
   teaspoons skimmed milk powder
1 teaspoon crème fraîche (*optional*)

Equipment
1 ovenproof dish
2 heavy-based saucepans
1 wooden spoon
1 skimmer
1 liquidizer
large needle and coarse thread

1   Scale the fish, cut off the fins and spines, then wash and gut it. Keep the liver.

2   Heat the olive oil in a heavy-based saucepan. Soften the chopped onion for two minutes without letting it brown, then add the diced mushrooms, chervil and tarragon and cook on for two minutes more. Add the finely chopped liver of the rascasse. Stir it in with the onion mixture, let it cook one minute more, then take the pan off the heat and let it cool.

3   Season the fish inside with salt and pepper, fill it with the cooled stuffing and sew up the opening.

4   Scatter the chopped shallot over the bottom of the oven dish, place the

stuffed rascasse on top, and moisten it with the fish fumet and white wine.

Braise the fish in the oven (220°C/425°F/Mark 7) for forty minutes, basting frequently.

5 At the end of the cooking lift out the fish with a fish-slice or skimmer and keep it hot.

6 Put the mushroom purée, skimmed milk dissolved in water, and the crème fraîche, if used, into the liquidizer and blend thoroughly. Thin it with the cooking liquid from the fish, which is first reduced by one-third of its volume. Return this sauce to the oven dish, add the chopped tomato pulp and heat thoroughly. Taste for seasoning.

7 Remove the skin from the top side of the fish, remove the flesh in two flat boneless fillets, then turn it over and remove the two remaining fillets in the same way – it is easiest done with a palette knife.

Arrange the fillets on the four plates. Cover them lightly with very hot sauce. Put the stuffing all round in spoonfuls. Sprinkle with freshly-chopped chervil. Serve the remaining sauce separately in a sauceboat.

Note for Australia Schnapper will be found to be an excellent substitute for rascasse in this recipe.

---

91. *Peppered John Dory with Sabayon sauce*
SABAYON DE SAINT-PIERRE EN INFUSION DE POIVRE

For four people

Main ingredients
1 John Dory weighing 1 kg (2¼ lb)
180 ml (⅓ pint) fish fumet (No 3)
1 teaspoon coarsely crushed
  peppercorns
half a chopped shallot
salt, pepper

Equipment
1 saucepan
1 conical strainer
1 small bowl
1 small whisk
1 ovenproof dish
4 hot plates

Ingredients of the Sabayon sauce
2 egg yolks
3 tablespoons water

1 Scrape the fish, cut off the fins and spines and gut it. Preheat the oven to 220°C/425°F/Mark 7.

2 Scatter the chopped shallot over the bottom of the oven dish, place the John Dory on top, season it with salt and pepper and moisten it with the fish fumet.

3   Cover the dish with a sheet of aluminium foil and braise the fish in the oven for twenty minutes. Baste the fish frequently with the cooking liquid and juices while it cooks.

4   Remove the fish and lay it on a hot serving dish. Strain the cooking liquid onto a small saucepan through a conical strainer. Add the pepper, bring it to the boil and reduce by one-third of its volume.

5   Meanwhile remove the skin of the fish and lift off the flesh in four unbroken fillets. Keep them hot.

6   Put the egg yolks and cold water in the bowl and whisk until the mixture has increased in volume and become frothy and mousse-like. Then pour this mixture into the boiling cooking liquid, whisking all the time.

7   Arrange the fillets of John Dory on hot plates and coat them lightly with the sauce.

---

92. *Bass cooked in seaweed*
BAR AUX ALGUES
   (*schnapper*)

For two people

Main ingredients
1 sea-bass weighing 800 g (1¾ lb)
2 large handfuls of seaweed
7 tablespoons water
salt, black pepper

Accompanying sauce
4 tablespoons Sauce vierge (No 34)

Other ingredients
2 whole freshwater crayfish **or**
   Dublin Bay prawns (*optional*)
2 tablespoons watercress purée (No 135)

Equipment
1 oval casserole with a lid
2 hot plates

1   Clean the fish and cut away its sharp dorsal fin. Don't scale it; the scales contain a salty deposit which intensifies the fish's savour of the sea as it cooks underneath its seaweed blanket, and also makes it easier to skin once it is cooked.

2   Put a layer of half the seaweed in the bottom of the casserole and pour in the water; season the bass inside and lay it on top, together with the two freshwater crayfish or Dublin Bay prawns, if used. Blanket with the remaining seaweed. Cover the casserole and cook it over a fast heat for twenty minutes.

3   Meanwhile heat the Sauce vierge and the watercress purée separately in the bain-marie.

4   When the cooking time is up, serve the fish in the casserole and lift the lid in front of your guests so that they can inhale the smell of the sea. Then, remove the skin, complete with scales, in one piece. Lift off the fillets, season them with salt and pepper and place them on the hot plates, on to which you have poured the Sauce vierge.

On either side of the fillets put a spoonful or two of the watercress purée, the deep green of which can be heightened by placing a cooked crayfish or Dublin Bay prawn on each plate.

I find this a thoroughly satisfactory way of cooking salt-water fish; it gives an incomparable depth and richness to the flavour. To increase the savour and give an added freshness, you can replace the black pepper with freeze-dried green peppercorns crushed in a peppermill.

EDITOR'S NOTE   For a discussion of seaweeds suitable for this recipe see page 29.

Note for Australia Several fish could be substituted for sea bass, but in this recipe the size and shape of the fish are important, and schnapper would provide the best results.

---

93. *Saffron-steamed turbot studded with anchovies*
TURBOTIN CLOUTÉ D'ANCHOIS À LA VAPEUR DE SAFRAN
(*flounder or schnapper*)

For four people

Main ingredients
1 young (chicken) turbot or halibut weighing about 1 kg 200 g (a good 2½ lb)
2 whole salted anchovies **or** 8 tinned anchovy fillets

Ingredients for the cooking liquid
1 litre (1¾ pints) fish fumet (No 3)
1 pinch whole saffron

Ingredients for the sauce
1 tablespoon mushroom purée (No 132)

1 teaspoon crème fraîche
4 handsome spinach leaves
1 tablespoon of raw diced tomato (No 138)
(*optional*)

Equipment
1 turbot-kettle or other fish-kettle with a rack and lid
1 small saucepan
1 liquidizer
1 metal palette knife
4 hot plates

Note for Australia No Australian fish is very close in taste and texture to turbot. Turbot has rather clear, white flesh, which is not oily. You may wish to experiment with fish other than the schnapper and flounder we tentatively suggest.

Preparing and cooking the fish

1   Ask the fishmonger to skin and clean the fish and remove its fins.

2   If using whole anchovies put them under running water for ten
minutes to desalt them. Remove the bones and divide them up into fillets.
Cut each fillet in half lengthwise and then across, so that you now have
sixteen small pieces of anchovy. If using tinned anchovies simply cut each
fillet in half.

3   Stud the turbot on both sides with pieces of anchovy, making small
deep incisions with the point of a kitchen knife. Season the fish with
pepper and a very little salt (the anchovies are already salty).

4   Pour the fish fumet, in which you have put the saffron, into the turbot-
kettle; it should just reach the level of the grill. Place the turbot on the
grill just above the liquid so that the fish is not poached but cooked in
steam. Put the lid on the kettle and cook the fish gently for thirty-five
minutes. At the end of the cooking take out the turbot and keep it hot.

Preparing the sauce

5   Pour the 250 ml (scant $\frac{1}{2}$ pint) of the cooking liquid into the liquidizer.
Blend with the mushroom purée and the crème fraîche. Put this sauce
into a saucepan to heat through.

6   Wash the spinach and remove the stalks. Cut the leaves into wide
ribbons, and poach in boiling water for one minute. Drain and add them
to the sauce.

Serving the dish

7   With a metal spatula or a broad knife lift the flesh of the turbot away
from the backbone. The two upper fillets are removed first, the backbone
is removed in one piece, and the lower fillets can then be lifted too.

8   Lightly cover the plates with the sauce. Place a turbot fillet on each
and sprinkle with raw diced tomato, if liked.

94. *Poached seafood with baby vegetables*
COURT-BOUILLON DE TOUS LES POISSONS AUX LÉGUMES NOUVEAUX

For four people

Main ingredients
12 oysters
16 mussels
120 g (4 oz) angler **or** monk fish
120 g (4 oz) fillets of sole
4 scallops
100 g (3½ oz) lobster **or** tinned crab
  meat

Ingredients for the cooking liquid
1 chopped shallot
2 tablespoons dry white wine
8 tablespoons fish fumet (No 3)
4 tablespoons water and 2 teaspoons
  skimmed milk powder

Ingredients for the sauce
4 tablespoons sauce Américaine (No
  10)

1 tablespoon mushroom purée (**No
  132**)
8 handsome spinach leaves
60 g (2 oz) carrots
60 g (2 oz) turnips
30 g (1 oz) French beans
30 g (1 oz) fresh peas
a few asparagus spears (*optional*)

Equipment
2 small saucepans
1 large shallow pan
1 skimmer
1 liquidizer
4 hot soup plates

See the **Note for Users in Australia** for suggested equivalents to European fish.

Preparing the fish
1 Clean the scrape the mussels meticulously. Open the oysters and loosen them from the shells. Do the same with the scallops. Keep the liquid from both the oysters and the scallops, filtering it through a muslin cloth. Cut the angler-fish into eight small pieces. Slice up the sole into eight miniature fillets. Cut the lobster meat in dice 1 cm (½ in) across. Cut the scallops across horizontally into two rounds.

Cooking the vegetables
2 Clean and prepare the vegetables. Bring salted water to the boil in one of the two small saucepans, cook the carrots and turnips cut in large sticks for ten minutes, then add the asparagus, peas and French beans and cook for a further five minutes. Keep them all hot in their cooking water. Boil the washed and destalked spinach leaves for one minute separately.

Cooking the fish
3 Put white wine, fish fumet and chopped shallot into the second small saucepan and bring to the boil. Throw in the mussels, and cook covered for six minutes or until they have all opened.

4   Strain the cooking liquid from the mussels through a fine muslin cloth and add it to the strained shellfish liquid together with the skimmed milk. Stir and season with pepper. Put it in the large flat pan. Poach the lobster, angler-fish, sole and scallops in this cooking liquid for one-and-a-half minutes. Add the oysters, which need no more than fifteen seconds on each side, and the shelled mussels, and immediately take the pan off the heat.

5   Liquidize the mushroom purée with the sauce Américaine and the cooking liquid from the fish. Check the seasoning.

Serving the dish
6   Put two spinach leaves into each soup plate, scatter the pieces of fish and the shellfish loosely over them. Cover them lightly with the sauce and strew the vegetables over the top.

---

95. *Seafood pot-au-feu*
LE GRAND POT-AU-FEU DE LA MER

For four people
Main ingredients
1 bass weighing 400 g (scant 1 lb)
4 small red mullet weighing about
   100 g (3½ oz) apiece
4 slices angler **or** monk fish of 50 g
   (2 oz) each
8 Dublin Bay prawns
16 medium-sized mussels
4 oysters (*optional*)
salt, pepper

Ingredients for the various cooking liquids
300 ml (good ½ pint) fish fumet (No 3)
300 ml (good ½ pint) nage or court-
bouillon (No 77)
4 tablespoons red wine
4 tablespoons dry white wine
100 g (3½ oz) fresh parsley
1 chopped shallot
1 small bouquet garni
4 peppercorns

Other ingredients
8 miniature turnips
8 miniature carrots
(made by cutting up ordinary
   vegetables into large sticks or they
   can be 'turned' to olive shapes)
12 asparagus tips
4 small leeks
half a cucumber cut in four thick
   slices, channelled with a special
   channelling knife

Accompanying sauces
180 ml (⅓ pint) Sauce vierge (No 34)
180 ml (⅓ pint) Red wine Sabayon
   sauce (No 46)
180 ml (⅓ pint) Parsley sauce (No 41)

Equipment
1 large oval oven dish **or** gratin dish
4 small saucepans
1 medium-sized saucepan
1 skimmer
4 large hot plates
3 sauceboats

1 Cook the vegetables in boiling salted water, the carrots, turnips and leeks for ten minutes, the asparagus and cucumber for five minutes. Keep them hot in the water in which they were cooked.

Preparing and cooking the fish

2 Scale, clean and wash the bass and red mullet, leaving in the livers of the latter. Scrape and wash the mussels meticulously. Preheat the oven to 220°C/425°F/Mark 7.

3 Strew the chopped shallot over the bottom of the oven dish or gratin dish and cover it with a thick bed of parsley. Lay the fish, seasoned with salt and pepper, on top, and cover it with more parsley. Moisten it with two ladles of fish fumet and cook, covered, in the oven for twelve minutes. Skin the fish, lift off the fillets and keep hot.

4 In one of the saucepans, put the red wine, eight tablespoons of fish fumet, bouquet garni and peppercorns, bring it to the boil and let it reduce for five minutes. Poach the angler-fish in this liquid for one minute, then take the pan off the heat and leave the fish in its liquid.

5 Next, poach the Dublin Bay prawns in the boiling nage for one-and-a-half minutes. Drain them, then poach the red mullet in the same liquid for four minutes. Keep both hot.

6 In a separate saucepan bring to the boil the dry white wine, four tablespoons fish fumet and the chopped shallots. Throw in the mussels. Season with pepper, cover and cook for about six minutes or until the mussels open their shells. Take the pan off the heat, remove the mussels, take them out of their shells, and keep hot.

7 Poach the oysters in their own liquid, brought to a gentle simmer. Keep them hot in the liquid.

8 Heat the three accompanying sauces separately.

Serving the dish

9 Arrange the fish and shellfish around each dish in the following order: a red mullet, a piece of angler-fish, four mussels, a fillet of bass, two Dublin Bay prawns, an oyster. Leave a little daylight between each and intersperse the vegetables so that the dish looks altogether generous, and the colours are as prettily arranged as possible. Cover the angler-fish with some of the Sabayon sauce, the bass with parsley sauce, and the red mullet with Sauce vierge. Serve the sauces which are left, separately, in hot sauceboats.

See notes on fish in the Note for Users in Australia.

Meat, Poultry and Game

96. *Grilled steak with herb relish*
GRILLADE DE BŒUF AUX APPETITS

For four people

Main ingredients
4 tournedos steaks each weighing
   120 g (4 oz)
1 teaspoon olive oil

Ingredients for the 'herb relish'
2 tablespoons parsley
1 shallot
half a clove of garlic

juice of half a lemon
2 teaspoons olive oil
salt, pepper
a hint of grated nutmeg.

Equipment
1 wire grill
1 small bowl
4 hot plates

1   Chop the 'relish' ingredients together (parsley, shallot and garlic). Put them in a bowl together with the lemon juice, olive oil, and seasoning of salt, pepper and nutmeg.

2   Brush the tournedos steaks with olive oil and grill them according to taste. (For the method *see pages 45–8*.) After cooking wipe with absorbent paper to remove excess fat, and season with salt and pepper.

3   Spread the relish over each steak and serve them on very hot plates. They can be accompanied by an apple gratin (No 143).

97. *Steak grilled on coarse salt*
GRILLADE DE BŒUF AU GROS SEL

1   Spread a layer of coarse salt over the bottom of a heavy frying-pan with a metal handle and put it into a very hot oven (250°C/500°F/Mark 10) until the salt starts rustling.

2   Place the steak on this saline base, put the pan over a fierce heat, and cook the steak on it in the usual way.

98. *Steak with green peppercorns*
GRILLADE DE BŒUF AU POIVRE VERT

Tournedos steaks are grilled as in the recipe for Grilled Steak with Herb Relish but without the relish, and placed on plates which have been covered with Sauce au poivre vert (No 118).

99. *Beef stew with baby vegetables*
ESTOUFFADE DE BŒUF AUX PETITS LÉGUMES

For two people

Main ingredients
300 g (10½ oz) stewing beef – with all fat and sinews removed, and cut in pieces weighing 30 g (1 oz)
1 litre (1¾ pints) chicken stock **(No 2)** or stock made with stock cubes
250 ml (scant ½ pint) red wine

Accompanying vegetables
8 miniature carrots
4 miniature cucumbers
8 miniature turnips
(obtained by cutting ordinary vegetables into sticks or by 'turning' them into olive shapes)
4 cauliflower florets
8 pickling onions

Flavouring ingredients
50 g (2 oz) of the white part of leek, 70 g (2½ oz) carrots, 80 g (3 oz) onions, 50 g (2 oz) button mushrooms (sliced)
1 small bouquet garni
1 heaped teaspoon salt
a pinch of pepper

Ingredients for making the sauce
2 tablespoons fromage blanc
1 teaspoon crème fraîche
½ teaspoon freshly chopped parsley

Equipment
1 small enamelled iron or earthenware casserole
1 non-stick frying-pan

1 Bring the red wine to the boil in the casserole and reduce it by half to eliminate the alcohol almost completely.

2 Sauté the pieces of meat without fat in the non-stick frying-pan to seal them.

3 Put them into the casserole with the wine and add the chicken stock and all the flavouring ingredients. Simmer, covered, for one-and-a-half hours either on the top of the stove or in the oven (200°C/400°F/Mark 6), which I think produces a better result.

4 Meanwhile cook the accompanying vegetables in boiling salted water – the onions for fifteen minutes, the carrots, turnips and cauliflower for ten minutes.

5 When it is tender remove the meat from its gravy with a skimmer and keep it hot. Strain the gravy through a conical strainer. Reserve one tablespoon of the strained vegetables from the gravy for making the sauce.

6 Put the tablespoon of vegetables into the liquidizer and purée them, adding the hot strained gravy, the crème fraîche and the fromage blanc.

7 Pour this mixture into the casserole. Put in the pieces of meat. Add seasoning if necessary.

8 Serve the estouffade in the casserole, scattering the accompanying vegetables – well drained – over the top, and embellishing it with chopped parsley.

---

100. *Pot-au-feu served like a fondue*
POT-AU-FEU DE VIANDE EN FONDUE

For four people

Main ingredients
150 g (5 oz) leg of veal
150 g (5 oz) beef fillet
150 g (5 oz) leg of lamb
2 litres (3½ pints) beef bouillon (light beef stock made as described in No 1)
1 tablespoon soy sauce

Ingredients for flavouring the bouillon
16 miniature carrots
16 miniature turnips
8 miniature cucumbers
(obtained by cutting ordinary vegetables into sticks or by 'turning' them into olive shapes)
4 small leeks

8 pickling onions
1 small celery stalk
1 unpeeled clove of garlic
1 bouquet garni
1 clove

Accompanying sauces
5 tablespoons tomato sauce (No 38)
5 tablespoons parsley sauce (No 41)
5 tablespoons béarnaise sauce (No 36)

Equipment
1 saucepan with a lid
2 deep dishes
1 fondue set with forks
4 hot plates
4 small bowls

1 Prepare the sauces and keep them hot.

2 Bring the beef bouillon to the boil, together with all the flavouring

ingredients, and simmer, covered, for fifteen minutes. Season with salt. Remove and drain the vegetables and keep them hot.

3 Meanwhile cut all the meat into cubes 2 cm ($\frac{3}{4}$ in) across. Put them to marinate in a deep dish with the tablespoon of soy sauce.

4 Put the two dishes on the table, one containing the meat and the other the vegetables. Pour one litre ($1\frac{3}{4}$ pints) of the now well-flavoured bouillon into the fondue pan placed over its lamp in the middle of the table.

Each guest cooks his own meat as he likes it, dipping it into the boiling bouillon and then into the various sauces and finally seasoning it.

The remaining bouillon can be served at the same time in small soup bowls.

---

101. *Scarlet tongue with onion sauce*
LANGUE DE BŒUF À LA FONDUE D'OIGNONS

For six people

Main ingredient
1 small ox-tongue

Ingredients for the cooking liquid and sauce
1 kg ($2\frac{1}{4}$ lb) onions
500 ml (scant 1 pint) red wine
500 ml (scant 1 pint) chicken stock (No 2) **or** stock made with stock cubes
3 tomatoes, skinned
1 bouquet garni

1 unpeeled clove of garlic
1 tablespoon freshly chopped chervil
1 tablespoon freshly chopped tarragon
salt, pepper

Equipment
2 stainless-steel saucepans
1 oval enamelled iron casserole
1 skimmer **or** slotted spoon
1 liquidizer
1 oval serving dish

1 Plunge the tongue into unsalted boiling water for fifteen minutes.

2 Cut the tomatoes in half and press them in the palm of your hand to squeeze out pips and excess juice. Peel the onions and slice them finely.

3 Bring the wine to the boil in a stainless-steel saucepan and reduce it to half its volume.

4 Preheat the oven to 200°C/400°F/Mark 6. Skin the tongue, season it with salt and pepper and put it into the casserole. Bury it with the onions and tomato halves and add the unpeeled clove of garlic, the bouquet garni and half the chopped chervil and tarragon.

5   Cover with the reduced red wine and chicken stock. Taste for seasoning, cover, and cook in the oven for two hours.

6   At the end of the cooking take out the tongue and keep it hot. Remove the bouquet garni and purée the vegetables and gravy in the liquidizer.

7   To serve the dish, slice the tongue and then put the slices back together as near as possible to their original shape on an oval serving dish. Pour the sauce round the tongue and sprinkle with the remaining chopped chervil and tarragon.

---

102. *Grilled veal chop in a waistcoat*
CÔTE DE VEAU 'GRILLÉE EN SALADE'

For four people

Main ingredients
4 best veal chops each weighing 110 g
   (4 oz) with all fat removed

Other ingredients
130 g (4½ oz) carrots
130 g (4½ oz) mushrooms
100 g (3½ oz) onions
⅛ teaspoon thyme
salt, a pinch of pepper
1 teaspoon olive oil
1 tablespoon coarsely chopped tomato
   pulp (No 138)
1 teaspoon freshly chopped parsley
12 handsome lettuce leaves

Ingredients for the liaison
30 g (1 oz) mushroom purée (No 132)
200 ml (⅓ pint) veal stock (No 1)

Accompanying sauce
200 ml (⅓ pint) Tomato sauce (No 38)

Equipment
1 wire grill
1 heavy-based saucepan with a lid
1 oval oven dish
1 sauceboat

1   Heat the olive oil in the saucepan and add the vegetables, cut in tiny dice, in succession; the carrots go in first, after four minutes add the onions and after a further four minutes add the mushrooms. Allow to cook for four minutes more, making twelve minutes cooking in all. Season with salt, pepper and thyme and cover the pan.

2   Cook the seasoned vegetables for two minutes more before adding half the veal stock, tomato pulp and chopped parsley, then allow to simmer for ten minutes.

3   Add the mushroom purée and stir it in delicately with a fork taking care not to crush the vegetables. Allow to cool.

4   Grill the chops briefly, giving them a criss-cross pattern or 'quadrillage' (*see page 46*). They should still be very pink inside. This is to impart a slight fragrance of grilled meat to the chops.

5   Preheat the oven to 200°C/400°F/Mark 6.

6   Blanch the lettuce leaves in boiling water for one minute, then spread them on a cloth in groups of three.

7   Cover each veal chop with two-and-a-half tablespoons of the vegetables and enclose them completely in a waistcoat of lettuce leaves.

8   Pour the remaining seven tablespoons of veal stock into the oven dish and put in the chops. Bake for fifteen minutes in the oven.

9   Serve straight from the oven and offer a tomato sauce separately, in a sauceboat.

---

103. *Grilled veal escalopes with artichoke sauce*
ESCALOPE DE VEAU GRILLÉE AU COULIS DE CULS D'ARTICHAUTS

For four people

Main ingredients
4 veal escalopes each weighing 100 g
  (3½ oz)
1 tablespoon arachide oil

Ingredients for the garnish
16 miniature carrots
16 miniature turnips
8 miniature cucumbers
(obtained by cutting ordinary
  vegetables into sticks or by 'turning'
  them into olive shapes)

16 pickling onions
1 tablespoon chopped parsley

Accompanying sauce
250 ml (scant ½ pint) Artichoke sauce
  (No 40)

Equipment
1 grill
1 saucepan
4 hot plates

1   Cook the vegetables in boiling salted water, the onions for fifteen minutes, the carrots and turnips for ten minutes, the cucumbers for two minutes. Keep them hot in their cooking water.

2   Brush the escalopes with arachide oil and grill for about two minutes on each side to give a criss-cross pattern or 'quadrillage' (*see page 46 for method*). Wipe off the excess oil with absorbent paper and season with salt and pepper.

3   Spoon artichoke sauce on to the heated plates and arrange the grilled

escalopes on top, surrounded with vegetables and sprinkled with freshly chopped parsley.

---

104. *Veal blanquette*
BLANQUETTE DE VEAU À LA VAPEUR

For two people

Main ingredients
300 g (11 oz) of shoulder of veal trimmed of all fat and sinew and cut into large cubes
1.25 litres (2¼ pints) chicken stock (No 2) or chicken stock made with stock cubes

Ingredients for the garnish
4 miniature carrots
4 miniature turnips
4 miniature cucumbers
(obtained by cutting ordinary vegetables into chunks and then 'turning' them into olive shapes)
4 cauliflower florets
4 pickling onions
4 button mushrooms

Flavouring ingredients
50 g (2 oz) the white part of leek

70 g (2½ oz) carrots
50 g (2 oz) mushrooms
20 g (¾ oz) celery
(all sliced coarsely into rounds)
1 small bouquet garni, salt, a pinch of pepper

Ingredients for the sauce
1 teaspoon Sauce Périgueux (No 11) (*optional*)
½ teaspoon crème fraîche
a pinch of chopped tarragon
2 teaspoons fromage blanc

Equipment
2 small saucepans, one with a lid **or** for second method, a steamer
1 wire sieve, 1 liquidizer, 2 hot plates

The veal for the blanquette can either be (A) cooked in the stock or (B) steamed over the stock.

A

1   Put the veal, flavouring vegetables, bouquet garni, seasoning and chicken stock into a saucepan and simmer gently for one-and-a-half hours.

2   In a separate saucepan cook the vegetables for the garnish in boiling salted water, giving the carrots and turnips ten minutes and the cucumbers only two minutes. Test them with a sharp knife to see if they are cooked – they should still be rather firm. Keep them hot in their cooking water, and drain only when you are ready to serve them.

3   When the veal is cooked, remove it from the cooking liquid with the skimmer and keep it hot. Strain the cooking liquid through a wire sieve and keep one tablespoon of the vegetables and 150 ml ($\frac{1}{4}$ pint) of the liquid for making the sauce.

4   Purée the tablespoon of cooking vegetables in the liquidizer, add the tarragon, fromage blanc, crème fraîche and, if used. Sauce Périgueux, and blend for one minute. Moisten the sauce with 150 ml ($\frac{1}{4}$ pint) of cooking liquid and heat through.

5   Put the veal on to the plates and cover lightly with the sauce. Scatter the hot, well-drained vegetables on top.

B

1   Take a small steamer or a saucepan with a rack on legs which fits into it. Put the chicken stock into the pan together with the flavouring vegetables, bouquet garni and seasoning. Put in the rack and place the pieces of meat on top. If using a couscoussier put the vegetables and stock in the bottom and the meat in the top. Simmer gently for two hours.

2   Finish the dish in exactly the same way as (A), cooking the vegetables for the garnish in plain salted water, and making the sauce as described in A.

105. *Stewed shin of veal with orange sauce*
JARRET DE VEAU AUX ORANGES

For four to five people

Main ingredients
1 whole shin of veal with the bone
1 tablespoon olive oil

Ingredients for the marinade
100 g (3$\frac{1}{2}$ oz) onions
1 sprig basil
1 pounded clove
1 small bouquet garni
juice of 2 oranges
juice of 1 lemon
salt, pepper

Ingredients for the sauce
7 tablespoons chicken stock (No 2) or chicken stock made with stock cubes

4 tablespoons wine vinegar, sugar substitute equal to 1 tablespoon sugar (for the sharp sauce)
1 orange

Equipment
1 deep dish
1 oval enamelled iron casserole
2 small saucepans
1 small whisk
1 liquidizer
1 oval serving dish

1   Peel the onion and slice it finely. Put it with all the other marinade ingredients into a deep dish. Let the shin of veal marinate in this mixture for twelve hours, turning it two or three times.

2   Preheat the oven to 220°C/425°F/Mark 7.

3   Drain the veal, wipe it dry and coat it with a tablespoon of olive oil.

4   Heat the casserole and put in the shin to seal and brown to a pale golden colour.

5   Pour on the marinade. Cover the casserole and cook in the oven for one-and-a-half hours.

6   Meanwhile, prepare the sharp sauce. Boil the vinegar and sugar substitute together until the mixture turns chestnut brown and becomes syrupy.

7   Peel the orange with a potato-peeler and cut the zest into fine julienne strips the size of pine-needles. Bring them to the boil, refresh in cold water and drain. Cut all the pith off the orange with a sharp knife, cut through the transparent inner skin of each section and remove the flesh.

8   Take the shin of veal out of the casserole and keep it hot.

9   Put the cooking juices into the liquidizer with the chicken stock. Blend and return to a saucepan to heat through, then whisk in the sharp sauce and add the orange peel and skinned orange sections.

10   Carve the shin into thin slices and lay them on the serving dish 'on horseback' over the bone. Pour the sauce round the meat.

Note for Australia Knuckle of veal is sometimes called osso buco by Australian butchers. This is simply by association with the Italian dish in which it is used.

106. *Veal kidney in a green waistcoat*
ROGNON DE VEAU 'EN HABIT VERT'

For two people

Main ingredients
1 veal kidney
4 large spinach leaves
4 large lettuce leaves
salt, pepper

Ingredients for the braising liquid
white part of a leek, half an onion,
   1 carrot, (cut in rounds)
1 small bouquet garni
200 ml ($\frac{1}{3}$ pint) of veal stock (No 1)
1 teaspoon olive oil

Ingredients for the liaison
1 teaspoon mushroom purée (No 132)
$\frac{1}{2}$ teaspoon fromage blanc
$\frac{1}{2}$ teaspoon Dijon mustard

Equipment
1 small oval casserole with a lid
1 liquidizer
2 hot plates

See colour illustrations between pages 128 and 129

1   Blanch the lettuce and spinach leaves in boiling water for one minute.

2   Remove every trace of fat from the veal kidney, season it with salt and pepper and wrap it in the spinach and lettuce leaves.

3   Heat the olive oil in the casserole, and brown the leeks, onion, carrot and bouquet garni for a moment before placing the kidney on top. Moisten with the veal stock. Braise, covered, for thirty minutes, basting often with the cooking liquid (*for braising method see pages 64–5*). The kidney should still be rosy inside.

4   Take the kidney out of the casserole. Strain the cooking liquid through a conical strainer. Blend the liquid in the mixer together with the mushroom purée, fromage blanc and mustard. Taste for seasoning and heat through without allowing to boil.

5   Lift off the green waistcoat of lettuce and spinach enclosing the kidney and spread on the two plates. Slice the kidney into fine slices, removing the core, and lay the slices over the lettuce and spinach. Pour a thread of sauce delicately round the outside.

107. *Steamed calf's liver with leeks in sweet-sour sauce*
FOIE DE VEAU À LA VAPEUR AUX BLANCS DE POIREAUX EN AIGRE-DOUX

For six people

Main ingredients
900 g (2 lb) calf's liver in a piece
500 ml (generous ¾ pint) chicken
  stock (No 2) **or** stock made from
  stock cubes

*Ingredients for the chopped mushroom
  coating*
1 teaspoon olive oil
40 g (1½ oz) dried morels
40 g (1½ oz) dried mousserons (millers)
  or Chinese mushrooms
120 g (4 oz) button mushrooms
100 g (3½ oz) meat from a cooked and
  boned pig's trotter
2 chopped shallots
a pinch of thyme, salt, pepper

1 tablespoon port
3 tablespoons veal stock (No 1)

*Vegetables and ingredients for the
  accompanying sauce*
24 tender young leeks
8 tablespoons sherry **or** wine vinegar
1 tablespoon olive oil
sugar substitute equivalent to
  1 tablespoon sugar

Equipment
1 saucepan
1 couscoussier **or** steamer
1 enamelled iron casserole with a lid
1 large sheet of aluminium foil
1 oval serving dish

See colour illustrations between pages 128 and 129

1   Clean and wash the leeks thoroughly. Cut off the tops leaving about
8 cm (3 in) of the white part.

  Soak the morels and mousserons or Chinese mushrooms for quarter of
an hour in cold water. Change the water several times, and rub the mushrooms briskly between the palms of your hands to remove every trace of
earth or sand.

  Peel, wash, and dry the button mushrooms and cut into quarters.

2   Heat the teaspoon of olive oil in the saucepan, add the chopped shallots, mushrooms and the chopped meat from the trotter; season with a
pinch of thyme, and cook for four minutes. Add the port, and three
tablespoons of veal or chicken stock and season with salt and pepper.
Cook, covered, for ten minutes. At the end of the cooking time, chop all
these ingredients finely with a sharp knife and let them cool, spread out on
a plate.

3   Place the seasoned calf's liver on a sheet of aluminium foil. Cover it
completely with the chopped mushroom mixture, and enclose it in the
foil, compressing it slightly to make it the shape of a rolled joint.

  Pour the chicken stock into the steamer or couscoussier. Place the liver, in its foil, on the rack of the steamer or in the top part of the couscoussier. Cook, covered, for twenty-five minutes and then allow to rest for a further fifteen minutes. Reserve 200 ml (⅓ pint) of the stock for the sauce.

4   Meanwhile, heat the tablespoon of olive oil in the casserole and cook the leeks until they are lightly browned. Season them with pepper and salt, and allow to cook, covered, for twenty minutes. Sprinkle with the sherry or wine vinegar, add the sugar substitute, and simmer until half the liquid has evaporated.

5   Remove the foil and chopped mushrooms from the liver. Cut it into nice slices, then put it back together as near as possible to its original shape and place it on the serving dish.

Arrange the leeks crossed over each other in pairs on top.

Put the chopped mushroom mixture into the reduced vinegar in which the leeks have cooked, add 200 ml (⅓ pint) of cooking liquid from the liver, allow to boil for one minute, taste for seasoning and spoon the sauce all round the edge of the liver.

108. *Sweetbreads with wood mushrooms*
GÂTEAU DE RIS DE VEAU AUX MORILLES

For four people

Main ingredients for the farce (forcemeat)

220 g (8 oz) uncooked chicken breast
30 g (1 oz) trimmed uncooked sweetbreads
half an egg white
1 teaspoon crème fraîche (*optional*)
1 teaspoon glace de viande (No 1)
1 teaspoon salt, a pinch of pepper and nutmeg
33 g (1 oz) skimmed milk powder dissolved in 300 ml (½ pint) water

Other ingredients

180 g (6½ oz) trimmed uncooked sweetbreads
25 g (1 oz) morels or Chinese mushrooms
100 g (3½ oz) button mushrooms
1 teaspoon glace de viande (No 1)
1 teaspoon truffle juice

Ingredients for the accompanying sauce

200 ml (⅓ pint) of the braising liquid from the sweetbreads
80 g (3 oz) button mushrooms
10 g (⅓ oz) dried morels or Chinese mushrooms (dried mushrooms are extremely light)
1½ teaspoons skimmed milk powder dissolved in 3 tablespoons water
4 slices of truffle

Equipment

1 non-stick frying-pan, 1 saucepan
1 pastry brush, 1 liquidizer
4 small porcelain or earthenware dishes
1 serving dish or 4 hot plates

1 *Preparing the farce*

Put the chicken breast, 30 g (1 oz) of sweetbreads and seasoning, salt, pepper and nutmeg, into the liquidizer and blend for one minute. Add half an egg white and blend for one minute more. Add the crème fraîche, if wanted, glace de viande and skimmed milk powder dissolved in the water, and give the mixture a quick final blend.

Pour this somewhat liquid forcemeat into a bowl and chill.

2 *Preparing the sweetbreads and morels*

Braise the 180 g (6½ oz) of sweetbreads (*for the method see page 189*). Soak the dried mushrooms in lukewarm water.

Cut the dried mushrooms, button mushrooms and braised sweetbreads into cubes 1 cm (½ in) across. Put them into the non-stick frying-pan and sweat them 'à sec', without any oil or fat, so that they release their juices. Season and add the truffle juice and the glace de viande.

Stir the mixture and put it on one side to cool.

3 *Accompanying sauce*

Coarsely chop the soaked dried morels and button mushrooms. Put the 200 ml (⅓ pint) of braising liquid from the sweetbreads and the skimmed milk into the saucepan and cook the chopped mushrooms gently until tender. Purée the mixture in the liquidizer. Keep the resulting sauce hot.

4 *Preparing the moulds*

Preheat the oven to 200°C/400°F/Mark 6. Brush the insides of the small dishes or moulds with a pastry brush dipped in cold water, to prevent them from sticking when they are turned out. Half fill them with the forcemeat, then put a tablespoon of the sweetbreads and mushrooms on top. Fill to the top with the remaining forcemeat.

Cook in a bain-marie in the oven for twenty–thirty minutes.

5 *Serving the dish*

Turn out the sweetbreads either on to a serving dish or on to individual plates. Decorate each with a slice of truffle and spoon the sauce over the top. Serve very hot.

109. *Eugénie mushroom and sweetbread ragoût*
RAGOÛT FIN D'EUGÉNIE

For two people

Main ingredients
170 g (6 oz) veal sweetbreads
15 g (½ oz) dried morels, washed and
  soaked
100 g (3½ oz) button mushrooms
2 teaspoons chopped shallot
70 g (2½ oz) veal kidney
salt, pepper
8 tablespoons chicken stock (No 2) or
  chicken stock made with stock cubes

Ingredients for the garnish
4 miniature carrots
4 miniature cucumbers
4 miniature turnips
(made by cutting up ordinary
  vegetables into sticks)
4 cauliflower florets
4 pickling onions

Flavouring ingredients
half carrot, coarsely chopped
quarter onion, coarsely chopped
1 small bouquet garni
1 tomato washed and quartered

Ingredients for the sauce
5 tablespoons braising liquid from the
  sweetbreads
1 tablespoon Sauce Périgueux (No 11)
1 dessertspoon truffle juice
30 g (1 oz) mushroom purée (No 132)
2 tablespoons fromage blanc
½ teaspoon of crème fraîche

Equipment
1 saucepan, 1 casserole
1 non-stick frying-pan

Preparing and cooking the sweetbreads
1   Soak the sweetbreads in a bowl under a slowly running tap for two
hours, to eliminate every trace of blood.

2   Blanch them by putting them into a saucepan of cold water, bringing
them to the boil and boiling for two minutes. Refresh in cold water, drain
in a wire sieve, then remove the outside membrane.

  Wrap them in a clean tea-towel and put beneath a weighted board to
press out any remaining water and give them an even shape.

  Sweetbreads can be braised straight away without being blanched. The
juices will add a certain amount of extra flavour to the braising liquid but
blanching perhaps makes the flavour purer.

Braising
3   Heat a teaspoon of olive oil in a casserole just large enough to hold the
sweetbreads. Season them with salt and freshly ground pepper and put
them into the casserole. Add the chopped carrots and onions. If you prefer
to cook the dish without the oil, use a non-stick pan.

Brown the sweetbreads all over for five minutes together with the vegetables.

Add the bouquet garni, tomato and the white wine, and reduce by three-quarters to evaporate the alcohol. Add the chicken stock and simmer gently, covered, for ten minutes.

4 Cook the little vegetables for the garnish in boiling salted water (*see recipe for blanquette de veau* No 104). Keep them hot in the water in which they were cooked and drain them just before serving the dish.

5 Peel the button mushrooms and cut them into dice 1 cm ($\frac{1}{2}$ in) across. Cut the morels into quarters and chop the shallot. Put them all into the non-stick saucepan and allow to cook for five minutes.

6 Take the cooked sweetbreads out of the casserole and cut them into cubes like the mushrooms. Strain the braising liquid and keep it on one side.

7 Put the button mushrooms, morels and sweetbreads into the casserole in which the sweetbreads were cooked. Add the truffle juice, Sauce Périgueux, if used, and five tablespoons of the braising liquid from the sweetbreads. Heat through.

8 Stir in the mushroom purée, fromage blanc and, if used, the half teaspoon of crème fraîche.

9 Season the veal kidney and cut it into cubes like the mushrooms and sweetbreads. Sauté it rapidly in the non-stick saucepan. It should still be rosy inside. Lightly mix the kidney cubes and little vegetables into the casserole with the sweetbreads and serve very hot in the casserole in which they were cooked.

Other dried mushrooms may be used instead of morels – see **Note for Users in Australia**.

Le gigot d'agneau cuit dans le foin

110. *Leg of lamb cooked in hay*
GIGOT D'AGNEAU CUIT DANS LE FOIN

For six people

Main ingredients
1 small leg of milk-fed lamb on the
  bone weighing about 1.2 kg (2 lb
  10 oz)
7 tablespoons water
salt, pepper
2 large handfuls hay
1 sprig thyme
half a bayleaf
1 sprig wild thyme (*optional*)

Ingredients for making the gravy
12 tablespoons gravy from a previously
  roasted leg of lamb

1 teaspoon tarragon
2 mint leaves
  or substitute a fresh tomato sauce
  (No 38)

Equipment
1 oval enamelled-iron casserole with a
  lid
1 hot serving dish
1 sauceboat

1   Preheat the oven to 220°C/425°F/Mark 7. Put a layer of hay in the bottom of the casserole, flavour it with thyme, bayleaf and, if you can obtain it, wild thyme.

Place the leg of lamb, seasoned with salt and pepper, on top, and cover it over with another handful of hay. Moisten the hay with seven tablespoons of water, cover the casserole, and cook for forty minutes in the oven.

2   Meanwhile put the chopped tarragon and mint leaves into the gravy (from a leg of lamb eaten previously, skimmed of all fat, and reheated).

3   Bring the lamb to the table in the casserole, still surrounded with hay.

4   Take it out, and carve it into fine slices. Arrange the slices on the hot serving dish and serve with the herb-flavoured gravy or fresh tomato sauce in a separate sauceboat.

It can be accompanied by one or two vegetable purées.

111. *Parslied chicken*
VOLAILLE 'TRUFFÉE' AU PERSIL

For four people

Main ingredient
1 chicken weighing 1 kg (2¼ lb)

Other ingredients
5 tablespoons chopped parsley
1 tablespoon chopped chives
1 tablespoon chopped tarragon
2 chopped shallots
50 g (2 oz) button mushrooms, chopped
1 tablespoon fromage blanc
1 teaspoon arachide oil
salt, pepper

Ingredients for the gravy
180 ml (⅓ pint) concentrated chicken stock (No 2)
1 tablespoon chopped parsley
1 unpeeled clove of garlic

Equipment
1 roasting-tin
1 conical strainer
1 mixing bowl

1   Preheat the oven to 240°C/475°F/Mark 9.

2   Put the ingredients for preparing the chicken into a bowl: parsley, chives, tarragon, mushrooms, fromage blanc, salt and pepper, and work them together with a fork until they form a smooth paste.

3   Lift the skin away from the breast and legs of the chicken (by sliding your fingers between the skin and the flesh) so that you can insert the parsley mixture, patting it into an even layer over the breast and thighs.

4   Season the chicken inside with salt and pepper and roast it in a hot oven, having brushed the outside with a teaspoon of arachide oil.

5   When it is cooked, remove the chicken from the roasting-tin and keep it hot. Put the flattened clove of garlic and the chopped parsley into the hot juices in the roasting pan. Moisten with the concentrated chicken stock and bring to the boil, scraping the bottom of the pan thoroughly with a fork to detach the caramelized juices. Reduce this gravy by one-third and taste for seasoning.

6   Carve the chicken into four serving pieces, put them on a large hot dish, and carefully moisten each piece with some of the gravy poured through a conical strainer.

This recipe is also suitable for guinea fowl or pheasant.

112. *Chicken cooked with lime blossom*
POULET AU TILLEUL EN VESSIE

For four people

Main ingredients
1 chicken weighing 1 kg (2¼ lb)
1 litre (1¾ pints) light chicken stock
   (No 2) **or** stock made with stock
   cubes
20 g (¾ oz) tilleul – dried lime
   blossom
400 g (14 oz) onions, sliced
1 tablespoon dry vermouth
salt, pepper

Ingredients for the sauce
1 teaspoon glace de viande, meat
   glaze, (No 1) (*optional*)
1 teaspoon crème fraîche

half an apple, half a grapefruit,
20 g (¾ oz) pimento (cut into little dice)

Equipment
1 saucepan
1 large enamelled-iron casserole with
   a lid
1 liquidizer
1 hot serving dish
1 pig's bladder or the nearest thing, a
   transparent roasting bag (*see pages
   61–2*)
string

1   Put 10 g (about ⅓ oz) of dried lime blossom inside the chicken, and truss it. Slide it into the cleaned, and turned inside-out, pig's bladder or the transparent roasting bag.

2   Boil the light chicken stock in a saucepan until it is reduced by three-quarters of its volume and has become slightly syrupy.

3   Pour the concentrated stock into the bag or bladder in which you have put the chicken, together with 10 g (⅓ oz) of dried lime blossom, the onions, vermouth, salt and pepper. Seal up the bag hermetically by tying it tightly with string. If using a pig's bladder, prick it several times with a needle to make little safety valves.

4   Half fill the casserole with hot water and put in the chicken in its bag. Cover and simmer over a gentle heat for one and a quarter hours.

5   Open the bag and take out the chicken. Remove the lime blossom and put the onions, and concentrated stock into the mixer together with the crème fraîche and glace de viande, if wanted, and blend to a sauce. Pour into a saucepan, adding the cubes of apple, grapefruit and pimento. Heat through.

6   Quickly skin the chicken. Cut it in four and decorate with one or two dried lime blossoms. Pour the sauce over the bottom of a very hot serving dish and place the pieces of chicken on top.

EDITOR'S NOTE   Dried lime blossom can be obtained from health food stores and herbalists.

Note for Australia Lemon-scented thyme has been found to produce delicious results where lime blossom is not available.

---

113. *Chicken with freshwater crayfish*
POULET AUV ÉCREVISSES
    (*chicken with yabbies*)

For four people

Main ingredients
1 chicken cleaned and trussed
   weighing 1 kg (2¼ lb)
12 small freshwater crayfish **or**
   Dublin Bay prawns or yabbies or
   King prawns
2 litres (3½ pints) chicken stock
   (No 2) or stock made with stock
   cubes
1 teaspoon freshly-chopped parsley
½ teaspoon freshly-chopped tarragon

80 g (3 oz) onions
80 g (3 oz) carrots
1 small bouquet garni

Accompanying sauce
250 ml (scant ½ pint) hot lobster
   sauce (No 46)

Equipment
1 casserole
1 skimmer
1 hot serving dish

1   Put the chicken stock in a casserole large enough to hold the chicken, together with the bouquet garni, sliced onions and carrots cut into rounds. Bring to the boil and plunge the chicken into the stock. Simmer gently for twenty-five minutes.

2   At the same time, together with the chicken, throw in the well-washed crayfish or Dublin Bay prawns and poach for two minutes. Remove them and keep hot.

3   While the chicken is cooking make the lobster sauce (*see* No 46).

4   Lift the chicken out of its cooking liquid with a skimmer, and cut it into four pieces, two wings and breasts and two legs. Skin them.

5   Put the pieces on a hot serving dish and coat them lightly with the hot lobster sauce. Arrange the crayfish or prawns round the outside with their claws in the air. Scatter finely chopped parsley and tarragon over the sauce.

114. *Chicken served in a soup bowl with crayfish*
POULET EN SOUPIÈRE AUX ÉCREVISSES

For four people

Main ingredients

1 chicken, cleaned and trussed,
weighing 1 kg (2¼ lb)

8 small freshwater crayfish **or** Dublin
Bay prawns or yabbies or King
prawns

2 litres (3½ pints) chicken stock
(No 2) **or** stock made with stock
cubes

280 g (10 oz) mangetout peas (sugar
peas)

Ingredients for the accompanying sauce

240 ml (scant ½ pint) hot lobster
sauce (No 46)

8 tablespoons chicken stock (No 2) **or**
stock made with stock cubes

Equipment

2 saucepans

1 skimmer

4 individual deep ovenproof porcelain
soup bowls

4 rounds of aluminium foil, 15 cm (6
in) across

1   Poach the chicken for fifteen minutes in the simmering chicken stock.
Cut it into four and take off the wings and breasts, and the legs.

2   In the same stock cook the mangetout peas for ten minutes – they
should be 'al dente'; still slightly crisp. Drain them.

3   Bring a pan of salted water to the boil and plunge in the well-washed
crayfish. Let them poach for thirty seconds.

4   Make or reheat the lobster sauce and mix it with the eight tablespoons
of chicken stock. Preheat the oven to 240°C/475°F/Mark 9.

5   Put some mangetout peas in the bottom of each soup bowl, keeping a
few to decorate the dish. Place a piece of chicken and two crayfish on top
and cover with the hot lobster sauce.

6   Cap the bowls with the rounds of silver foil tied in place with string
like a pot of home-made jam.

Cook in a hot oven for fifteen minutes.

Bring them to the table as they are and let the guests inhale the delicious
aromas as they take off the covers.

EDITOR'S NOTE   This can be made more economically if you use crab
instead of lobster for the sauce (No 46).

115. *Chicken drumsticks steamed with marjoram*
GIGOT DE POULETTE CUIT À LA VAPEUR DE MARJOLAINE

For four people

Main ingredients
4 drumsticks from young roasting chickens
3 branches fresh marjoram
750 ml (1¼ pint) chicken stock (No 2) or stock made with stock cubes

Ingredients for the stuffing
220 g (8 oz) uncooked sweetbreads, trimmed
40 g (1½ oz) uncooked chicken breast
45 g (1¾ oz) onions, chopped
30 g (1 oz) halved button mushrooms
50 g (2 oz) dried morels or Chinese mushrooms
5 tablespoons chicken stock
2 tablespoons port
2 tablespoons olive oil
1 heaped teaspoon salt, a pinch of pepper

Ingredients for the sauce
40 g (1½ oz) mushroom purée (No 132)

150 ml (¼ pint) cooking liquid from the chicken drumsticks
1 teaspoon watercress purée (No 135)
2 teaspoons fromage blanc
2 teaspoons crème fraîche (*optional*)

Vegetables for decorating the dish
80 g (3 oz) carrots
20 g (¾ oz) celeriac
80 g (3 oz) asparagus
60 g (2 oz) French beans
30 g (1 oz) dried morels or Chinese mushrooms
12 pickling onions

Equipment
1 saucepan
1 steamer
1 hot oval serving dish or
4 hot plates

Preparing the forcemeat (farce)
1   Wash the dried morels several times in clean, cold water and put them to soak in warm water.

2   Heat the olive oil in a saucepan. Add the onions, button mushrooms and morels.

3   Sweat the vegetables gently for one minute then add the trimmed sweetbreads and uncooked chicken and season with salt and pepper.

4   Let them simmer for two minutes then pour in the port and let it reduce by three-quarters before adding the chicken stock.

Preparing the drumsticks and their cooking liquid
5   With a small sharp knife remove the bone from each drumstick.

6   Make an infusion by pouring the boiling chicken stock on to the branches of marjoram and letting it draw.

7 Allow the sweetbreads, chicken and mushrooms to cool in their cooking liquid, then take them out and chop them into tiny dice, 5 mm ($\frac{1}{4}$ in) across. Mix them together with one dessertspoon of their cooking liquid.

8 Season the insides of the boned drumsticks and fill them with the forcemeat, pressing it in well.

9 Close the chicken round the forcemeat stuffing and fasten it with a wooden cocktail stick or sew it together with thread.

Cooking the dish

10 Prick the stuffed chicken legs with a fork to prevent them from bursting during cooking.

11 Arrange them in the top of the steamer in which you have brought the marjoram-flavoured chicken stock to the boil. Cover the pan and steam gently for thirty minutes.

12 Meanwhile cook the vegetables in boiling salted water (*see recipe for blanquette de veau* No 104), and keep them hot.

Preparing the sauce

13 Put the mushroom purée, watercress purée, fromage blanc, optional crème fraîche and 150 ml ($\frac{1}{4}$ pint) of the marjoram-flavoured cooking liquid into the liquidizer and blend briefly. Taste the sauce for seasoning and keep it hot.

Serving the dish

14 Pour the sauce, which should be a delicate pale green, over the bottom of the hot serving dish or plates. Arrange the drumsticks on top and decorate with marjoram leaves. Scatter the different coloured strips of vegetables and the onions all round.

Le gigot de poulette cuit à la vapeur de marjolaine

116. *Grilled guinea fowl with limes*
PINTADEAU GRILLÉ AU CITRON VERT
(*chicken or small turkey*)

For four people

Main ingredient
1 guinea fowl of 900 g (2 lb)

Ingredients for the marinade
100 g (3½ oz) onions, finely sliced
7 tablespoons chicken stock (No 2) or
  stock made with stock cubes
3 tablespoons fresh lime juice
1½ tablespoons orange juice

Ingredients for the sauce
1 teaspoon glace de viande (meat
  glaze) (No 1)
1 teaspoon crème fraîche
4 tablespoons wine vinegar
sugar substitute equivalent to 1
  tablespoon of sugar

Other ingredients
1 lime (skin and pith removed with a
  sharp knife)
the zest of half the lime, the zest of
  quarter of an orange (cut in fine
  julienne strips and blanched in
  boiling water)

Equipment
1 large sharp knife
1 steak-beater
1 deep dish for the marinade
2 saucepans, 1 wire grill
1 liquidizer, 4 hot plates

1   The day before the dish is to be served, prepare the guinea fowl 'à la crapaudine' by making an incision along the back, and sliding the blade of a knife carefully between the bone and the flesh so as to expose the whole vertebral bone. Remove this bone completely leaving the breastbone in place, and flatten the bird with the steak-beater. The ends of the leg bones are tucked away by pressing them down into slits made in the sides of the bird. (This ensures that the bones do not burn.)

2   Mix together all the ingredients of the marinade and marinate the guinea fowl for twelve hours.

3   Remove the bird and cook the marinade over a gentle heat for twenty minutes.

4   While it is cooking, prepare the sweet-sour sauce by boiling the vinegar and sugar substitute together in a small pan until the mixture becomes chestnut brown and syrupy.

5   Blend the cooked marinade in the liquidizer with the glace de viande, the crème fraîche, and the sweet-sour sauce. Taste the resulting sauce, season if necessary and keep it hot. Separate the sections of the peeled lime and skin them.

6   Grill the guinea fowl for twenty minutes, ten minutes on each side, giving it a criss-cross pattern or 'quadrillage' (*see page 46 for method*) with the wire grill. Do not forget to prick the skin with a needle, to allow the fat to run out. When the bird is cooked, carve it into quarters.

7   Pour the hot sauce on to the four heated plates, put a quarter of the guinea fowl on each plate and decorate it with skinned slices of lime and the blanched orange and lime zest.

Note for Australia Guinea fowl is occasionally available, fresh or frozen, in Australia. This recipe would also be excellent for a chicken, young turkey or even a duckling.

---

117. *Fillets of duck breast with fresh figs*
AIGUILLETTES DE CANETON AUX FIGUES FRAÎCHES

For four people

Main ingredients
2 ducks each weighing 1.5 kg (3¼ lb)
12 fresh figs

Ingredients for the accompanying sauce
5 tablespoons concentrated veal stock (No 1)
1 tablespoon mushroom purée (No 132)
5 tablespoons milk used in the cooking of the mushroom purée

2 teaspoons crème fraîche **or 2** teaspoons fromage blanc
150 ml (¼ pint) red wine
sugar substitute equivalent to 1 tablespoon sugar
salt, pepper

Equipment
1 roasting pan
1 saucepan
1 whisk
1 hot serving dish

1   Preheat the oven to 250°C/500°F/Mark 10. Roast the two ducks, having first removed the legs which can be used for another recipe. The skin should be pricked all over with a fork beforehand so that the fat can run out. They will only take fifteen to twenty minutes in a very hot oven. The meat should still be rosy.

2   Put the red wine, sweetened with the sugar substitute into a small pan with the fresh figs. Cover and cook for two minutes. Lift out the figs and reduce the cooking liquid by a quarter.

3   Whisk all the ingredients for the sauce, including the reduced cooking liquid from the figs, together. Taste the resulting sauce for seasoning and keep hot in a bain-marie.

4 Remove the skin from the ducks. Take off the breasts and cut them lengthwise into very fine strips. Arrange them on the hot serving dish, pour over the hot sauce, and decorate with the figs cut open to look like open flowers.

The duck legs can be cooked for a separate meal in the following way: Skin them, make an incision in the upper part of the leg and slide out the thigh bone, leaving the drumstick bone in place. Flatten lightly with a beater and then treat in the same way as the guinea fowl in No 116, serving with the same sauce. The carcases can be used to make the golden poultry stock described on page 73.

EDITOR'S NOTE For this dish and the one that follows, M. Guérard recommends Challans or Rouennais ducks, which are killed in a special way to conserve their blood. Most cooks outside France, however, will have to be content with ordinary ducks.

---

118. *Fillets of duck breast with green peppercorns*
AIGUILLETTES DE CANETON AU POIVRE VERT

For four people

Main ingredients
2 ducks each weighing 1.5 kg (3¼ lb)
2 apples (Cox's Orange Pippin or other sweet eating apple)
2 apricots (fresh or tinned without sugar)

Ingredients for the sauce
3 tablespoons armagnac
8 tablespoons white wine
3 tablespoons water which has been used to rinse a tin of green peppercorns (the liquid in the tin is too strong)
8 tablespoons concentrated duck stock with all the fat removed (No 2)

20 g (¾ oz) green peppercorns
20 g (¾ oz) red pimento cut into tiny cubes

Ingredients for the liaison of the sauce
1½ tablespoons fromage blanc
30 g (1 oz) button mushrooms
250 ml (scant ½ pint) water
25 g (1 oz) skimmed milk powder

Equipment
1 oval roasting dish or gratin dish
2 saucepans
1 sieve
1 liquidizer
1 serving dish

1 Preheat the oven to 250°C/500°F/Mark 10. Roast the ducks, having first removed legs and thighs in one piece, which can be used as suggested in No 117. Prick the skin of the birds before cooking so that the fat can

run out. Cook fifteen to twenty minutes in the hot oven. The flesh of the duck should still be rosy. Set aside in a warm place.

2 Turn down the oven to 180°C/350°F/Mark 4 and bake the peeled, cored and halved apples, each half covered with half an apricot, in a dish moistened with a little water, for twenty minutes.

3 Boil the armagnac and white wine until almost completely evaporated. (The alcohol evaporates, leaving only the flavour of wine.)

4 Add the liquid obtained by rinsing the green peppercorns, and the concentrated duck stock and simmer, gently, for half an hour.

5 Meanwhile, in a separate pan, cook the mushrooms in the milk powder dissolved in the water for ten minutes. Purée the mushrooms in the liquidizer with half their cooking liquid and the fromage blanc, and mix with the wine and stock, the green peppercorns and red pimento.

6 Remove the skin from the ducks. Carve off the breasts and slice them lengthwise into very fine slivers, or fillets. Place them on a hot dish, and coat them lightly with the green peppercorn sauce. Decorate with the apples.

---

119. *Salmi of goose hearts*
BROUET DE CŒURS D'OIE

For two people

Main ingredients
8 goose hearts **or** 12 chicken hearts,
   with fat removed
1 teaspoon olive oil

Vegetables for the sauce
10 pickling onions
10 small button mushrooms
8 small cauliflower florets
40 g (1½ oz) French beans

Ingredients for the accompanying sauce
7 tablespoons veal stock (No 1)
5 tablespoons red wine
100 g (3½ oz) onions, finely sliced
1 teaspoon chopped parsley
a sliver of garlic (*optional*)

Equipment
1 saucepan
1 non-stick saucepan
2 hot plates

1 Cook all the vegetables for the sauce, all in the same pan of boiling water, the onions for fifteen minutes, the cauliflower florets for ten minutes and the mushrooms and French beans for five minutes. Keep hot in their cooking liquid.

Preparing the sauce

2 Sauté the sliced onions 'à sec', without fat or oil in the non-stick pan (their own juices will prevent them from sticking). When they are becoming tender and transparent add the red wine and reduce by three-quarters of its volume. Add the veal stock, season and cook on a low heat for twenty minutes. Purée this mixture in the liquidizer.

3 Strain the vegetables and put them into the pan with the red wine and onion sauce. Mix them together lightly with the sauce.

4 Heat the teaspoon of olive oil in the first saucepan and put in the hearts, seasoned with salt and pepper and brown them all over. Let them cook for eight minutes stirring them all the time.

5 Divide the sauce and vegetables between the two hot plates and arrange the hearts, cut in two, on top. Sprinkle with freshly chopped parsley (and a tiny piece of garlic, chopped, if liked).

---

120. *Grilled pigeon with creamy garlic sauce*
PIGEON GRILLÉ À LA CRÈME D'AIL
  (spatchcock)

For four people

Main ingredients
4 pigeons

Other ingredients
80 g (3 oz) pickling onions
1 medium carrot
50 g (2 oz) celery
150 g (5 oz) spinach
80 g (3 oz) French beans
1 teaspoon butter
4 tablespoons water
sugar substitute equivalent to 1
  teaspoon of sugar

Accompanying sauce
12 tablespoons creamy garlic sauce
  (No 42)

Equipment
1 steak-beater
2 saucepans
1 wire grill
4 large hot plates

1 Make the garlic sauce and keep it hot.

2 Prepare the pigeons 'à la crapaudine' in the same way as the guinea fowl with limes (No 116), removing the vertebral bones, beating the birds flat, and then tucking the ends of the leg bones into slits made in the flesh.

3   *Preparing the vegetables*

Cut the peeled carrot and the celery into strips 4 cm (1½ in) long and 5 mm (¼ in) thick. Top and tail the French beans and cut them in half. Cook all the vegetables in boiling salted water, the onions for fifteen minutes, the carrot and celery for ten minutes, the beans and spinach for four minutes. Drain them all except the spinach.

4   *Glazing the vegetables*

Heat the teaspoon of butter in a saucepan, and sauté all the vegetables except the spinach. Moisten with four tablespoons of water in which you have dissolved the sugar substitute. Cook the vegetables gently in the liquid, turning them over carefully from time to time with a fork. Let them simmer until the liquid has almost evaporated and coats the vegetables with a glossy syrup.

5   Grill the pigeons quickly on a very hot grill giving them five minutes on each side. When they are cooked, remove the skin, and cut off the legs and the breasts with the wings attached. Season with salt and pepper. Slice the breasts finely.

6   *Serving the birds*

Drain the spinach and make it into four little flat cakes. Put one on the side of each plate and decorate it with the vegetables. Reassemble the pigeons as near as possible to their original shapes and place them beside the vegetables. Coat them lightly with the garlic sauce.

Apple sauce (**No 43**) would be just as delicious as the garlic sauce.

Note for Australia Spatchcock can be prepared in the same way as pigeon, and will produce similar results in this recipe.

121. *Pigeon pots*
PIGEON EN SOUPIÈRE
(*spatchcock*)

For two people

Main ingredient
A young pigeon

Other ingredients
80 g (3 oz) lettuce hearts
50 g (2 oz) miniature carrots (made with ordinary carrots either cut in strips or else 'turned' to make olive shapes)
16 g ($\frac{1}{2}$ oz) celery cut in strips
20 g ($\frac{3}{4}$ oz) the smallest button mushrooms
15 g ($\frac{1}{2}$ oz) French beans
20 g ($\frac{3}{4}$ oz) artichoke hearts cut into large dice
30 g (1 oz) raw ceps or dried ceps, soaked in water and squeezed dry

2 tablespoons fresh peas
2 teaspoons truffles cut in julienne strips or dried morels soaked in water and squeezed dry

Ingredients for the sauce
8 tablespoons chicken stock (No 2) or stock made with stock cubes
salt and pepper
1 tablespoon sauce Périgueux (*optional*) (No 11)

Equipment
1 saucepan
2 deep white porcelain soup bowls
2 rounds of aluminium foil, 15 cm (6 in) across

1   Roast or, better still, poach the pigeon for seven minutes (*for poaching method see recipe* No 113). Let it cool and remove the breasts with the wings attached, and the legs.
2   Cook all the vegetables except the ceps, button mushrooms and truffles, in boiling salted water, keeping them slightly under-done and firm.
3   Preheat the oven to 240°C/475°F/Mark 9.
4   Divide half the cooked vegetables, and all the mushrooms, raw ceps and truffles between the two soup bowls. The fungi – mushrooms, ceps and truffles – will cook in the bowl and give the dish a fine bouquet.
5   Put a pigeon breast, carved into thickish slices, and a leg into each bowl. Cover with the remaining vegetables and add the chicken stock and, if liked, the sauce Périgueux.
6   Cover each soup bowl with a round of aluminium foil and fasten it in place with string. Cook in a hot oven for ten minutes.
7   Serve the soup bowls 'bonneted' so that the guests can have the pleasure of lifting the lids and savouring the delicious smells that waft out.

Note for Australia Spatchcock can be prepared in the same way as pigeon, and will produce similar results in this recipe.

122. *Saddle of young rabbit steamed with hyssop*
BARON DE LAPEREAU À LA VAPEUR D'HYSOPE

For four people

Main ingredient
The saddle and hindlegs of a young
  rabbit

Ingredients for the cooking liquid
500 ml (scant 1 pint) chicken stock
  (No 2) or stock made with stock
  cubes
5 sprigs hyssop or 3 branches thyme
  and 3 branches tarragon

Ingredients for the sauce
1 teaspoon glace de viande (No 1)
1 tablespoon fromage blanc
1 tablespoon watercress purée
  (No 135)

Equipment
1 steamer
1 liquidizer
1 sauceboat

1 Simmer the hyssop, or other herbs, and chicken stock, in the bottom half of the steamer.

2 Put the saddle of rabbit with the legs attached in the top half of the steamer over the simmering infusion of stock and herbs. Strew with a few of the chosen herbs. Steam, covered, for twenty minutes.

3 At the end of the cooking remove the rabbit and keep it hot.

4 Blend the watercress purée in the liquidizer, together with the glace de viande, fromage blanc, 250 ml (scant ½ pint) of the cooking liquid and the herbs. Taste the resulting sauce and season if necessary with salt and pepper.

5 Carve the meat off the saddle and legs in fine slivers. Put them back in place on the bones and serve on a heated dish. Serve the sauce in a sauceboat.

EDITOR'S NOTE Hyssop (*hyssopus officinalis*), also known as the butterfly bush, is an easily-grown culinary herb, making an attractive evergreen bush. The blue flower spikes are used as well as the leaves.

Note for Australia Many rabbit recipes can be adapted to yearling veal. Rabbit, in Australia, might well prove too tough and strong-tasting in this recipe.

123. *Rabbit in jelly with fresh herbs and golden plums*
GÂTEAU DE LAPIN AUX HERBES ET AUX MIRABELLES

For five people

Main ingredients
The hindquarters of a rabbit (the saddle and hindlegs) taken off the bone
20 small golden plums (fresh or preserved without sugar)

Ingredients for the marinade
1 tablespoon chopped parsley
1 tablespoon chopped chervil
1 tablespoon chopped shallot
1 teaspoon chopped tarragon
8 tablespoons dry white wine
salt and pepper

Ingredients for the cooking liquid
500 ml (scant 1 pint) chicken stock (No 2) or stock made with stock cubes

1 teaspoon mirabelle eau-de-vie (a colourless liqueur similar to kirsch)
4 sheets leaf gelatine or 4 level teaspoons powdered gelatine

Accompanying sauce
Cooked coarsely chopped tomato pulp (No 139)

Equipment
1 deep dish for the marinade
1 saucepan
1 oval earthenware terrine, 30 cm long by 10 cm deep (12 in by 4 in) with a lid
1 sauceboat

1   Start two days before you want to serve the dish. Put the rabbit meat with the marinade ingredients in a deep dish, and let it soak overnight.

2   The next day, start by soaking the sheets of leaf gelatine in cold water until they become soft and swell up. Stone the plums and sprinkle them with the mirabelle eau-de-vie.

3   Drain the pieces of rabbit, pour the marinade into a saucepan, put it over a moderate heat and let it reduce to half its original volume and evaporate the alcohol in the wine. Add the softened gelatine and the chicken stock and mix thoroughly.

4   Put the pieces of rabbit and the plums into the terrine, and pour the herb and white wine mixture over the top.

5   Cook covered in a bain-marie in a slow oven (150°C/300°F/Mark 2) for two-and-a-half hours.

6   Allow to chill in the refrigerator for twenty-four hours.

7   Serve the rabbit straight from the terrine with a serving spoon and accompany it with a sauceboat of chilled cooked tomato.

EDITOR'S NOTE   This recipe can also be made with chicken. You will need about 450 g (1 lb) of meat.

---

124. *Saddle of hare with beetroot*
RÂBLE DE LIÈVRE AUX BETTERAVES

For two people

Main ingredients
1 saddle of hare weighing about
   400 g (14 oz)
1 teaspoon olive oil

Ingredients for the marinade
250 ml (scant ½ pint) red wine
1 small bouquet garni
1 carrot chopped into cubes 1 cm (½
   in) across
1 onion chopped into cubes 1 cm (½
   in) across
4 juniper berries
2 cloves

Accompanying vegetables
200 g (7 oz) beetroot, freshly cooked
1 tablespoon wine vinegar

Ingredients for the sauce
4 tablespoons veal stock (**No 1**)
1 chopped shallot
1 tablespoon wine vinegar
½ teaspoon Dijon mustard
1 tablespoon mushroom purée (**No
   132**)
4 tablespoons water
1 teaspoon skimmed milk powder

Equipment
1 deep dish for the marinade
1 oval oven dish
1 non-stick frying-pan
1 liquidizer
2 hot plates

1   The day before you want to serve the dish, remove the translucent skin which covers the saddle of hare, with a sharp fine-bladed knife. Let it marinate for twenty-four hours in a deep dish with all the ingredients for the marinade. Turn it from time to time.

2   At the end of this time drain the saddle and wipe it dry with kitchen paper. Strain the marinade, keeping only the liquid.

3   Preheat the oven to 250°C/500°F/Mark 10. Heat the olive oil in the oven dish, seal the saddle of hare in it and let it brown all over, then roast in a very hot oven for twelve minutes.

4   Take it out of the oven and keep it hot on a serving dish, to allow it to settle (*see the notes on roasting, page* 51) and to give it an even rosy colour.

5   Skim the fat from the roasting dish, add the chopped shallot and let it soften for a minute, before adding the vinegar. Bring to the boil and dissolve the caramelized juices on the bottom of the pan, reducing almost

to nothing. Add the strained marinade, bring to the boil once more and reduce by three-quarters to evaporate the alcohol.

6   Blend the mushroom purée, mustard, veal stock and the skimmed milk powder dissolved in the four tablespoons of water in the liquidizer, together with the reduced marinade. Taste for seasoning, and heat through.

7   Slice the beetroots fairly thinly and sauté them in the non-stick frying-pan, moistening them with a tablespoon of vinegar. This turns them a beautiful deep ruby-red and gives them a perfect flavour.

8   With a long-bladed knife carve the saddle into thin strips parallel to the backbone. Spread half of them out like a fan on each hot plate, lightly coat them with the very hot sauce. Finally, arrange the beetroot all round.

Vegetables

125. Celeriac and parsley puree
PURÉE-MOUSSE DE CÉLERI-RAVE AU PERSIL

For four people

Main ingredients
500 g (1 lb 2 oz) celeriac
100 g (3½ oz) parsley
1 litre (1¾ pints) water
100 g (3½ oz) skimmed milk powder
salt, pepper

Equipment
1 heavy-based saucepan
1 wooden spoon or spatula
1 liquidizer

1 Peel the celeriac and cut into chunks. Blanch for two minutes in boiling salted water to eliminate any bitterness and drain.

2 Stir the skimmed milk powder into the cold water in the heavy-based pan. Season with salt and pepper, bring to the boil, add the celeriac and simmer for thirty minutes. Stir from time to time with a wooden spoon or spatula to prevent it from sticking.

3 Remove the stalks from the parsley, wash and dry it, and ten minutes before the end of the cooking time, add to the pan with the celeriac.

4 Strain off the liquid or lift out the parsley and celeriac with a skimmer and blend them in the liquidizer, adding just enough of the cooking liquid to give the purée a light mousse-like consistency. Taste for seasoning. Either keep the purée hot in a bain-marie ready to serve, or store in the refrigerator until needed.

EDITOR'S NOTE   In this section the recipes are enough to serve the number of people suggested, as a vegetable dish accompanying a meat or fish dish, but some of the purées – for instance Mushroom Purée (No 132) – and the tomato recipes No 138 and No 139, occur so frequently as ingredients that it is worth making them up in quantity when you are planning a course of Cuisine Minceur.

126. *Leek purée*
PURÉE-MOUSSE DE POIREAUX

For four people

Main ingredients
600 g (1 lb 6 oz) the white part of
   leeks
3 tablespoons chicken stock (No 2)
   or stock made with stock cubes
a pinch of pepper
a knob of butter (*optional*)

Equipment
1 heavy-based saucepan
1 liquidizer
1 hair sieve or fine-meshed wire sieve

1   Slice the leeks into rounds and wash thoroughly under running water.
Drain.

2   Sweat them 'à sec' – without fat or liquid – in the heavy-based pan for
five minutes to evaporate some of their juices.

3   Moisten with the chicken stock, season with salt and pepper and cook
gently, uncovered, for about thirty minutes.

4   Purée the mixture in the liquidizer long enough to break down all the
fibres. If you can't obtain a completely smooth fibre-free purée, the
mixture can be sieved through a hair sieve, but you will lose about 20 per
cent of it.

5   Just before serving you can add a walnut-sized knob of butter, either
plain or 'noisette' ('noisette' butter is butter heated until the foam sub-
sides and you can no longer hear it singing, when it turns a beautiful
golden colour).

127. *Cauliflower purée*
PURÉE-MOUSSE DE CHOUX-FLEURS

For four people

Main ingredients
1 cauliflower of about 750 g (1 lb
   11 oz) or 500 g (just over 1 lb) of
   cauliflower florets
1 litre (1¾ pints) water
100 g (3½ oz) skimmed milk powder

salt, pepper
a pinch of grated nutmeg

Equipment
1 stainless-steel saucepan
1 liquidizer

1 Prepare the cauliflower by removing the leaves, thicker stalks and branches, leaving virtually just the florets. Divide them up and wash thoroughly in plenty of water.

2 Dissolve the skimmed milk powder in the water in the stainless-steel pan and add the salt, pepper and nutmeg. Cook the cauliflower for about thirty minutes.

3 Drain the cauliflower and blend in the liquidizer, adding if necessary a little of the liquid in which it was cooked, to give the purée the consistency of a light mousse. Taste for seasoning.

4 Keep hot in a bain-marie ready to serve, or keep in the refrigerator until needed.

---

128. *Purée of French beans*
PURÉE-MOUSSE DE HARICOTS VERTS

For four people

Main ingredients
500 g (just over 1 lb) fresh French beans
1 teaspoon butter
1.5 litres (2½ pints) water

35 g (1¼ oz) coarse salt

Equipment
1 stainless-steel saucepan
1 liquidizer

1 Top and tail the beans and rinse them in cold water. Throw them into a large pan of boiling salted water. Let them cook, uncovered, at a fast boil for ten minutes. Drain thoroughly and refresh in cold water for fifteen seconds. Drain again and blend in the liquidizer, until you have obtained a smooth purée. Add a little of the cooking liquid if necessary.

2 Pour the purée into a small pan, add the butter and let it melt. Heat through.

3 Taste for seasoning and keep hot in a bain-marie ready to serve, or keep in the refrigerator until needed.

129. *Pear and spinach purée*
PURÉE-MOUSSE DE POIRES AUX ÉPINARDS

For four people

Main ingredients
400 g (14 oz) fresh spinach
100 g (3½ oz) pears
coarse salt
pepper

Equipment
1 saucepan
1 liquidizer

1   Peel, quarter and core the pears and cook for fifteen minutes in boiling water.

2   Wash the spinach and destalk it, before cooking for three minutes in very salty boiling water (3 heaped teaspoons of salt per litre of water.) Refresh the spinach in cold water and drain thoroughly.

3   Blend spinach and pears together in the liquidizer. Taste for seasoning.
  This purée is best made just before it is wanted, when it is a beautiful delicate green.

130. *Carrot purée*
PURÉE-MOUSSE DE CAROTTES

For four to six people

Main ingredients
650 g (1½ lb) carrots
2 litres (3½ pints) water
coarse salt
pinch of pepper
1 teaspoon noisette butter (*optional*)

Equipment
1 saucepan
1 liquidizer

1   Peel the carrots with a potato-peeler. Cut them in quarters.

2   Cook them in the saucepan of boiling salted water for twenty minutes.

3   Strain and liquidize.

4   Reheat the purée in the saucepan, adding pepper and, if liked, the 'noisette' butter (*for method see* No 126).

131. *Sorrel and watercress purée*
PURÉE-MOUSSE DE CRESSON ET D'OSEILLE

For two or three people

Main ingredients
2 bunches watercress
200 g (7 oz) fresh sorrel
sugar substitute equivalent to 1
   tablespoon of sugar
2 tablespoons wine vinegar

salt, pepper
1 teaspoon crème fraîche (*optional*)

Equipment
1 heavy-based saucepan with a lid
1 wooden spoon or spatula
1 liquidizer

1 Remove the stalks from the sorrel, wash it well in running water and dry it in a cloth. Pick over and wash the watercress.

2 Heat the saucepan, put in the sorrel and watercress and let them sweat gently, stirring with a wooden spoon or spatula, until all the water which is given off has completely evaporated.

3 Add the sugar substitute, wine vinegar, salt and pepper and continue to cook in the covered pan for five minutes. Purée the mixture in the liquidizer. Before serving, this sweet-sour purée can be lightly bound with a teaspoon of crème fraîche.

For a note on the use of sugar substitutes see page 20–21.

132. *Mushroom purée*
PURÉE-MOUSSE DE CHAMPIGNONS

For four people

Main ingredients
420 g (15 oz) button mushrooms
1.25 litres (2¼ pints) water
125 g (4½ oz) skimmed milk powder
1 heaped teaspoon salt
pinch of pepper

hint of grated nutmeg
1 tablespoon lemon juice

Equipment
1 saucepan
1 liquidizer

1 Trim the mushrooms, cutting off the earthy parts of the stalks. Wash them in plenty of water, rubbing them well between the palms of your hands.

2 Drain the mushrooms, cut them in half and toss them quickly in the lemon juice to keep them white.

3 Put the water in which you have dissolved the skimmed milk powder, into the saucepan, and bring to the boil. Add the mushrooms cut in half and season with salt, pepper and nutmeg. Simmer uncovered for twenty minutes.

4 Drain the mushrooms and purée them very finely in the liquidizer. Moisten with 150 ml (¼ pint) of the cooking liquid and taste for seasoning.

Keep the rest of the cooking liquid to use instead of chicken stock in certain recipes where it would be suitable, for example, Fillets of Duck Breast with Fresh Figs (No 117).

EDITOR'S NOTE This purée, so important in Cuisine Minceur, especially as a liaison ingredient, can be made in quantity and either frozen, or stored in sealed jars in the refrigerator for up to a week.

133. *Globe artichoke purée*
PURÉE-MOUSSE D'ARTICHAUTS

For four people

Main ingredients
6 globe artichokes weighing about
    300 g (10½ oz) each
1.5 litres (2½ pints) water
1 lemon

1 teaspoon crème fraîche
35 g (1½ oz) coarse salt

Equipment
1 large stainless-steel saucepan
1 liquidizer

1 Snap the stalks of the artichokes and pull them off by hand. Cook them in a large pan of boiling salted water, acidulated with lemon juice, for forty-five minutes.

2 Let them cool, then remove leaves and choke.

3 The hearts, now completely bare, are cut in quarters and puréed in the liquidizer with the crème fraîche and 150 ml (¼ pint) of the water in which they were cooked. Taste for seasoning.

For this recipe I prefer to cook the artichokes whole, to conserve the full flavour of the hearts.

EDITOR'S NOTE Removing the stalks by hand rather than cutting them off draws out the coarser fibres from the heart.

134. *Onion purée*
PURÉE-MOUSSE D'OIGNONS

For four people

Main ingredients
800 g (1¾ lb) onions
1 litre (1¾ pints) chicken stock (No 2)
  or stock made with stock cubes
2 teaspoons salt

pinch of pepper

Equipment
1 saucepan
1 liquidizer

1   Peel the onions, cut them in quarters and simmer for twenty-five minutes in the chicken stock. Season with salt and pepper.

2   Drain the onions and purée them in the liquidizer.

3   Reheat the purée and let it reduce by a third of its original volume.
  The cooking liquid can be used for another purpose – for making soup, etc.

135. *Watercress purée*
PURÉE-MOUSSE DE CRESSON

For three or four people

Main ingredients
4 bunches watercress
1.5 litres (2½ pints) water
3 heaped teaspoons coarse salt
½ teaspoon lemon juice

1 teaspoon crème fraîche

Equipment
1 stainless-steel saucepan
1 liquidizer

1   Remove the coarser stalks from the watercress. You will have about 250 g (9 oz) left.

2   Bring the water to the boil, add the salt and plunge in the watercress, blanching for three minutes.

3   Drain the cress and plunge immediately into iced water to prevent it cooking any further.

4   Drain it and purée in the mixer.

5 Pour the resulting purée into the stainless-steel pan and reheat, adding lemon juice and cream.

Served immediately, this purée is a beautiful delicate green, but after a few hours it fades and turns a yellowish-green.

---

136. *Onions cooked in sherry vinegar*
MARMELADE D'OIGNONS AU JEREZ

For four people

Main ingredients
1 kg (2¼ lb) onions
sugar substitute equivalent to
  2 teaspoons of sugar
salt

½ teaspoon pepper
1 teaspoon olive oil
4 tablespoons sherry vinegar

Equipment
1 heavy-based saucepan with a lid

1 Peel the onions and slice them finely.

2 Heat the olive oil in the heavy-based pan, add the onions, sugar substitute, salt and pepper.

3 Cover the pan and allow the onions to brown slowly, stirring from time to time with a wooden spoon.

4 After three-quarters of an hour, pour in the sherry vinegar and allow to cook gently for a further three-quarters of an hour, stirring occasionally. The onions slowly turn into a transparent 'jam'.

Dried fruit (muscatel raisins, prunes, apricots, etc.), previously washed, soaked and plumped in water can be added with the vinegar.

EDITOR'S NOTE This can be eaten on its own as a first course or with grilled or roast pork, beef or lamb.

137. *Tante Louise's stuffed onions*
OIGNONS TANTE LOUISE

For four people

Main ingredients
8 medium-sized onions
8 tablespoons chicken stock (No 2) or
   stock made with stock cubes
salt

Other ingredients
250 g (9 oz) courgettes
60 g (2 oz) fresh ceps (or tinned 'au
   naturel')
1 small bouquet garni
1 teaspoon olive oil
salt, pepper

Ingredients for the liaison
1 egg
2 heaped teaspoons skimmed milk
   powder
4 tablespoons water

Accompanying sauce
Fresh tomato sauce (No 38)

Equipment
1 heavy-based saucepan with a lid
1 teaspoon
1 bowl
1 wooden spoon or spatula
4 hot plates

1   Skin the courgettes with a potato-peeler. Chop them coarsely and brown them in the olive oil in a heavy-based pan. Add the ceps and bouquet garni, season with salt and pepper, and cook covered for fifteen minutes, stirring from time to time with a wooden spoon or spatula.

2   Peel the onions and cook them, whole, in boiling salted water for twenty minutes. Drain them, refresh in cold water, drain again, and hollow out the middles with a small teaspoon.

3   When the ceps and courgettes are cooked, take out the ceps and chop them coarsely. Purée the courgettes in the liquidizer.

4   Beat the egg with a fork, and mix in the skimmed milk powder dissolved in water, the courgette purée and the chopped ceps. Season the mixture and use it to stuff the onions.

5   Place them on an oven dish, pour in the chicken stock and bake in the oven (220°C/425°F/Mark 7) for twenty minutes. Heat the tomato sauce.

6   To serve the dish, pour hot tomato sauce on to the heated plates and put two stuffed onions on each.

EDITOR'S NOTE   If you have no tomato sauce already made, you should start preparing it while the courgettes and onions are cooking.

138–9. *Coarsely-chopped tomato pulp*
TOMATE FRAÎCHE CONCASSÉE

For four people

Main ingredients
1.5 kg (3¼ lb) tomatoes
2 finely-chopped shallots
2 whole cloves of garlic, unpeeled
1 bouquet garni
salt, pepper
1 teaspoon olive oil

Equipment
2 saucepans
1 earthenware pot **or** stainless-steel
   bowl

138   Uncooked Version

1   Remove the stalks from the tomatoes.

2   Bring a pan of water to the boil and drop the tomatoes in for fifteen seconds.

3   Scoop them out and plunge them straight into very cold water, letting the cold tap run over them to stop them from cooking any further. The tomatoes are now easily peeled.

4   Peel the tomatoes and cut them in half. Squeeze each half gently in the hollow of your palm to press out the pips and excess liquid. Chop the tomato pulp coarsely with a knife and season with salt and pepper. Alternatively, the tomato halves can be cut into small dice.

139   Cooked Version

5   Follow steps 1 to 4 above. Soften the chopped shallots in olive oil in a saucepan and add the raw chopped tomato pulp. Add the unpeeled garlic cloves and bouquet garni and taste for seasoning.

6   Cook for thirty minutes until the juice of the tomatoes has evaporated.

7   Remove the cloves of garlic and put the cooked tomato pulp, poured into an earthenware or stainless-steel container, in a cold place until it is needed.

140. *Leeks simmered with wild mint*
EMINCÉ DE POIREAUX À LA MENTHE SAUVAGE

For two to three people

Main ingredients
600 g (1¼ lb) of the white part of leeks
2 tablespoons chopped wild mint **or** garden mint
2 mint leaves
3 tablespoons chicken stock (No 2) or stock made with stock cubes **or** white wine

salt
pinch of pepper

Equipment
1 non-stick saucepan with a lid

1   Slice the leeks finely into rounds. Wash them in plenty of water and drain thoroughly.

2   Put leeks and chopped mint in the saucepan and let them sweat gently 'à sec' to evaporate their water for five minutes, stirring from time to time.

3   Pour in the chicken stock or white wine and season with salt and pepper.

4   Simmer very gently for about thirty minutes.

5   Just before serving, decorate with the mint leaves.

141. *Confit bayaldi*

For four people

Main ingredients
200 g (7 oz) courgettes
360 g (13 oz) tomatoes
240 g (8½ oz) aubergines
180 g (6½ oz) button mushrooms
½ teaspoon thyme
2 teaspoons olive oil

half clove of garlic, chopped
1 teaspoon salt, a pinch of pepper

Equipment
4 small enamelled-iron oven dishes, 14 cm (5½ in) across
1 sheet of aluminium foil

1   Preheat the oven to 200°C/400°F/Mark 6. Peel the courgettes and aubergines along their length with a potato-peeler, leaving strips of skin about 1 cm (⅓ in) wide all the way round to give a striped effect. Cut them into thin slices.

2   Clean and peel the mushrooms and cut into thin slices.

3   Cut the unpeeled tomatoes into thin slices.

4   Arrange all the vegetables in the little dishes, overlapping them and alternating the colours (i.e. aubergines, mushrooms, tomatoes, courgettes).

5   Sprinkle half a teaspoon of olive oil and a pinch of thyme flowers and chopped garlic over each dish and season with salt and pepper. Cover with aluminium foil.

6   Bake in a moderate oven for thirty minutes.

---

142. *Maman Guérard's vegetable stew*
CONFITURE DE LÉGUMES DE MAMAN GUÉRARD

For four people

Main ingredients
200 g (7 oz) finest tinned petits pois **or** 200 g (7 oz) shelled fresh garden peas
2 lettuces
1 medium carrot
1 medium cep (fresh or tinned 'au naturel') or other mushrooms
20 pickling onions
1 teaspoon olive oil

sugar substitute equivalent to 2 teaspoons of sugar
8 tablespoons chicken stock (No 2) or stock made with stock cubes
salt, pepper

Equipment
1 stainless-steel saucepan
1 cast-iron casserole

1   *Preparing the vegetables*
Peel the carrot and the cep and cut into small cubes.

Take off the outside leaves of the lettuce. Separate the remaining leaves and wash them in cold water.

If using fresh peas, cook them for five minutes in boiling, salted water and drain.

2   *Cooking the vegetables*
Heat the olive oil in the casserole and sauté the carrot, covered, for three minutes without allowing to brown. Season with salt and pepper. Add the small onions, peeled, and the diced cep. Cook three minutes more. Finally, add the peas and the sugar substitute dissolved in a little chicken stock and cover everything with the lettuce leaves. Moisten with the remaining chicken stock and season with salt and pepper.

Allow to simmer, covered, over a gentle heat for one-and-a-quarter hours; make sure that there is always about the same quantity of liquid and add a little more water when necessary.

3   Bring it to the table in the casserole, lifting the lid at the last moment. This melting dish of vegetables is exactly the reverse of vegetables cooked 'al dente'.

---

143. *Normandy apple gratin*
GRATIN DE POMMES DU PAYS DE CAUX

For two people

Main ingredients
1 apple weighing 100 g (3½ oz)
1 whole artichoke weighing 300 g (11 oz)
1 apricot weighing 70 g (2½ oz), **or** 2 tinned apricot halves preserved without sugar
1 teaspoon olive oil
juice of 1 lemon

Ingredients of the liaison
1 egg
2 level tablespoons skimmed milk powder

7 tablespoons water
1 teaspoon salt
a pinch of pepper
a hint of grated nutmeg

Equipment
1 heavy-based saucepan
2 individual oven dishes, 14 cm (5½ in) across

1   *Preparing the vegetables*
Peel the apple and core with an apple-corer.

With a small sharp knife, remove all the artichoke leaves; cook it in boiling salted water with the juice of a lemon. When it is cooked and cooled, remove the hairy choke.

Blanch the apricot, if fresh. Cut the apple, artichoke heart and apricot in cubes.

2   *Cooking the vegetables*
Heat the teaspoon of olive oil in the heavy-based pan. Put in the apples, and, when they are three-quarters cooked (still slightly resistant when pierced with a needle), add the artichoke and apricot and cook until almost tender.

3   Prepare the liaison: beat the egg lightly with a fork to break down the white, add the skimmed milk powder dissolved in the water, and season with salt, pepper and nutmeg.

4   Put the cubed apple, artichoke and apricot into the two oven dishes and cover them with the liaison mixture. Bake in the oven (225°C/425°F/Mark 7) for fifteen minutes, and take the dishes straight to the table as they are.

This recipe is somewhat reminiscent of clafoutis and is an excellent accompaniment to various birds, duck for example, and game such as pheasant.

---

144. *Ratatouille Niçoise*

For four people

Main ingredients
140 g (5 oz) courgettes
140 g (5 oz) aubergines
160 g (6 oz) onions
70 g (2½ oz) green peppers
400 g (14 oz) tomatoes
2 crushed cloves of garlic
1 sprig of thyme

half a bayleaf
salt, pepper
3 tablespoons olive oil

Equipment
1 frying-pan
1 oval iron terrine **or** earthenware dish
1 sheet of aluminium foil

1   Peel the courgettes along their length with a potato-peeler leaving alternate stripes of green skin about 1 cm (½ in) wide all the way round, to give a striped effect. Cut the courgettes and the unpeeled aubergines in half lengthwise. Slice them finely.

2   Deseed the green peppers and cut into thin slices.

3   Peel the tomatoes, having first removed the stalks, and cut them into eight pieces.

4   Slice the onions finely.

5   Preheat the oven to 200°C/400°F/Mark 6. Heat half the olive oil in a frying-pan and brown the onions, garlic and green pepper. Add the aubergines and let them brown, then the courgettes, and finally the tomatoes. Season with salt and pepper.

6   Put the whole mixture into an earthenware terrine or oval baking dish, add the thyme and bayleaf, and bake covered with aluminium foil for thirty minutes. Serve hot or chilled.

Desserts

145. *Fresh strawberry, raspberry or blackcurrant sauce*
SAUCE COULIS DE FRAISES, FRAMBOISES OU CASSIS

For five people

Main ingredients
200 g (7 oz) strawberries or raspberries
   or blackcurrants
7 tablespoons water
sugar substitute equivalent to 2–3
   tablespoons of sugar

juice of 1 lemon

Equipment
1 stainless-steel casserole
1 conical strainer, 1 liquidizer
1 small ladle, 1 bowl

1   Dissolve the sugar substitute in the water. Bring to the boil in a saucepan and simmer, uncovered, until the liquid becomes syrupy.

2   Pulp the strawberries, raspberries or blackcurrants in the liquidizer. Strain the resulting purée through a conical strainer, pressing it with a small ladle to help it through.

3   Mix the fruit purée with the syrup and lemon juice. Pour into a bowl and keep, covered, in the refrigerator ready for use.

Uses   Iced Stuffed Apples (No 156)
       Caramelized Orange (No 162)
       Iced Stuffed Melon (No 163)
       Floating Island with Fresh Blackcurrant Sauce (No 106)
       Iced Pineapple with Wild Strawberries (No 167)
       Little Strawberry Soufflés (No 170)

146. *Apricot sauce*
SAUCE COULIS D'ABRICOTS

For five people

Main ingredients
25 fresh apricot halves, **or** 25 apricot
  halves tinned, without sugar
4 tablespoons water
sugar substitute equivalent to 1–2
  tablespoons of sugar

1 vanilla pod

Equipment
1 heavy-based saucepan
1 liquidizer
1 bowl

1   Put the apricots in the saucepan together with the water, sugar substitute and vanilla pod. Allow to reduce by one-third of its volume to a thickish purée.

2   Take out the vanilla pod, blend the sauce in the liquidizer. Pour into a container and keep in the refrigerator ready for use.

Uses   Light Apple Tart (No 159)
       Apple Snow (No 157)
       Bananas en papillote (No 161)

EDITOR'S NOTE   See page 20–21 for a note on the use of sugar substitutes in this and the following recipes.

147. *Lime sorbet with grapefruit*
SORBET CITRON VERT AU PAMPLEMOUSSE

For five people

Main ingredients
500 ml (scant 1 pint) of water
sugar substitute equivalent to 6
  tablespoons sugar, or to taste
3 limes
half an egg white
1 grapefruit

Equipment
1 small saucepan
1 whisk
1 sieve
1 electric ice-cream maker (*optional*)
5 champagne 'flutes' chilled in the
  refrigerator

EDITOR'S NOTE   Domestic sorbetières, or electric ice-cream making machines, are available fairly widely, but it is important to note that some may take considerably longer to thicken and freeze the ice cream or sorbet mixture than is suggested in these recipes or in their instructions. The champagne flutes used to serve the sorbets are tall and narrow glasses, as opposed to the shallow type. If you are not using an electric ice-cream maker the half-frozen purée can be broken up in the liquidizer instead of with a fork to obtain a smoother result.

1 A Day Ahead Dissolve the sugar substitute in the water in the saucepan. Boil until it becomes syrupy. Then remove it from the heat.

Peel the limes with a potato-peeler, keeping the finely peeled zest. Squeeze the limes, and put juice and zest into the syrup and leave to macerate overnight.

2 Making the Sorbet Beat the egg white briefly with a whisk until it froths, mix it into the lime syrup, strain the mixture through a wire sieve and pour it into the ice-cream maker. The egg white helps to lighten the texture.

3 Let the sorbet freeze while you peel skin and pith off the grapefruit with a sharp knife. Skin the segments, collecting the juice.

4 To serve, fill the champagne 'flutes' with the lime sorbet piled up and rounded into a dome with a teaspoon. Decorate with grapefruit segments arranged like flowers and sprinkle with the grapefruit juice.

Normally sorbets are made with an electric ice-cream maker. However, if you do not happen to have this particular gadget, it is quite possible to make them in the freezing compartment of the refrigerator. Simply put in the prepared mixture and let it freeze, whisking it several times with a fork as it thickens to obtain a smooth sorbet free of large ice crystals.

---

148. *Melon sorbet*
SORBET AU MELON

For five people

Main ingredients
1 medium **or** 2 small melons
7 tablespoons water
sugar substitute equivalent to 5
    tablespoons sugar, or to taste

To decorate the sorbets
15 little melon balls made with a
    melon-baller
5 fresh mint leaves

Equipment
1 small saucepan
1 melon-baller
1 wire sieve
1 liquidizer
1 electric ice-cream maker (*optional*)
5 champagne 'flutes' chilled in the
    refrigerator

1   Dissolve the sugar substitute in the water. Put the mixture in the saucepan and boil until it becomes syrupy. Remove the pan from the heat and put the syrup in a cool place to get cold.

2   Cut the melons in half and scoop out the seeds and fibres.

3   If you have a melon-baller scoop out fifteen little balls from the inside of the melon halves, and put them in the refrigerator to chill.

4   Spoon the rest of the flesh from the melon and blend it in the liquidizer. There should be about 200 ml ($\frac{1}{3}$ pint) of purée. Strain.

5   Stir the melon purée into the cold syrup, pour the mixture into the ice-cream maker and let it run until the sorbet starts to thicken.

6   To serve the dish, fill the champagne 'flutes' with melon sorbet, shaping the tops into domes with a spoon. Decorate with the small melon balls and fresh mint leaves.

EDITOR'S NOTE   Ogen or Charentais melons are best for this recipe. Choose very ripe and heavily scented ones. If you do not possess a melon-baller cut the flesh into elegant cubes.

---

149. *Strawberry or raspberry sorbet*
SORBET À LA FRAISE OU À LA FRAMBOISE

For five people

Main ingredients
300 g (11 oz) fresh hulled strawberries
  or raspberries
150 ml ($\frac{1}{4}$ pint) water
sugar substitute equivalent to 5
  tablespoons sugar, or to taste
juice of 1 lemon

To decorate the sorbets
5 strawberries or 10 raspberries with
  their stalks

5 mint leaves

Equipment
1 small saucepan
1 conical sieve
1 liquidizer
1 electric ice-cream maker (*optional*)
5 champagne 'flutes', chilled in the
  refrigerator

1   Dissolve the sugar substitute in the water. Put the mixture in a saucepan and boil until it becomes syrupy. Remove from the heat and put the syrup in a cool place to get cold.

2   Choose very ripe and perfect strawberries or raspberries with a strong

perfume. Put the five whole strawberries or ten raspberries in the refrigerator to chill, together with the 'flutes'.

3   Put the hulled fruit into the liquidizer and purée. It should make about 400 ml (⅔ pint) of purée. Strain if you want a very smooth sorbet.

4   Stir the purée and the lemon juice into the cooled syrup, pour the mixture into the ice-cream maker and let it run until the mixture thickens.

5   To serve the dish, fill the champagne 'flutes' with strawberry or raspberry sorbet, shaping the tops into domes with a spoon. Decorate with the whole berries, kept for the purpose, and the fresh mint leaves.

---

150. *China tea sorbet*
SORBET AU THÉ

For four people

Main ingredients
3 large tablespoons China Tea
300 ml (½ pint) water
sugar substitute equivalent to 5
   tablespoons sugar, or to taste
juice of 1 lemon

Equipment
1 saucepan with a lid
1 conical strainer
1 electric ice-cream maker (*optional*)
4 champagne 'flutes'

To decorate the sorbets
Ice-crystals made from 4 tablespoons
   of the infusion of tea
4 fresh mint leaves

1   Dissolve the sugar substitute in the water and bring to the boil in the saucepan. Add the tea and leave in the covered pan to infuse for three hours.

2   Strain four tablespoons of the infusion and pour it into a flat dish; slip it into the freezer and stir it occasionally with a fork as it sets to break up the mixture into crystals.

3   Strain the remaining 240 ml (scant ½ pint) of the infusion through the conical sieve and pour it into the ice-cream maker, together with the lemon juice.

4   To serve, fill the champagne 'flutes' with the tea sorbet, shaping the tops into domes with a spoon. Sprinkle with the crystallized flakes of tea and decorate with a fresh mint leaf.

151. *Bitter chocolate granita*
GRANITÉ DE CHOCOLAT AMER

For four people

Main ingredients
400 ml (⅔ pint) water
40 g (1½ oz) skimmed milk powder
sugar substitute equivalent to 6
　tablespoons sugar, or to taste
60 g (2 oz) of unsweetened cocoa
　powder
half vanilla pod
1 tablespoon crème fraîche

To decorate the sorbets
Frozen crystals of coffee made with 4
　tablespoons of strong sweet black
　coffee

Equipment
1 saucepan
1 whisk
1 electric ice-cream maker (*optional*)
4 champagne 'flutes' chilled in the
　refrigerator

1　Dissolve the milk powder and cocoa powder in a little of the water, then add the rest, whisking with a small wire whisk.

　Bring the mixture to the boil in the saucepan, and add the sugar substitute and the vanilla pod. Remove from the heat and put in a cool place to get cold.

2　Prepare the coffee for the crystals. Pour it into a small flat dish and put it in the freezing compartment of the refrigerator. Stir it from time to time with a fork while it freezes to form ice crystals.

3　Add the teaspoon of crème fraîche to the cooled cocoa mixture, whisk it well, pour it into the ice-cream maker and let it run until the mixture starts to freeze and thicken.

4　To serve the dish, fill the champagne 'flutes' with the chocolate ice, shaped into domes with a spoon. Sprinkle the tops with the iced coffee crystals.

152. *Little orange custard creams*
PETITS POTS DE CRÈME À L'ORANGE

For four people

Main ingredients
30 g (1 oz) skimmed milk
    powder
300 ml (½ pint) water
sugar substitute equivalent to 5
    tablespoons sugar, or to taste
2 whole eggs
1 orange

Equipment
2 bowls
1 small saucepan
1 whisk
1 conical strainer
4 small earthenware or porcelain pots
1 bain-marie

1   Peel the orange with a potato-peeler. Blanch the zest in boiling water for ten minutes, drain and chop finely into tiny dice.

2   Preheat the oven to 150°C/300°F/Mark 2. Dissolve the skimmed milk powder and sugar substitute in the cold water.

3   In a separate bowl, beat the eggs, mix them into the milk mixture and strain through the conical strainer. Add the finely chopped orange zest. Pour the mixture into the little ovenproof dishes and cook them in a bain-marie in a slow oven for one hour, then allow to get cold and chill in the refrigerator.

4   Meanwhile peel skin and pith from the orange. Skin the segments, catching the juice that runs out in a bowl.

5   To serve, turn out the small pots on to a plate, decorate them with the skinned orange segments and sprinkle them with orange juice. Serve very cold.

153. *Little custard creams with fresh fruit*
PETITS POTS DE CRÈME AUX FRUITS FRAIS

'Petits pots' with fresh fruit are made in the same way as the orange custard creams, replacing the orange zest with fruits in season (strawberries, raspberries, cherries, pears) cut in little dice ½ cm (¼ in) across. Decorate with the same fruits, whole if using soft fruits, or finely sliced if using tree fruits such as pears.

154. *Little coffee creams*
PETITS POTS DE CRÈME AU CAFÉ

For four people

Main ingredients
30 g (1 oz) skimmed milk powder
300 ml (½ pint) black coffee
sugar substitute equivalent to 2
  tablespoons sugar
2 eggs

For decorating the dish
frozen coffee crystals made with
4 tablespoons strong sweetened black
  coffee

Equipment
2 bowls
1 small shallow dish
1 small whisk
1 conical strainer
4 small ovenproof pots
1 bain-marie

1 Pour the coffee for the crystals into a small shallow dish and freeze in the freezing compartment of the refrigerator, stirring from time to time with a fork to break it up into crystals.

2 Preheat the oven to 150°C/300°F/Mark 2. Dissolve the skimmed milk powder and the sugar substitute in 300 ml (½ pint) of black coffee.

3 In a separate bowl beat the eggs, then pour them into the coffee mixture and whisk. Strain the resulting liquid through a conical strainer.

   Fill the pots with the mixture and cook in a bain-marie in a slow oven for one hour. Allow to cool.

4 These creams can either be served as they are in their little pots or turned out on to small plates. Either way they are sprinkled with coffee crystals at the last moment.

155. *Apple compôte with apricots*
COMPÔTE DE POMMES À L'ABRICOT

For two people

Main ingredients
3 apples, preferably russets or pippins
4 fresh apricots **or** 8 tinned apricot
    halves (without sugar)
sugar substitute equivalent to $1\frac{1}{2}$
    tablespoons sugar

1 tablespoon water

Equipment
1 heavy-based saucepan with a lid
1 liquidizer
1 small deep bowl

1   Peel, quarter and core the apples.

2   Put the tablespoon of water and sugar substitute in a saucepan with the apples and four apricot halves. Simmer, covered, for fifteen minutes.

3   Meanwhile cut the remaining apricots into little dice.

4   After cooking, purée the apples and apricots in the liquidizer. Spoon the purée into a small deep china bowl and stir in the diced apricots. Serve chilled.

156. *Iced stuffed apples*
POMMES EN SURPRISE

For two people

Main ingredients
2 apples, russets, pippins or other
    sweet eating apples
An assortment of 3 or 4 fresh fruits
    according to the season (strawberries,
    melon, peaches, figs, mango, oranges,
    grapefruit, etc.)
juice of 1 lemon
4 fresh mint leaves

Accompanying sauce
7 tablespoons fresh raspberry **or**
    blackcurrant sauce (No. 145)

Equipment
1 melon-baller
2 dessert plates

1   Decapitate the apples and keep the tops.

2   Scoop out the insides with a melon-baller, making small even balls. Macerate them, together with the tops which you have just cut off, in lemon juice and chill.

3   Fill the apples with the diced fruit mixed with the little apple balls.

4   Put the stuffed apples on to plates. Moisten them inside and round the base with the fresh raspberry or blackcurrant sauce and cover with the tops stuck with two mint leaves. Chill thoroughly in the refrigerator before serving.

---

157. *Apple snow*
POMMES À LA NEIGE

For four people

Main ingredients
4 apples, preferably russets or pippins
2 egg whites
sugar substitute equivalent to 3
    tablespoons sugar
1 lemon
1 leaf **or** 1 level teaspoon gelatine
8 fresh mint leaves

Accompanying sauce
150 ml (¼ pint) Apricot Sauce chilled
    (No 146)

Equipment
1 deep dish
1 saucepan
2 salad bowls
1 balloon whisk
1 liquidizer
4 dessert plates

1   Preheat the oven to 150°C/300°F/Mark 2. Put the whole unpeeled apples into a baking dish which has been very sparingly brushed with water, to prevent them from sticking, and bake for thirty minutes.

2   Dissolve the gelatine in a little hot water.

3   Peel the lemon with a potato-peeler, collect the zest and chop finely, blanch for fifteen minutes in boiling water, and drain. Squeeze the lemon and reserve the juice.

4   When they are tender reserve the tops from the apples, and keep them on one side. Then hollow out the skins. Blend the cooked apple pulp in the liquidizer with half the sugar substitute, the dissolved gelatine and lemon juice. Pour the mixture into a bowl. Keep the empty apple skins.

5   Beat the egg whites to a soft snow with the remaining sugar substitute, crushed, in a separate bowl.

6   Fold the beaten whites and lemon zest lightly with the apple mixture

and fill the apple skins with the mixture, put the tops back on and chill for one hour in the refrigerator.

7 Put an apple on each plate, stick two fresh mint leaves in the top of each, and pour apricot sauce all round.

---

158. *Apple clafoutis*
CLAFOUTIS AUX POMMES D'AURÉLIA

For six to eight people

Main ingredients
250 ml (½ pint) water
25 g (1 oz) skimmed milk powder
sugar substitute equivalent to 5
   talespoons sugar
1 vanilla pod
4 apples
half a banana
2 eggs
2 egg whites

3 level tablespoons olive oil
3 level tablespoons self-raising flour
half a lemon

Equipment
2 bowls
1 whisk
6–8 small oven dishes in earthenware,
   enamelled iron or porcelain

1 Preheat the oven to 240°C/475°F/Mark 9. Dissolve the skimmed milk powder and the sugar substitute thoroughly in the water. Bring this liquid to the boil together with the vanilla pod. Allow to cool.

2 Peel, quarter and core the apples and cut into slices ½ cm (¼ in) thick. Put them into a bowl together with the sliced banana and sprinkle with the juice of half a lemon.

3 Beat the eggs and egg whites briefly in the second bowl to break them down. Add the milk mixture and the oil. Lastly, still beating, incorporate the flour.

4 Distribute the sliced apples and bananas between the four dishes. Pour on the batter.

5 The clafoutis are then cooked in two stages, first ten minutes in the hot oven, then for twenty minutes at 180°C/350°F/Mark 4.

6 Serve straight from the oven in their enamelled iron, earthenware or porcelain dishes.

159. *Light apple tarts*
TARTE FINE AUX POMMES CHAUDES

For four people

Ingredients for the shortcrust pastry
125 g (4½ oz) flour
80 g (3 oz) unsalted butter
1 tablespoon cold water
pinch of salt

Equipment
1 liquidizer
1 rolling pin
1 baking sheet
4 hot plates

Ingredients for the filling
4 medium-sized apples
5 tablespoons apricot sauce (No 146)

See colour illustrations between pages 128 and 129

1 Make the pastry in the mixer, put in flour, butter, water and salt, and blend to a lightly adhering mass. Put it on a floured board. Crush the mixture with the heel of the palm to obtain a homogenous paste. Roll it into a ball and put in a polythene bag in the refrigerator to rest for thirty minutes.

2 Preheat the oven to 220°C/425°F/Mark 7. Cut the pastry into four pieces and flatten them with the rolling pin to make four rounds 12 cm (4½ in) across.

3 Peel, quarter and core the apples and cut into slices ½ cm (¼ in) thick. Arrange them overlapping in circles on the pastry rounds, so that the pastry is completely covered.

4 Put the tarts with their apples on to the baking sheet in the oven and cook for twenty minutes.

5 Take the tarts from the oven and cover them with hot apricot sauce. Serve on very hot plates.

160. *Fresh fruit steeped in red wine*
FRUITS AU VIN ROUGE DE GRAVES

For four people

Main ingredients
A variety of fresh fruit: pears, peaches, grapes, oranges, cherries, strawberries, raspberries, melon, redcurrants, etc., depending on what is in season
300 ml (a good ½ pint) red Graves or other red Bordeaux wine
150 ml (¼ pint) water

sugar substitute equivalent to 4 tablespoons sugar
1 vanilla pod
8 fresh mint leaves

Equipment
1 saucepan
1 deep china bowl **or** compotier
4 large chilled balloon glasses

1   Put the wine in the saucepan and bring it to the boil; reduce it by half (to evaporate as much alcohol as possible). Add the water, sugar substitute and split vanilla pod, bring briefly to the boil, then cool and chill.

2   Peel or skin the tree-fruits such as pears, peaches, and oranges, and the melons. Cut them into little crescents. Leave the soft fruits whole, strawberries, raspberries, cherries, etc.

Mix all the different fruits together in a deep china bowl and leave them to steep in their own juices for an hour in the refrigerator.

3   To serve the dish, half fill the balloon glasses with fruit and pour some of the red-wine syrup into each glass. Decorate with small sprigs of mint and the vanilla pod, cut in four.

161. *Bananas en papillote*
BANANES EN PAPILLOTE

For four people

Main ingredients
4 small well-ripened bananas
8 tablespoons apricot sauce (No 146)
2 vanilla pods
4 drops bitter almond essence (*optional*)
sugar substitute equivalent to 2 tablespoons sugar
4 tablespoons water

Equipment
1 small saucepan
1 small whisk
4 pieces of aluminium foil, 25 cm by 15 cm (9 in by 6 in)
4 hot plates

1 Preheat the oven to 220°C/425°F/Mark 7. Bring the water and sugar substitute to the boil in the saucepan. Take it off the heat, add the apricot sauce and almond essence, if wanted. Whisk the mixture lightly.

2 Fold the sheets of aluminium foil into shallow boat shapes. Place a peeled banana in each. Sprinkle it with the apricot sauce and put half a vanilla pod split lengthwise alongside each banana.

3 Fold up the edges of each papillote to seal it hermetically and bake in a hot oven for twenty minutes. When they are cooked put a little parcel on each plate and let your guests open them for themselves.

This recipe can equally well be made with apples.

See colour illustrations between pages 128 and 129

---

162. *Caramelized oranges*
ORANGE À L'ORANGE

For two people

Main ingredients
2 blood oranges
2 kiwis (*optional*)
250 ml (½ pint) water
sugar substitute equivalent to 2
  tablespoons sugar

Accompanying sauce
6 tablespoons fresh strawberry **or**
  blackcurrant sauce (No 145)

Equipment
1 small stainless-steel saucepan
2 small plates

1 Peel the oranges with a potato-peeler and cut the zest into very fine julienne strips (about the size of pine-needles).

2 Dissolve the sugar substitute in the water in a small saucepan and bring to the boil.
 Throw in the julienne of orange peel and allow to simmer very gently for one-and-a-half to two hours. The orange zest will almost have become caramelized in their syrup. Allow to cool.

3 Peel the pith from the skinned oranges and take off all the inner skin with a very sharp knife. Cut through the flesh to detach it from the inner skins and take out the skinned segments. Do this over a bowl to collect the juices.

4 Cut the kiwis (if used) in half lengthwise and slice thinly.

5 *To serve the dish*

Arrange the segments of orange like the petals of a flower on each plate, and cover with the caramelized peel; moisten with orange juice and arrange the slices of kiwi all round. Coat very lightly with the chosen fresh fruit sauce.

Note for Australia Since the sauce accompanying this dish is red in colour it is not necessary to insist on blood oranges, which are often difficult to obtain.

---

163. *Iced stuffed melons*
MELON EN SURPRISE

For four people

Main ingredients
4 very small Ogen melons

Other ingredients
1 orange
1 grapefruit
strawberries, raspberries, grapes,
    pears, etc.
8 fresh mint leaves

Accompanying sauce
240 ml (scant ½ pint) fresh raspberry
    sauce (No **145**)

Equipment
1 china dish
4 small plates

1 Carefully cut the tops off the melons and keep them on one side. Scoop out the seeds with a teaspoon. With the same teaspoon carefully scoop out the flesh in thin pieces, leaving the skins whole.

2 Peel the orange and the grapefruit: and skin the segments.

3 Put the pieces of melon flesh in a bowl with the strawberries, raspberries, grapes, peeled pears cut in thin slices and orange and grapefruit segments, and chill for an hour in their own juice in the refrigerator.

4 To serve the dish put the melons on the plates, fill them with the chilled fruit. Pour the fresh fruit sauce over the top, replace the lids and decorate each with two mint leaves.

For an even more special pudding the melons can be filled with Melon Sorbet (No **148**) as well as fruit.

Note for Australia Wild strawberries are not easily available. When substituting cultivated strawberries, it is important to choose the smaller varieties.

164. *Strawberries chantilly*
FRAISES À LA CHANTILLY

For four people

Main ingredients
250 g (9 oz) strawberries
1 tablespoon kirsch
6 tablespoons whipping cream **or**
    4 tablespoons double cream stirred
    with 2 tablespoons iced water
2½ egg whites
sugar substitute equivalent to 4
    tablespoons sugar
1 drop vanilla essence

4 handsome fresh mint leaves

Equipment
1 bowl
2 deep stainless-steel dishes
1 whisk
1 wooden spoon **or** spatula
4 wide topped glasses or 'coupes'
    chilled in the refrigerator

1   Hull the strawberries and put them in a china bowl with the kirsch. Put to macerate in the refrigerator.

2   Put the egg whites and the sugar substitute, pounded to a powder if necessary, in a large bowl. Place the bowl over a pan of just simmering water and whisk for ten minutes. The mixture will whiten, thicken and then become stiff. Put this meringue in the refrigerator.

3   Whisk the cream, flavoured with a drop of vanilla essence, in a large bowl. Beat gently at first, and then more briskly to incorporate the maximum amount of air. Stop whisking when the cream stiffens.

4   Fold the whipped cream very lightly into the chilled meringue with a spatula.

5   Put the strawberries steeped in the kirsch into the 'coupes' with a tablespoon and cover them with a soft mound of Chantilly cream. Decorate each with one large strawberry flanked with one mint leaf. Serve chilled.

165. *Almond jelly with fresh fruit*
GELÉE D'AMANDE AUX FRUITS FRAIS

For four people

Main ingredients
200 ml (⅓ pint) water
20 g (¾ oz) skimmed milk powder
2 sheets leaf gelatine or 2 level
  teaspoons powdered gelatine
2 drops bitter almond essence

Other ingredients
400 g (14 oz) of different coloured
  fruits. According to the season,
  choose from: whole soft fruits
(strawberries, raspberries, cherries,
currants, etc.) or larger fruits cut in
fine slices (pears, peaches, pineapple,
oranges, etc.)

Equipment
2 bowls
1 saucepan
1 wide round dish
1 biscuit or pastry cutter (*optional*)
4 chilled plates

1   Soak the leaves of gelatine in cold water to soften and swell them.

2   Dissolve the skimmed milk powder in the cold water. Bring to the boil, remove from the heat and add the two drops of almond essence and the drained soaked gelatine. Mix until the gelatine has dissolved and pour into a wide round dish. Chill in the refrigerator and let it set into a round flat jelly about 1 cm (⅓ in) deep.

3   Prepare all the fruits, put them into a china bowl and let them steep in their own juice.

4   Take the jelly out of the refrigerator and cut it into any shapes you like, diamonds, lozenges, or rounds, either with a knife or a biscuit cutter.

5   Put the almond jelly shapes in the middle of the plates and arrange the fruits round them, moistened with their own juice, arranging the colours to look as pretty as possible. Serve chilled.

166. *Floating islands with fresh blackcurrant sauce*
BLANCS À LA NEIGE AU COULIS DE CASSIS

For four people

Main ingredients
5 egg whites
sugar substitute equivalent to 2
  tablespoons sugar
250 ml (scant ½ pint) fresh
  blackcurrant sauce (No **145**)

For poaching the egg whites
2 litres (2½ pints) water
¾ teaspoon salt

Equipment
1 large wide saucepan
1 bowl
1 balloon whisk
1 skimmer
1 spatula
4 cold plates

1   Bring the water with the salt to a very slow simmer in the large wide saucepan.

2   Whisk the egg whites in a bowl. Beat slowly at first to break down their resistance, then increasingly briskly as they start to thicken. Add the sugar substitute, ground to a powder if necessary. Bring the whites back to a good even stiff consistency by whisking with a steady stirring movement.

3   Cook the egg whites. Make little mounds of egg white 3 cm (just over 1 in) high on the skimmer, shaping them smoothly with the spatula. Rest the skimmer on the surface of the very gently moving water, when the egg white will detach itself and float away on the top of the water. Repeat this operation four times, to make four little light rounded islands of egg white. With the water barely simmering, poach the islands for fifteen minutes, turning them over gently half-way through. Lift them carefully and drain them on a cloth.

4   Pour the fresh blackcurrant sauce on to the plates and place the islands on top.

  If you like they can be decorated with fine slices of tropical fruit such as mangoes, kiwis, etc., embellished with fresh mint leaves.

167. *Iced pineapple with wild strawberries*
ANANAS GLACÉ AUX FRAISES DES BOIS

For eight people

Main ingredients
1 medium pineapple
150 ml (¼ pint) water
sugar substitute equivalent to 5
   tablespoons sugar

Other ingredients
250 g (9 oz) wild or alpine
   strawberries
1 tablespoon kirsch

Accompanying sauce
250 ml (scant ½ pint) fresh raspberry
   sauce (No 145)

Equipment
1 small saucepan
1 bowl
1 liquidizer
1 electric ice-cream maker (*optional*)
1 serving dish
1 sauceboat

1   Dissolve the sugar substitute in the water in a small saucepan. Bring to the boil and simmer until it becomes syrupy. Remove from the heat and allow to cool.

2   Cut off the bottom of the pineapple so that it will stand firmly on its base. Cut off the top and keep the plume of leaves for later. Remove the flesh of the pineapple by sliding a long-bladed knife between flesh and skin. Take out the cylinder of pineapple, cut it in half lengthwise and remove the central core from each piece.

3   Cut up enough of the pineapple flesh to give four large tablespoons of small dice ½ cm (¼ in) across. Put these dice in the bowl with the strawberries and the kirsch and allow to steep in their own juice.
   Chill the dice and the pineapple shell in the refrigerator.

4   Blend the remaining pineapple flesh in the liquidizer together with the syrup. Pour the mixture into the ice-cream maker and allow to run until it starts to freeze and thicken.

5   Line the bottom and sides of the pineapple shell generously with the sorbet and put the strawberries and pineapple cubes in the centre. Finish by filling up to the top with sorbet and put the top back on the pineapple.

6   Bring to the table standing on a folded napkin on a round serving dish and serve the chilled fresh raspberry sauce separately in a sauceboat.

168. *Paris-Brest coffee ring*
PARIS-BREST AU CAFÉ

For six people

Ingredients for the choux paste
1 teaspoon skimmed milk powder
4 tablespoons water
25 g (1 oz) butter
pinch of salt
sugar substitute equivalent to 1½
  teaspoons sugar
35 g (1¼ oz) flour
1 beaten egg
1 beaten egg for brushing the pastry
icing sugar (*optional*)

Crème Chantilly
Made as in recipe No 164, with 1
  tablespoon instant coffee powder

Equipment
1 small heavy-based saucepan
1 spatula
1 bowl
1 baking sheet
1 sheet of baking paper
1 pastry piping bag with a nozzle 2 cm
  (¾ in) across
1 round serving dish
1 saw-bladed knife

EDITOR'S NOTE This pastry is more easily made if you double the quantities, so make a larger amount of pastry, put it all into the piping bag, and use it to make as many crowns as you can. Cook what you need and keep the rest in the freezer for another day.

Preparing the choux pastry
1   Bring the water, skimmed milk powder, butter, sugar substitute and salt to the boil in the small heavy-based saucepan.

2   Take it off the heat as it comes to the boil and stir in the flour with a wooden spatula. Put it back on the heat and cook, stirring for one minute to dry the mixture.

3   Transfer to the warmed bowl and mix in half the egg, beating lightly with a fork. After a few seconds add the second half of the egg, and stop beating as soon as the pastry has become supple and smooth.

Making the Paris-Brest ring
4   Preheat the oven to 220°C/425°F/Mark 7.

5   Lightly grease the baking sheet or, better, cover it with a sheet of baking paper. Mark out a 20 cm (8 in) circle on the baking sheet or paper.

6   Fill the piping bag with the choux pastry and pipe over your mark, to make a circular ring of pastry. Brush it with a light glaze of beaten egg, to give a good colour.

Cooking the Paris-Brest ring

7   Bake in a hot oven for fifteen minutes with the door propped open a crack with a spoon. When the pastry has risen well, reduce the heat to 200°C/400°F/Mark 6, and cook for a further fifteen minutes with the door closed.

8   Take the ring out of the oven, allow to cool, then cut the Paris-Brest ring horizontally into two halves.

Finishing the ring

9   Fill the bottom ring with the Crème Chantilly, flavoured with the coffee powder, which is added to the egg whites before you start to whisk them.

If your guests are particularly greedy you can double the amount of cream.

Put the top ring on the cream and powder with a light cloud of icing sugar if liked. Serve on a round dish.

---

169. *Little pear soufflés*
SOUFFLÉ LÉGER AUX POIRES

For eight people

Main ingredients
3 *very ripe* pears, each weighing about 120 g (4 oz)
½ teaspoon eau-de-vie de poire (pear liqueur)
sugar substitute equivalent to 4 tablespoons sugar
2 egg yolks
7 egg whites
20 g (¾ oz) softened butter

Ingredients for the syrup
750 ml (1¼ pints) water

sugar substitute equivalent to 5 tablespoons sugar
1 vanilla pod, cut in half lengthwise

Equipment
2 bowls
1 saucepan
8 small soufflé dishes, 9 cm across by 4 cm deep (3½ in by 1½ in)
1 liquidizer
1 balloon whisk
1 spatula

1   Put the ingredients for the syrup in the saucepan and bring to the boil.

2   Peel the pears with a potato-peeler, cut them into quarters and core them, then poach them in the syrup for fifteen minutes.

3   Drain the pears and blend them in the liquidizer with the sugar substitute and pear liqueur.

4 Pour the mixture into a bowl and add the egg yolks.

5 Use the softened butter to brush the insides of the individual soufflé dishes. Preheat the oven to 220°C/425°F/Mark 7.

6 Beat the egg whites to a soft snow. Mix one quarter into the pear purée. Gradually add the rest of the egg whites, folding them in carefully with a spatula.

7 Fill the soufflé dishes right up to the top with the mixture. Level the surface with the back of a knife or a palette knife.

Push the mixture away from the edges of each dish with your thumb to help the soufflés to rise.

8 Cook for about eight minutes in the oven. Serve the minute they are taken out of the oven.

---

170. *Little wild strawberry soufflés*
SOUFFLÉ LÉGER AUX FRAISES DES BOIS

For eight people

Main ingredients
200 g (7 oz) wood **or** alpine
  strawberries
sugar substitute
  equivalent to 4 tablespoons sugar
a squeeze of lemon juice
1 tablespoon fresh raspberry purée
  (No 145) (*optional*)
½ teaspoon kirsch
2 egg yolks

7 egg whites
softened butter

Equipment
2 bowls
8 small soufflé dishes, 9 cm across by
  4 cm deep (3½ in by 1½ in)
1 liquidizer
1 balloon whisk
1 spatula

1 Blend the strawberries in the liquidizer together with the sugar substitute, kirsch, raspberry purée, if used, and the lemon juice.

2 Pour the resulting purée into a bowl and stir in the egg yolks.

3 Lightly brush the insides of the soufflé dishes with butter and preheat the oven to 200°C/400°F/Mark 6.

4 Beat the egg whites to a soft snow. Take one quarter of the egg whites and mix into the strawberry purée. Now gradually incorporate the rest of the egg whites, folding them in lightly with a spatula.

5 Fill the soufflé dishes right to the top with the mixture. Level the

surface with the back of a knife or palette knife. Push the mixture away from the edges of each dish with your thumb to help the soufflés to rise.

6   Cook for about eight minutes in a moderate oven. Serve the minute they are taken from the oven.

Note for Australia Wild strawberries are not easily available. When substituting cultivated strawberries, it is important to choose the smaller varieties.

171. *Little coffee soufflés*
SOUFFLÉ LÉGER AU CAFÉ

For eight people

Main ingredients	*Equipment*
2 tablespoons strong black coffee	2 bowls
sugar substitute equivalent to 4 tablespoons sugar	1 small saucepan
3 egg yolks	1 liquidizer
7 egg whites	1 balloon whisk
softened butter	1 spatula
	8 small soufflé dishes, 9 cm across by 4 cm deep (3½ in by 1½ in)

1   Dissolve the coffee powder and sugar substitute in the water in a small pan. Bring to the boil then take off the heat and allow to cool. Mix in the egg yolks.

2   Lightly brush the insides of the soufflé dishes with the softened butter and preheat the oven to 200°C/400°F/Mark 6.

3   Beat the egg whites to a soft snow. Take one quarter of the egg whites and stir into the coffee mixture. Now gradually incorporate the rest of the egg whites, folding them in lightly with a spatula.

4   Fill the soufflé dishes right to the top with the mixture. Level the surface with the back of a knife or palette knife. Push the mixture away from the edges of each dish with your thumb, to help the soufflés to rise.

6   Cook for about eight minutes in a moderate oven and serve the minute they are ready.

Index

Suppliers of utensils and kitchen equipment

Brisbane
The Kitchen Shop, City

Sydney
Accoutrement, Mosman
The Bay Tree, Woollahra
Hamden Cuisine, Epping

Canberra
The Provincial Kitchen, City

Melbourne
Cooking Co-ordinates, South Yarra
Culinarion, East Hawthorn

Hobart
Ornamo, City
Just The Thing, Sandy Bay

Adelaide
North Adelaide Cookshop,
   North Adelaide
Colonial Galleries, Fullarton

Perth
Lady Kitchener, Nedlands